Representative democracy?

Manchester University Press

Representative democracy?

Geography and the
British electoral system

Ron Johnston, Charles Pattie and
David Rossiter

Manchester University Press

The right of Ron Johnston, Charles Pattie and David Rossiter to be identified as the authors of this work has been asserted by them in accordance with the Copyright, Designs and Patents Act 1988.

Published by Manchester University Press
Altrincham Street, Manchester M1 7JA
www.manchesteruniversitypress.co.uk

British Library Cataloguing-in-Publication Data
A catalogue record for this book is available from the British Library

ISBN 978 1 5261 3989 4 paperback
ISBN 978 1 5261 5181 0 hardback

First published 2021

The publisher has no responsibility for the persistence or accuracy of URLs for any external or third-party internet websites referred to in this book, and does not guarantee that any content on such websites is, or will remain, accurate or appropriate.

Typeset by Servis Filmsetting Ltd, Stockport, Cheshire

Contents

Figures

Figures

Tables

Tables

Preface

Either individually or together, we have been studying aspects of the UK's electoral system for more than four decades, focusing in particular on how parliamentary constituencies have been defined and the impact of that geography on election results. This has resulted in two major monographs, an overview volume, and a substantial number of academic papers, reports, blogs and other publications.[1] Given that output, why another book?

There are two reasons. The first is that a lot has happened in the last twenty years, especially since the Conservatives achieved a significant change to the rules by which constituency boundaries are determined in 2011. Although we have written extensively on those changes and their potential implications – they have not yet been finally implemented – that material has not been drawn together in a single volume. It is now, in a series of chapters that outlines how the electoral system has evolved since 1832, with major decisions concerning its form made in 1885, 1944 and – perhaps, if the changes ever finally go through – in 2011. The book thus provides, in its central chapters, an outline history of what the British call redistributions – the redrawing of constituency maps – over nearly two centuries.

The second reason for this book is that in our earlier work the political implications of those redistributions have only been lightly addressed. The United Kingdom has what is generally known as a representative democratic form of government. But what is understood by that, what should a representative system deliver, and how well does the system that has evolved since 1832 meet those criteria? Does the electoral system, and in particular its geographical elements – the academic discipline through which, in various forms, all three of us emerged – impede that goal? When we were initially contemplating this book (at about half the length it now fills!) the suggested title was *(un?)Representative democracy*, but we then simplified it to *Representative democracy?* with the question mark key. Hence, more so than in our other books, we address the issues of representation in some detail, ask to what extent the electoral system influences the achievement of a representative democracy, and also ask whether other electoral systems – other geographies – might be better suited to that end.

As we wrote this book, political events intervened and made us reconsider some of its contents. With the basic rules for constituency redistributions having been rewritten in 2011, we expected to be able to evaluate that change. Its implementation had been delayed by political decisions in 2013, when a nearly completed redrawing of the constituency map was halted. Another redistribution began three years later and was completed in autumn 2018 – but a now minority Conservative government was unwilling or unable to take the final step and implement the changes that the Boundary Commissions proposed. The general election of December 2019 was thus fought on pre-existing boundaries, and, following a clear Conservative victory, the new government chose to shelve the Commissions' 2018 recommendations and instead introduced a new Parliamentary Constituencies Bill 2019-21, retaining many of the key changes of the 2011 legislation but reverting to 650 seats and moving from a 5-year to an 8-year redistricting cycle. While we have endeavoured to include analysis of the 2019 election in our analyses, as this manuscript goes to press the Bill is still wending its way through Parliament. Its provisions are not yet final – during the course of its passage an amendment to add another protected seat, Ynys Mon, has been accepted by the government, for example – and are not yet law. That said, as the new Bill does not change the basic principles of the 2011 legislation, our analyses of the 2011 Act are likely to apply to it too. The book is as up to date as we could make it in the autumn of 2020.

During this forty-year journey we have benefited greatly from the assistance, involvement and support of a large number of people, not least former graduate students David Cutts, Ed Fieldhouse, Andrew Russell and Andrew Schuman. Danny Dorling was closely involved in our work at a critical stage, along with Ian McAllister and Helena Tunstall, as have been Galina Borisyuk, Colin Rallings and Michael Thrasher. Along the way we have collaborated with Justin Fisher, Todd Hartman, Kelvyn Jones and David Manley, and many others have provided help and support without which we could not have achieved what we have. Our work on the Boundary Commissions has been much aided by their Commissioners and, especially, their staffs who have generously provided material and other assistance; we have also gained much from political party officials, notably Greg Cook and Roger Pratt, and from politicians, not least Lords Rob Hayward, David Lipsey, Chris Rennard and Paul Tyler. To them and many others who have encountered us on the way our deepest thanks, along with the patient and helpful staff at Manchester University Press who have seen the project through its final stages.

Ron Johnston was, as ever, absolutely central to researching and writing this book. Sadly, he died suddenly just before we received the proofs. So David and Charles dedicate the book to Ron, our much-loved friend, colleague and mentor, as a paltry thanks for many very happy years working together.

1
Introduction

Two party leaders were happy on the morning after the United Kingdom's 12 December 2019 general election; another resigned immediately, one vowed to establish a new party, and the Leader of the Opposition acknowledged that his days as leader were numbered. Their responses reflected not only how successful their parties had been in winning votes but also how the electoral system had translated those votes into seats, in large part because of geography.[1] Geography matters in so many aspects of life; the creation of a representative legislature – in this case the UK House of Commons – is a clear example of that.

Of the contented party leaders, none was more so than the Prime Minister, Boris Johnson. His Conservative Party's share of the vote had only increased by a modest 1.1 percentage points (to 43.6) but this was sufficient to take the number of Conservative MPs to 365, an increase of 5.7 percentage points compared with 2017 and delivering in his words 'a stonking majority'. The disproportionate return was a reflection in part of the demise of his main opposition, but also of the shift in the party's geographical support. The UK's electoral system typically bestows a winner's bonus on the most popular party and a further bonus on those whose supporters are in the right places.

Nicola Sturgeon, leader of the Scottish National Party (SNP), was the other happy leader, and for similar reasons. The SNP won 45 per cent of the vote in Scotland, well ahead of the Conservatives (25 per cent), Labour (19 per cent) and the Liberal Democrats (10 per cent). This translated to seat shares of 48, 6, 1 and 4 respectively, demonstrating not only how well the largest party is treated but also how capricious first-past-the-post (FPTP) can be (twice as many Labour as Liberal Democrat votes, a quarter as many MPs).

The failure of the Labour Party overall, however, could not reasonably be laid at the door of the electoral system. Under Jeremy Corbyn's leadership it had increased its support at the 2017 election, but in 2019 it went backwards in terms of both votes and seats. As one of the two main parties it consistently gets a higher level of representation than most European parties of the left, who operate under systems of proportional representation, but with just three victories in the last eleven general elections it is difficult to argue that it has benefited from FPTP.

Jo Swinson, leader of the Liberal Democrats, resigned immediately. She was not one of those Scottish Liberal Democrats who kept the SNP at bay and paid for that with her seat and her job. Across the UK the party had increased its share of the vote from 7.4 per cent to 11.6 per cent, but it actually went backwards in terms of MPs – from twelve to eleven. Even with targeted campaigning and appeals to tactical voting, the combination of underwhelming levels of support and the lack of a spatially concentrated core vote proved insuperable.

In the wake of the election the leader of the Brexit Party, Nigel Farage, confirmed that he intended to change his party's name to the Reform Party and campaign to change the UK's voting system. Previously leader of yet another party, the United Kingdom Independence Party (UKIP), he had good cause to want change. When leading that party in 2015 he secured the support of one in eight voters across the UK (3.88 m), achieved one MP, 120 runners-up, and the knowledge that at the same election to the same Parliament the SNP's 1.45 m votes had returned 56 MPs!

It seems that there is only a weak relationship between a party's share of the votes and seats at a UK general election, therefore. Furthermore, that relationship is far from consistent, as illustrated by the Conservative Party's experience at recent contests. In 2010 it won 36.1 per cent of the votes, which delivered it 307 seats – substantially short of the number needed for a majority over all other parties (326). Five years later, its vote share increased slightly to 36.9 per cent – and this time it achieved a majority of seats (331). At four earlier elections its vote share was close to its 2017 and 2019 totals, but its seat share varied: in 1979, 43.9 per cent of the votes delivered 339 MPs; in 1983 42.4 per cent (a decline in support) resulted in 397 Conservative MPs being elected; in 1987 it won 42.3 per cent – virtually the same again, but 21 fewer MPs (376); and then in 1992 its share in the number of seats (336) fell significantly more than its vote share (41.9 per cent).

* * *

That few parties get a similar percentage of the seats as the votes is a well-known feature of UK general elections. So is the general 'rule' that small parties are more likely to win seats in the House of Commons if they concentrate on building their support in a few constituencies. Gaining 10 (or even 20) per cent of the votes nationally is unlikely to lead to many MPs being elected to represent a party unless it wins at least 30 per cent in a few: 30 per cent is not guaranteed to win a seat, however;[2] 35 per cent is slightly better; 40 per cent is almost certain to ensure that your party provides the constituency's MP.[3] Once you have crossed that magic threshold, however, there is little point building up many more votes in those constituencies, since they will not deliver any more winning MPs. As a party becomes more popular it needs to win support more widely in a geographical sense: large majorities in some seats but losing fairly badly in the rest is a poor strategy. The parties realise this and construct their campaigning strategies accordingly, as reflected in their spending patterns and canvassing intensity preceding an election. They pay relatively little attention to seats they are sure to win, spend very little where they know they will lose, and focus much of their activity on an (increasingly small) number of marginal seats where victory or defeat is uncertain: at the 2019 general election only 67 seats were won with a margin of 5 percentage points of the votes cast or less, compared to 97 at the 2017 election.[4] Parties are much more interested in their potential supporters in some places than in others.[5]

The reason for this incommensurate translation of votes into seats that characterises UK general elections is the electoral system – technically defined as single-member plurality or more colloquially as 'first-past-the-post'; the winner in each constituency is the candidate with most votes there, irrespective of whether they constitute a majority of those cast let alone a majority of those that could be cast (i.e. if there were no abstentions). This system, of MPs being elected to represent discrete areas within the national territory, has its origins in the thirteenth century and was only marginally modified during electoral reforms linked to franchise extension in the early nineteenth century.[6] Its present format was largely in place after reforms in 1885, when single-member constituencies became the predominant feature. Since then the rules for defining constituencies have been formalised and procedures for their implementation institutionalised, but the basic features have only been tweaked – usually by a party in government wishing either to gain an advantage over its opponents or to reduce, if not remove, an advantage one or more of its opponents already has.

That system was not designed to ensure that each party – or at least each party that gains a significant share of the votes cast nationally – gains representation in the House of Commons commensurate with its vote share. The results are invariably disproportional. But how disproportional, and why? And does that disproportionality affect each party to the same extent, or is it biased, with one gaining more from a particular share of the votes than others? The answers to those questions lie in geography, in the spatial distributions of each party's support and the precise location of constituency boundaries. Again, as illustrated here, that argument is generally appreciated. It was formalised in a pioneering essay in spatial theory by two geographers, whose insights provide the foundations on which this book is based.[7]

British democracy is presented as representative, as one form of the general principle enunciated by Abraham Lincoln in his Gettysburg Address – 'government of the people, by the people, for the people'. Representation has a range of meanings, however – who is to be represented, by whom, and how are the elected held accountable by the electorate? We explore these issues in Chapter 2 as an introduction to our later exposition of the United Kingdom's means of implementing that principle.

Chapters 3 and 4 set out how the electoral system emerged and has been modified.[8] Chapter 3 covers the period from 1832 to 1918, when the system was modified four times in an ad hoc manner. Chapter 4 turns to the period since 1930 when a legal framework was established, setting out the procedures for defining parliamentary constituencies and their non-partisan implementation – procedures considerably 'tweaked' during the sixty years that followed their introduction but never substantially altered to tackle the issue of disproportional treatment of political parties.

The latest, most substantial, of those tweaks came about because of one party's concern over the system's operations at the 1997 and 2001 general elections. In 1997 the Conservatives suffered a landslide defeat by the Labour Party: they won 9,602,857 votes and 165 seats, giving a ratio of one seat gained for every 58,199 votes, whereas their principal opponent gained 418 seats with 13,516,632 votes – a ratio of one seat for every 32,336 votes. That disproportional treatment was repeated four years later: Labour won 412 seats at a ratio of one for every 26,031 votes, whereas the Conservatives' ratio for their 166 seats was 50,347. The latter party decided that something needed to be done to remove that unequal treatment and prepared legislation for when it next gained power. That happened in May 2010 and by February 2011 a new set of procedures was in place. Chapter 5 documents the passage of that legislation and its implementation in two boundary-redrawing exercises (the UK technical term is redistribution; Americans call it redistricting). The first was halted before completion following a political disagreement within the 2010–15 coalition; the second was completed and its recommendations for a new set of 600 constituencies delivered to Parliament in September 2018, but having lost its overall majority and facing significant backbench unease at the prospect of reducing the number of MPs, the government did not proceed to implementation. Instead they were rescued by the 2019 general election, the result of which delivered them the majority they needed to introduce fresh legislation to maintain 650 MPs as at present.[9] Indeed, as a consequence the 2019 general election, like the election before it, was fought in the constituencies defined using electoral data for the early 2000s.

The changes – mainly up to and including the 1944 legislation – and then the tweaks and their implementation by those given the task of defining constituency boundaries, all illustrate a basic tension within this part of the UK's electoral practice between an organic conception of representation which sees MPs as the representatives of distinct communities and an arithmetic conception which requires each MP to represent the same number of people. That tension underpins all of the changes to the system since 1944 as parties, basically those in power and able to use their parliamentary majorities to achieve their desired change, wrestle with the electoral consequences of giving one of those conceptions – organic or arithmetic – precedence over the other.

The UK's electoral system regularly produces both disproportional and biased outcomes, it seems – but how disproportional and how biased? Chapter 6 explores their measurement, illustrating the key role of geography in the unequal translation of votes into seats. But if that system is so likely to produce disproportional outcomes, favouring some parties and disadvantaging others, why has it not been replaced, with something that is more proportional, as in many European and other states?[10] Electoral reform has been discussed in the UK for almost two centuries but only rarely has it gained a prominent place on the public agenda.[11] The Liberal Democrats have long been committed to reform, believing that only a shift to a proportional system would deliver them representation in the Commons commensurate with their popular support – indeed, that support might increase if voters thought this would bring the party increased representation. It wanted to achieve that when it joined the coalition with the Conservatives in 2010 but its putative partner was adamantly against such a change; as a concession, the Conservatives agreed to hold a referendum on switching to the Alternative Vote (AV) system, which retains single-member constituencies and is unlikely to deliver a proportional outcome,[12] if the Liberal Democrats would support the proposed changes to the redistribution procedures. The AV system had been rejected by politicians in 1918, 1929 and again in 1944 but the Liberal Democrats accepted the concession as a small step towards their nirvana, despite their leader having previously described it as a 'miserable little compromise'.[13] The referendum was held in May 2011 and the proposed change was decisively rejected, by a ratio of 68:32 on a turnout of only 42 per cent.

But a wide range of other electoral systems is available; indeed, the UK has introduced a number of them for elections at the sub-national level in recent decades. Do they produce better outcomes in terms of disproportionality? We explore answers to that question in Chapter 7, looking not only at those systems deployed from 1999 to 2019 for elections to the European Parliament from the UK, but also elections to the Scottish Parliament, the Northern Ireland Assembly and the National Assembly for Wales, to the Greater London Assembly and local government elections in Scotland and Northern Ireland.

Representational democracy is at the heart of the UK's unwritten political constitution. But, as we ask in this book's title, is it truly representative? The answer depends on your definition of representative. The country's electoral system was not designed to ensure proportional representation for parties, even though by 1885 they dominated political life. Since then it has been modified in a variety of ways while retaining its basic features – unlike in some countries, such as Australia, New Zealand and South Africa, to which it was exported but has now been replaced; it remains in place in Canada and the United States, where recent elections have seen outcomes in which the winning candidate failed to obtain most votes – Donald Trump lost by some 3 million votes to Hillary Clinton in the 2016 US presidential election and in Canada's 2019 federal election the Liberal Party won 33.1 per cent of the votes and 157 seats whereas the

Conservatives, with 34.4 per cent of the votes, obtained only 121 seats. Whether it should be retained will continue to excite some desperate for change but substantial electoral reform is rare, especially in established democracies such as the UK's, and is only likely to be achieved when the 'political class' feels it has to respond to intensive political pressure.[14] What might produce such pressure in the UK is beyond the agenda set for this book, designed to provide a fuller appreciation of where we are now and how we got here. As to the future ...

2

Representation: of whom, what and where?

In a representative democracy like the UK, citizens cede control over policy decision-making power to elected representatives but retain the power to judge those representatives in periodic and regular elections, both on what they promise to do and on how effectively they are felt to have delivered. If we like what we hear, or feel our representatives are generally doing a good job, we can re-elect them when the time comes. But if we think they are taking us in the wrong direction, or are making a hash of government, we can choose, via the ballot box, to kick the rascals out. Our involvement, though limited, is consequential as our choices decide who governs on our behalf and (to some extent) what policies they adopt. Although referendums, citizen juries and so on are becoming more popular, and do allow for a degree of direct democracy, elections remain by far and away the most common and widespread means by which most citizens get involved in their government. The representative function – and the functions of our representatives – remains central.

But just what is it that is being represented, or that we expect or want our representatives to be like, and how might we best achieve a balance of representatives to fit our preferences? In practice, these questions raise some tricky issues. Moving closer to what people want from their representatives on one dimension may risk moving further away from what citizens want on some other. In this chapter we explore some of the challenges. We begin by considering a classic debate regarding the role of our elected representatives, before moving on to consider what sorts of attributes (political, moral, personal) we might want to see reflected in them, and whether those attributes really are being delivered.

Edmund Burke's old chestnut

One of the oldest questions regarding the role of elected politicians
– pre-dating extension of the franchise, the emergence of modern
political parties or concerns regarding whether MPs reflect the demographic diversity of the country – concerns how our MPs should act.
Should they be our delegates, acting as our messengers to Parliament
and doing exactly and minutely what we instruct them to do? Or
should they act as our representatives, being aware of our demands,
but exercising their independent judgment to act in what they see as
our best interests, even if that runs counter to our own preferences?
These were questions that faced a number of MPs at the 2017 and
2019 general elections; they personally favoured Remain but a majority of their constituents voted for Leave at the 2016 referendum on the
UK's membership of the EU.

In his 1774 election address to the voters of Bristol, the eighteenth-
century Irish politician and thinker Edmund Burke eloquently con-
trasted these opposing views of how the relationship between MPs
and voters should be conducted. While recognising the importance
of MPs knowing and taking seriously their constituents' preferences
and wishes, Burke famously argued that MPs should be independent-
minded representatives, not simple delegates:

> Certainly, gentlemen, it ought to be the happiness and glory of a
> representative to live in the strictest union, the closest correspond-
> ence, and the most unreserved communication with his constituents.
> Their wishes ought to have great weight with him; their opinion, high
> respect; their business, unremitted attention. It is his duty to sacrifice
> his repose, his pleasures, his satisfactions, to theirs; and above all,
> ever, and in all cases, to prefer their interest to his own. But his
> unbiased opinion, his mature judgment, his enlightened conscience,
> he ought not to sacrifice to you, to any man, or to any set of men
> living ... Your representative owes you, not his industry only, but his
> judgment; and he betrays, instead of serving you, if he sacrifices it to
> your opinion.
> ...
> Parliament is not a *congress* of ambassadors from different and hostile
> interests; which interests each must maintain, as an agent and advo-
> cate, against other agents and advocates; but parliament is a *deliberative*
> assembly of *one* nation, with *one* interest, that of the whole; where, not
> local purposes, not local prejudices, ought to guide, but the general
> good, resulting from the general reason of the whole. You choose a

member indeed; but when you have chosen him, he is not member of Bristol, but he is a member of *parliament*.[1]

For Burke, MPs were (or at least should be) in a better position to decide than were voters, as they were closer to the point of decision, had greater access to the evidence and arguments, and had greater experience and expertise in difficult affairs of state. True to his vision of the MP's role, Burke took positions on a number of issues (for instance, on policy towards the American colonies and, later, the United States, the abolition of slavery, trade and tolerance for Catholics) which ran counter to the interests and wishes of his Bristol constituents. By the 1780 election, it was becoming clear that they were unlikely to return him to Parliament (presumably they were unhappy that their MP had not proved more of a delegate), and he stood down as their MP.

In practice, his preference for independent-minded MPs has always been something of an ideal, often invoked, but also often flouted. In his own day, many MPs were elected (or returned unopposed) from pocket and rotten boroughs, their services and votes in effect bought by powerful landowners who 'owned' the constituency and directed its voters.[2] And with the emergence of modern political parties in Britain from the mid-nineteenth century onwards, MPs were increasingly answerable to their parties and party manifestos, and were routinely 'whipped' in Commons votes, supporting the measures approved by their parties rather than exercising their personal judgments. The picture is complicated, however. MPs elected on party tickets tend, not surprisingly, to agree on most issues with other members of their party. On many occasions, therefore, whipped votes produce results which are broadly similar to the likely outcome had MPs all been ideal Burkean representatives, following their own consciences and judgments.

That said, Burke's view has proved resilient. Writing in the mid-twentieth century, Joseph Schumpeter offered a recognisably Burkean analysis, arguing that ordinary citizens should have only a limited role in the democratic government of their countries.[3] They should, he argued, be able to choose their leaders via regular elections, where they could express support for particular programmes, and make judgments on the performance of politicians while in office. But, he went on, once elected, the government should be able to rule untrammelled by popular demands until the next election (so acting as representatives and not delegates), when voters would once again have the opportunity to express their continued support for, or opposition to, the government's programme. Nor is this a debate which is limited to the realms of political theory. It regularly resurfaces in the world of modern democratic politics. In many modern states, including the UK, public trust in politicians, never especially high, is falling.[4] Just after the UK's 2017 general election, for instance, the British Election Study found that only 24 per cent of British voters agreed that 'most politicians are trustworthy', 51 per cent felt that 'politicians don't care what people like me think', and an almost identical percentage agreed that 'politicians ignore the issues that are important to me': only around a quarter disagreed with these statements.[5] There is not much sign of voters feeling that their MPs are their parliamentary delegates, even though they would in some respects like their MPs to be closer to the delegate model.

But do voters really mean it when they say they would prefer their MPs to do their bidding? There are signs that a significant minority of voters do not. In 2002, John Hibbing and Elizabeth Thiess-Morse asked American voters what they really wanted from their relationships with their elected representatives.[6] A significant minority, who they dubbed the 'stealth democrats', did not welcome the prospect of being closely involved in politics and being regularly consulted by their representatives. Just as we would not expect to be asked by our plumber how best to fix our central heating, so stealth democrats did not want government to continually ask for their views. But if things went wrong, they wanted to retain the ability to vote the government out. Such views are not limited to the United States. For instance, about 39 per cent of British voters in 2011 scored high on stealth democracy.[7]

What is more, many voters recognise that their MPs have to balance the competing claims of being a delegate and a representative. While 47 per cent of British voters in 2010 thought 'represent(ing) the views of local people in the House of Commons' was one of the most important tasks for MPs, 41 per cent thought that 'representing the UK's national interests' was an important task too: these preferences were not mutually exclusive.[8] There is no clear dividing line between representing local preferences and representing the national interest: it is complicated – especially since most constituencies are divided on many, if not most, issues.

One further illustration of the voters' wish for their MPs to strike a balance between being representatives and delegates can be found in an ingenious experiment carried out by Nick Vivyan and Markus Wagner.[9] They presented British voters with a series of profiles of hypothetical MPs. Participants were asked to compare pairs of MPs. Each pair was carefully described to contrast each politician on a number of dimensions – their roles as representatives (for instance, whether they focused on national policy issues or on constituency work), their gender, their party, how rebellious they were in the Commons and how long they had served as MPs. The results were clear – but, in the terms of the debate sparked by Burke, oddly inconclusive. Not surprisingly, other things being equal, voters preferred MPs representing the party they supported to MPs from other parties (a point we return to). MPs' gender made no real difference, and their relative experience only a small difference (there was a very slight preference for longer-serving MPs). But voters expressed strong preferences for independent-minded MPs who were willing to disagree with their party leaderships (a win for the Burkean representative). They also preferred MPs who followed the wishes of their constituents (a blow in favour of a delegate model). And they wanted MPs who worked hard on constituency issues – but who also worked hard on national policy issues.

Elected politicians feel the rival 'pulls' of their roles as delegates and representatives too, as illustrated by the debate over how to implement the 2016 referendum decision for Britain to leave the EU (Brexit). By early 2019, with the initial deadline for Brexit fast approaching, MPs were split on whether they supported or opposed Brexit in general, or the particular Brexit deal negotiated with the EU by Prime Minister Theresa May – and these splits occurred both between parties and within them. Significant minorities of both Labour and Conservative MPs rebelled against their party's official position at various points during the Brexit debates. For some MPs, their position on Brexit – and how they voted in the Commons – was driven by political and ideological beliefs – for or against EU membership: to that extent, they acted as Burkean 'representatives'. In some cases, this was to the detriment of their parliamentary careers. Labour MP Paul Farrelly, for instance, was a convinced supporter of remaining in the EU and voted accordingly in the Commons, even though the Leave vote in his Newcastle under Lyme constituency was 62 per cent. In September 2019, he announced that he would not stand at the next election, a decision some of his constituents interpreted as 'jumping before he was pushed'![10]

But others justified their decisions (both for and against Brexit) on other grounds, often referring to their responsibility to represent the views of their constituents – the delegate view. For instance, justifying her decision to rebel against the Labour whip and to vote in favour of Mrs May's deal in February 2019, Caroline Flint MP pointed out that, as the MP for Don Valley, where 68 per cent voted for Brexit in 2016, she was duty-bound to deliver on what a majority of her constituents wanted.[11] Another Labour MP, Paul Sweeney backed a second referendum on Brexit, partly on the grounds that 67 per cent in his Glasgow North East constituency had voted to remain in the EU.[12] They were not alone.

None of this is to say that 'representative' orientations are 'better' than 'delegate' orientations (or vice versa). Nor is it to argue that the two are polar opposites. There will be times, for instance, when an MP might act in a way that is consonant both with the wishes of most of their constituents and with the MP's vision of what best serves the national interest, bringing the two roles into alignment. And even the most diligent constituency MPs will often not really know what the balance of opinion is among their constituents on a particular issue. Many decisions made in government are unlikely to have created so much as a ripple in public debate: voters are unlikely to have any view at all on such issues. Other issues may be more widely discussed by the public at large. But even then, it is not clear how most MPs could gauge the mood in a modern constituency (the average seat at the 2019 UK general election was home to over 73,100 voters, and reliable opinion polls at the constituency scale are very rare). MPs could rely on the messages sent them by constituents, or on what they hear in their surgeries, or on their conversations with their friends, contacts and party members in their seat – but all these sources are liable to be biased in unpredictable ways. Being a delegate is hard, not least as there is no easy way of receiving messages from voters on what they want one to do.

In practice, of course, there is another heuristic in modern politics which both voters and MPs use to guide them in what is being represented: party affiliation. What issues does that raise?

It's my party ...

Although Burke's address to his Bristol voters has been widely cited down the years, in many ways it is an echo from a lost political world. Modern politics is very different in many ways. Two changes are of particular importance here. First, the electorate has expanded massively, both in number and in coverage (as discussed in the following chapters). In Burke's time, very few people were enfranchised. On the eve of the 1832 Great Reform Act, only around 5 per cent of UK adults were entitled to vote. In many seats, an MP stood a good chance of at least meeting most of his electors, and so had the option of asking them directly for their views. Now, most adult UK citizens can vote; MPs represent large numbers of people in their constituencies and have no easy way of assessing the 'public mood' there.

Second, in contrast to Burke's day, modern MPs' potential for true independence is heavily constrained by their membership of political parties. Burke and his fellow eighteenth-century MPs did not encounter political parties in the modern sense. There were factions and groupings in Parliament, but MPs' allegiances were often fluid. And there were no party organisations in the country as a whole. Of course, in reality, there were constraints (for instance, the possibility of gaining patronage could tie MPs to one faction or another in the Commons). But in principle, each MP could decide for himself how to vote, and where to strike the balance between being a delegate and being a representative.

But in the wake of the political reforms which began with the 1832 Great Reform Act, recognisably modern political parties began to emerge, both to campaign for support from the expanding electorate, and to coordinate MPs' activities in Parliament.[13] Parties have evolved down the years, from elite-dominated organisations to mass-membership parties in the early and mid-twentieth century (drawing to a large degree on the support of particular economic classes) and then, with the decline of class voting in the later twentieth century, to catch-all parties, once again dominated by their leaderships, but appealing explicitly to the 'median voter'.[14] The development of a party system has altered MPs' relationships with their constituents in important ways, blurring Burke's distinction between delegates and representatives. Most politicians (and almost all MPs) now stand for election as part of an established party, campaigning on the party's manifesto, and (if elected) voting in Parliament in line with the party's command. As a consequence, modern MPs are not straightforward Burkean independent-minded representatives. On most issues, they follow the party line (except on so-called free votes, or – more rarely – when MPs rebel and vote against their party on an issue).[15] .

One consequence of parties (and their candidates) campaigning on the basis of published manifestos is that winning an election is taken as conferring a mandate for the party's manifesto. So does that therefore make party-based MPs Burkean delegates, following the wishes of their voters as expressed through the latters' endorsement of the party programme? In a sense, perhaps. But ultimately this won't do either. Voters have little or no say in the content of a manifesto, which is put together by groups within the party (often, but not always, close to the party leadership). Nor is it likely that all voters for a party will accept or support every measure in the party's manifesto (for instance, many Labour voters in 2005 supported much of the party's domestic agenda, but were deeply opposed to its position on conflict in the Middle East). Yet, with only one vote to cast, a voter for a party cannot pick and choose which aspects of its manifesto to endorse and which to reject: their vote is taken as endorsement for all it contains, whether liked or not. What is more, there is ample evidence that voters may decide what they think on an issue based on whether the party they identify with supports or opposes it: if my party backs a policy, then that policy is probably all right; if my party opposes it, the policy is probably mistaken.

Indeed, this party heuristic can extend even to non-political issues, as shown by a clever – and disturbing – experiment.[16] Survey respondents were shown a picture of a cat which lived at number 10 Downing Street, and were randomly assigned to one of two groups: the first group was told the cat belonged to Conservative Prime Minister Mrs Thatcher; the second was told it was Labour PM Tony Blair's cat. They were then asked how much they approved of the cat – and, amazingly, their reactions split along party lines. Conservative supporters thought more highly of the cat if told it was Mrs Thatcher's than if told it was Mr Blair's. Labour supporters broke the other way, thinking better of the cat if it was Blair's and worse of it if it were Thatcher's. In other words, it would be naive to think that voters' policy preferences are revealed by their votes. Often, it is quite the other way around, and their votes determine their preferences – a real problem for the 'delegate' model! Voters' instructions via the ballot box are imperfect, unclear – and largely involve choosing between predetermined options into which they themselves have had little input. For all the rhetoric of the electoral mandate as a form of delegated authority, this is a rather imperfect form of delegation, to say the least.

Not only that, but (as no manifesto writer has complete insight into the future, and as the unexpected happens, and has to be dealt with) much government business inevitably covers issues and policies which could not possibly have been put to the voters before the event. No major party, at the time of the 2005 UK general election, foresaw the 2008 financial crash. All assumed the continuation of economic growth. No major party had put a plan before the electorate for how to respond to the economic crisis. But when the crisis came, a response was urgently required. The parties (and their MPs) had to act without a direct delegate mandate from their voters.

What is more, individual MPs, at different points in their career, can play different roles.[17] Some backbench MPs may specialise in dealing with their constituents' concerns and worries. Others may focus on the scrutiny of legislation and of policy. And others, particularly those who take on front bench ministerial responsibilities for their party, may focus on policy development and implementation. Typically, MPs take on several of these roles at once – sometimes as a delegate, sometimes a representative, sometimes following a mandate from their constituents, sometimes following a mandate from their party.

For voters, however, much of this is beside the point. The most salient attributes of individual candidates standing for election to Parliament are their party, and (something we will return to) their work (whether actual for incumbent candidates or in prospect for challengers) for their constituency. Party serves as an efficient heuristic for voters, indicating what each candidate stands for on the major issues of the day.[18] Hence a primary function of modern electoral systems is to translate voters' party preferences into seats in Parliament: the number of MPs sitting for each party should bear some sort of resemblance to the balance of political opinion in the country as a whole.

Quite how precise that resemblance should be is moot. As we discuss in Chapter 7, much will depend on the electoral system. Where proportional representation systems are employed, the percentage of MPs elected for each party will closely match the party's vote share in the country (though it will rarely do so precisely: the exact rules used to convert votes into seats will have some bearing, as will the existence and size of minimum vote thresholds which parties may need to exceed in order to return MPs).

In FPTP elections to Westminster, however, the match is much more approximate. After an election, the rank order of the numbers of MPs elected for each major party normally reflects the rank order of the parties' votes in the country as a whole. The party with the largest vote share usually comes out of the election with the largest number of MPs and the second most popular party usually has the second largest number of MPs (though this does not always happen – in both the 1951 and February 1974 UK general elections, for instance, the two most popular parties came very close to each other on vote share, but the less popular of the two gained more MPs than the more popular).

But the exact match of votes to seats under FPTP rules can be very approximate, as we discuss in Chapter 6. FPTP tends to exaggerate the most popular party's parliamentary representation. Since 1945, no party has won a true majority of the vote (i.e. over 50 per cent) in any UK general election. But in the vast majority of elections, one party has gained a majority of MPs, and has been able to form a government on its own (only the February 1974, 2010 and 2017 elections did not produce an outright parliamentary majority). What is more, there is no simple relationship between vote and seat shares under FPTP. Parties can win much the same vote share in successive elections, yet their numbers of MPs can fluctuate quite substantially. For instance, at each election from 1979 to 1992, the Conservatives' vote share never fell outside a narrow range, from 41.9 per cent (in 1992) to 43.9 per cent (in 1979). But over the same period, the number of Conservative MPs elected varied between 336 (1992) and 397 (1983), as did the party's Commons majority (just 21 in 1992, it had been as high as 144 in 1983). A party can even substantially increase its vote share, only to see its share of seats fall. Just such a fate befell the Conservative Party in 2017. At the previous general election, it won 36.1 per cent of the votes and was rewarded with 330 MPs, an overall majority of 12. Just two years later, its vote share went up substantially, to 42.4 per cent, the largest percentage point increase in the Conservative vote since 1979, and the party's best vote share since 1983. But it won only 317 MPs (down 13 from the previous election) and lost its parliamentary majority in the process.

FPTP is even more erratic in translating smaller parties' vote shares into seats. Notoriously, at the 1983 general election the Liberal-SDP

Alliance took 25.4 per cent of the vote, just short of Labour's 27.6 per cent. But while the latter party returned 209 MPs, the Alliance had just 23. The Liberal Democrats (the Alliance's successor) gained their largest crop of MPs (62) in 2005. But this was less than 10 per cent of all MPs elected, even though the party won 22 per cent of the vote. And at the 2015, 2017 and 2019 elections, the SNP had the third-largest contingent of MPs in the Commons (56, 35 and 48 respectively), substantially more than the Liberal Democrats' 8, 12 and 11. Yet, in terms of UK-wide vote share, the Liberal Democrats outperformed the SNP in these contests (in 2015, they won 7.9 per cent of the vote to the SNP's 4.7 per cent; in 2017, the shares were 7.4 per cent and 3.0 per cent; and in 2019 they were 11.6 and 3.9). If one (important) yardstick of representation is how well the distribution of parties in Parliament reflects support for those parties in the country as a whole, therefore, we would have to conclude that FPTP elections to the UK's House of Commons perform badly. True, the most popular party tends to form the government. But the match of MPs to votes is neither consistent nor proportional.

Even so, although it could by no means be said that the British public is happy with its politicians (quite the contrary), there is little sign that voters see their governments as illegitimate or lacking in a clear mandate, despite the repeated failure of successive governments to win a majority of the votes. How happy voters are with a government tends to be in large part a function of whether they support the party (or parties) in power: those supporting the government party tend to think better of the government than those who oppose it. And this extends to their feelings on the state of democracy in the UK. Immediately after the 2017 general election 55 per cent of voters said they were satisfied or very satisfied with the way democracy worked in the UK.[19] This rose to 70 per cent among those who supported the Conservative government, but only 46 per cent of those who had voted for other parties in the election agreed. Even so, few voters expressed serious dissatisfaction with the state of democracy: only 13 per cent overall were very dissatisfied (as were 6 per cent of Conservative voters, and 17 per cent of those voting for other parties). This hardly suggests that voters see the party make-up of the House of Commons as unrepresentative.

To understand why British voters accept election results which only imperfectly match their party preferences, it is useful to look at the political philosopher Raymond Plant's distinction between two competing purposes of electoral systems.[20] They could be designed to achieve what he termed 'microscopic' representation, such that the elected assembly would contain a microcosm of the country as a whole, with all major political views (and all major groups – a subject we return to in Chapter 3)[21] represented in roughly the same proportions as in the population as a whole. Or they could be designed with Schumpeterian representation in mind – an assembly designed to create governments with clear legislative mandates and the capacity to carry their legislation (with elections as periodic devices to comment on how well the government is performing and, if need be, to replace it). The problem, Plant argued, was that these two models of representation could not readily be delivered simultaneously. Maximising microscopic representation would make it harder to achieve the one-party majority governments needed to maximise Schumpeterian representation, and vice versa. Decisions on which electoral system to adopt would depend on which model of representation was most desired: PR systems favoured 'microscopic' outcomes, while plurality and majoritarian systems (such as FPTP) favoured the Schumpeterian.

A clear majority of British voters favour Schumpeterian outcomes from their elections (or at least are not sufficiently exercised about FPTP to want change). Immediately after the 2017 election, the British Election Study asked voters whether the voting system for Westminster elections should be changed 'to allow smaller parties to get a fairer share of MPs' (a microscopic outcome), or should remain unchanged 'to produce effective government' (a Schumpeterian outcome): 61 per cent favoured the latter option.[22] Nor is there much public pressure for electoral reform in parliamentary elections. The 2011 Referendum on switching from FPTP to the Alternative Vote – albeit the latter is by no means a PR system – resulted in a substantial majority for maintaining the status quo (68 per cent of voters rejected the change). While people do want election results that reflect the public's party political preferences, they do not demand a precise mapping. Rather, in so far as people have thought this through at all, most seem to prefer a system that broadly approximates the state of public opinion while maximising the chance of the most popular party being able to form a majority government.

To see ourselves ...

Achieving broad representation in terms of the party make-up of the Commons is clearly very important. But that is not the only criterion by which our politicians' representativeness might be judged. Many argue that MPs, as well as being politically representative of the population, should be descriptively representative of it too.[23] When citizens look at their MPs, do they see people who not only understand their problems and concerns and represent their political preferences, but who also reflect the social and demographic balance of the country, in terms of important dimensions such as gender, ethnicity and social class? And does that concern voters, and does it matter?

Judged in terms of the social and demographic composition of the House of Commons, British MPs are not representative of the country as a whole.[24] Britain is a diverse society, yet our MPs do not reflect that diversity. MPs are disproportionately white, middle class, middle-aged, university-educated and male (Table 2.1). Many voters look at our MPs and do not see many people who look or sound like them, or who are likely to have any first-hand experience of the sorts of lives they lead.

This is problematic. It helps feed narratives of our politicians as out of touch, unconcerned or uninformed about the issues that face many people, and ultimately as a self-serving, self-satisfied elite. Such views are not entirely fair. There is no necessary reason why the interests of people from particular sections of society can only be understood or represented adequately by MPs drawn from the same groups. Nor is it inevitably the case that MPs drawn from those groups should or will be able to represent 'their' group's demands (or will even want to do so). Even so, there is a larger issue at stake here, which is the extent to which our politics is seen as inclusive or exclusive. For many voters, Parliament still looks very exclusive indeed, and not a place where people they might identify with are particularly welcome.

In some areas, of course, things have improved markedly (though they still have a long way to go). For instance, although women MPs were first elected to the Commons in 1918 (when Constance Markievicz was elected for Sinn Féin – though she did not take her seat), they made up under 5 per cent of MPs until the late 1980s. But since then, the proportion of women MPs in the Commons has risen substantially (reaching 31 per cent in 2017 and 34 per cent two years later – although whereas women formed a majority of Labour and

Table 2.1 The social make-up of the UK's MPs, 2017[A]

Gender	MPs		The public
	N	per cent	per cent
Male	447	68.8	49.4
Female	203	31.2	50.6
Age			
18–24	2	0.3	11.6
25–34	44	6.8	17.4
35–44	129	19.9	16.5
45–54	213	32.9	18.1
55–64	187	28.9	14.7
65+	72	11.1	21.8
Average age (years)	51		39
Education			
University graduates	533	82.0	42.0
Oxbridge-educated	156	24.0	1.0
Previous occupation[B]			
Professions (law, education/doctors/ architects etc.)	116	18.6	
Politics (councillors, party officials, Special Advisors, journalists, etc.)	246	39.4	
Business	155	24.8	
Other non-manual	101	16.2	
Manual	7	1.1	47.0
Ethnicity			
White	598	92.0	86.4
Black, Asian and minority ethnic	52	8.0	13.6

[A] *Sources:* R. Campbell and J. Hudson, 'Political recruitment under pressure: MPs and candidates', in P. Cowley and D. Kavanagh, *The British General Election of 2017*, Basingstoke: Macmillan, 2018; L. Audickas and V. Apostolova, *Ethnic Minorities in Politics and Public Life* (2017) House of Commons Library Briefing Paper No. SN01156.
[B] Based only on Conservative, Labour, Liberal Democrat and SNP MPs

Liberal Democrat MPs after the 2019 election they were only one-quarter of the Conservatives' total), as has the proportion of women standing for election for the major parties.[25] Similarly, the proportion of MPs from Black, Asian and minority ethnic (BAME) backgrounds has grown over time. As recently as 1987, only 4 MPs came from BAME communities. By 2017, this had grown to 52, around 8 per cent of the Commons. Of course, the proportions of female and BAME MPs still fall well short of the equivalent proportions in the population as a whole. But the direction of travel is towards more equal representation on these dimensions. In other areas, too, modern MPs look more like the population as a whole. There are more 'out' LGBT MPs now than ever before, for instance (though this does not necessarily mean the proportion has risen: in the past anti-gay prejudice and – before 1967 – legal discrimination meant many gay politicians previously kept their sexuality secret).

But while progress has been made in some areas, it has not in others. To take one example, manual workers have always been under-represented in Parliament, and things have if anything become worse in recent years. MPs were first paid salaries in 1911, partly to make it easier for people who did not have substantial private means to sit in Parliament. The Labour Party was created originally to rep-resent manual workers, and for much of the twentieth century many (though by no means all) of its MPs were drawn from working-class occupations (many having emerged through the trade union move-ment). Yet the proportion of MPs coming from manual working-class occupations (never high) has declined steeply from c.16 per cent in 1979 to just 1 per cent in 2017.[26]

Modern MPs are overwhelmingly university-educated. Whereas in 1979, around 63 per cent of MPs were graduates, this had risen to over 80 per cent by 2017 – both far higher than the equivalent propor-tions in the population as a whole. True, the rise in the proportion of graduates in Parliament over that period has not been as steep as the equivalent increase in the electorate. Yet in part this is a function of a 'ceiling effect': as the proportion of graduates in Parliament gets ever closer to 100 per cent, there is a structural limit on how much faster it can rise. Among recent prime ministers, neither Jim Callaghan (Labour, 1976–79) nor John Major (Conservative, 1990–97) had attended university. But as we move closer to almost all MPs holding a degree, the probability of another non-graduate entering Number 10, while still possible (among recent potential contenders for the job, Jeremy Corbyn, elected Labour leader in 2015, did not complete his degree and Angela Rayner, a senior member of his Shadow Cabinet, left education at 16) is declining.

Most striking of all is the rise in the proportion of MPs who have spent almost their entire adult lives in professional politics. By 2017,

Table 2.2 Voters' perceptions of the social backgrounds of MPs, May 2018

	Roughly what proportion of MPs in Westminster do you think are in the following groups? Average per cent	From which of the following groups, if any, would you most like to see more MPs in Parliament be drawn? Per cent
People from the area they represent	33.1	56.4
Working class people	23.5	43.7
Women	34.0	12.8
People with disabilities	12.6	9.3
Young people under 30	18.5	10.4
Ethnic minorities	22.9	6.0
Christians	49.0	6.0
LGBT people	17.7	5.1
Muslims	18.7	1.4
People with degrees	68.2	5.1
None of these	–	10.0
N (average)	5725	6526

Source: British Election Study Internet Panel Survey, Wave 14, May 2018.

almost 40 per cent of MPs had, prior to entering Parliament, worked in various politics-related jobs – as party officials, councillors, special advisers (SpAds) and so on. Unsurprisingly, many voters worry that their MPs exist in something of a political 'bubble', isolated from real world experiences and concerns.

Some sense of how voters feel about the social make-up of the Commons can be drawn from the May 2018 wave of the British Election Study (BES) Panel. Respondents were asked what percentage of MPs they thought came from particular groups. They were also asked which of those groups they would like to see more MPs drawn from (they were allowed to select up to two groups). Their answers are instructive (Table 2.2). While we should be cautious about putting too much trust in voters' estimates of the percentages of MPs in different groups (who among us, if we are honest, could answer most of these questions accurately?), it is noticeable that voters over-estimate the representation of some groups and underestimate the representation of others. Most notable among the groups over-estimated by the public are working class, BAME and Muslim MPs. On average, BES respondents thought about a quarter of MPs were working class (only 1 per cent of MPs are from manual occupations), 23 per cent were from BAME backgrounds (8 per cent in reality), and 19 per cent were Muslim (in fact, only 15 MPs, just 2 per cent of the total, are). But while voters thought a substantial majority of their MPs (68 per cent on average) were graduates, this underestimates the actual proportion after the 2017 election. Intriguingly, on average, voters got the proportion of female MPs in the 2017 Parliament about right, estimating that 34 per cent of MPs were women (though whether this had more to do with real knowledge than with lucky guessing is uncertain).

More telling, perhaps, are the percentages saying they want more MPs from particular groups. Very few people said they wanted more Christian or ethnic minority MPs (only around 6 per cent plumped for these groups), or more MPs drawn from either the LGBT community or from university graduates (only about 5 per cent wanted more MPs from these groups). And hardly any (only about 1 per cent) wanted to see more Muslim MPs – perhaps not unconnected to the substantial over-estimate of the number of Muslim MPs actually sitting in the Commons. Around 10 per cent each said there should be more women MPs (12 per cent), more young MPs (chosen by 10 per cent) and more disabled MPs (9 per cent).

But substantially more respondents say that more MPs should be elected from the remaining two groups. Voters may over-estimate substantially the proportion of working-class MPs currently siting in the Commons. But a strikingly large proportion, 44 per cent, of voters say they want more MPs from working-class backgrounds. And the same share say that they want more MPs to come from the areas they represent than is currently the case.

This fits well with experimental research which asks voters to choose between candidates with carefully manipulated and contrasting profiles, to test which dimensions of difference really matter to voters. We discussed Nick Vivyan and Markus Wagner's experiment earlier. In a similar study, Rosie Campbell and Philip Cowley presented survey respondents with descriptions of pairs of hypothetical candidates in which they manipulated the candidates' gender, age, religion, education, occupation and place of residence (they deliberately gave no information on candidates' party allegiances), and then asked respondents which candidate they though was the most approachable, experienced or effective, and which they would prefer as their MP.[27] Like Vivyan and Wagner (and in line with the BES results), they found that, other things being equal, candidates' gender, education, age and religion generally made only modest differences to what voters thought of each candidate. Female candidates were seen as being more approachable (but less experienced) than male candidates. Younger candidates were seen as less experienced than older ones. Interestingly, candidates who supposedly left education aged 18 were generally rated more highly than were candidates who had gone to university (though when voters were told a candidate had left school at 16, the minimum school leaving age in the UK, they rated the candidate less well than they rated one who left at 18 – though still better than a candidate with a PhD).

But (and again in line with the BES results), candidates' previous occupations made a difference to how they were seen. Voters warmed more to candidates they were told had been medical doctors than to candidates who had been solicitors. And candidates who came from 'political' occupations were given much stronger ratings for 'experience' than were solicitors – although they did not enjoy as large relative advantages on other dimensions.

At the heart of both Burke's account of British MPs' roles, and Britain's electoral system, however, is another dimension of representation which is not simply a function of either party preferences or of individual descriptive representation. That dimension is the representation of particular places: MPs, after all, are elected to represent 'their' constituency, a geographically defined territory, in Parliament. We explore the implications of this in the next section.

'All politics is local …'

Tip O'Neill, the long-serving Democrat Speaker of the United States House of Representatives, once famously said that 'all politics is local'. In a very practical sense, his claim describes an important truth about parliamentary representation in the UK. The only way to enter the House of Commons as an MP is to be elected to represent a particular place, a parliamentary constituency. And that carries with it a much deeper story about the importance of representing local communities in Parliament.

The notion that constituencies (and hence the MPs elected from them) represent distinct local communities has deep roots in the British electoral system. Reflecting this remains an important aim when drawing up constituency boundaries, though – as set out later in this book – one consequence of political reform from the nineteenth century onwards has been to introduce another goal into the process: achieving greater equality of electorates between constituencies. This presents the UK's independent Boundary Commissions charged with drawing up parliamentary constituencies with a balancing act between the 'organic' representation of communities and the 'arithmetic' representation of more-or-less equally sized groups of people. In Burke's day, the 'organic' principle dominated, and constituency electorates varied very substantially. In the modern era, legislation has placed much more emphasis on achieving a balance between the organic and the arithmetic. And, since 2011, the 'arithmetic' principle has had clear priority: any redistribution conducted under the new rules must ensure that all bar a specified handful of new constituencies will have electorates that are within ±5 per cent of the national average, or quota – although to date no new constituencies have been implemented on that basis. That said, the organic principle remains as an important criterion: once equal electorates have been achieved, the Commissions are enjoined to ensure, as far as they can, that constituencies still represent identifiable local communities (though this does undoubtedly raise substantial difficulties in practice).

The 'organic' principle matters to many voters. When parliamentary constituencies are periodically redrawn in the UK, a public consultation process allows citizens to comment on the Boundary Commissions' proposals, which may be altered in the light of that consultation. Most members of the public tend to be largely unaware when a boundary review is taking place, and relatively few engage in the consultation. But some constituency proposals do excite especially strong public comment, almost always when some local community is felt to be adversely affected by proposed changes. Indeed, most objections to the Commissions' proposals revolve around concerns over community representation. Perhaps a proposed boundary is thought to split an established community between two or more seats. Or a proposal might be claimed to lump two very different communities, with very different perceived interests, into the same seat. Community-based objections stretch even to the proposed names of new constituencies. In recent redistricting exercises, this has proved a very contentious topic. The symbolism of having one's community name-checked in the title given to one's constituency seems to matter to some people. And changing a proposed constituency name to accommodate such concerns is very easy for the Boundary Commissions to do: certainly easier than redrawing actual boundaries again, which can create substantial unintended knock-on consequences for other seats. Indeed, some British parliamentary constituency names are now long, to reflect the communities they contain, as with two current Scottish constituencies – East Kilbride, Strathaven and Lesmahagow; and Inverness, Nairn, Badenoch and Strathspey!

Not only do many voters value having their local community represented in Parliament, but many would prefer it to be represented by an MP with personal ties to the local area. Compared to an MP with no personal connections to the constituency, a local person might be expected to have both a better understanding of local problems and concerns and a stronger commitment to raising those issues in Parliament and fighting for their resolution.

In practice, while many MPs can claim local ties to their constituency, many others cannot. Three famous MPs make the point. Aneurin Bevan, one of the giants of the Labour left in the mid-twentieth century, was in some respects the epitome of an MP with strong local ties to his seat. Born in Tredegar, on the edge of the South Wales coalfield, he represented his local constituency, Ebbw Vale, from 1929 until his death in 1960. His successor as Labour MP for Ebbw Vale was Michael Foot (another prominent figure on the party's left). But he was neither a local nor even Welsh: he was born in Plymouth. On the other side of the aisle, Winston Churchill was born in his family's Oxfordshire ancestral home, Blenheim Palace, and from 1922 until his death his main home was at Chartwell in Kent. Over his long and remarkable parliamentary career, he represented a wide range of seats, scattered across the country: Oldham (1900–6); Manchester North West (1906–8); Dundee (1908–22); Epping (1924–45); and Woodford (1945–64). Beyond being for a time its MP, he had no local ties to any of these seats. The same contrasts recur again and again. Whether having local ties really makes people better MPs is a moot point. Many 'local' MPs are excellent, but many languish for years on the backbenches and make little if any impact, either in Parliament or in their constituency. And the same goes for 'incomer' MPs: some are assiduous constituency MPs, some less so; some rise to the top in politics (and in doing so may shed reflected glory on their seat) while others remain obscure.

Whatever the rights and wrongs of the matter, however, it is clear that (*pace* O'Neill) many British voters feel that not enough politics is local, at least when it comes to their MPs. It is striking just how consistently (other things being equal) voters express a strong preference for potential representatives who are local to the area they seek to represent over candidates who come from further away.[28] Almost 60 per cent of the 2018 BES respondents wanted to see more MPs who represented their home area. And this finding also comes through strongly in experimental studies like those conducted by Vivyan and Wagner and by Campbell and Cowley, where other factors and candidate attributes are held constant. What is more, this relative preference for more local candidates survived even when experiment participants were told about the party allegiance of each candidate (though it was not as strong as when no party cues were given).[29]

A preference for 'local' candidates is not universal, however. Analysis of British voters' preferences at the 2015 general election shows that some voters value representatives with local ties more than do others.[30] Not surprisingly, the stronger an individual's sense of local identity, the more likely they are to prefer a local candidate over an outsider. In parts of the country where nationalist parties stand for election – for instance, the Scottish National Party in Scotland – this effect can be over-ridden as those with strong regional/national identities have an alternative political outlet through which to express it. But other factors also influenced the preference for a truly local MP. Other things being equal, women were on average more likely to prefer candidates from the local area than were men. And the greater an individual's interest in the election, the higher their preference (on average) for being represented by a local person. But increasing levels of formal educational attainment are associated with weakening preferences for local MPs.

Even so, many voters, it seems, do want MPs who are 'like them'. But, in an electoral system which very much values the representation of places and of local communities, when push comes to shove, it seems 'an MP like me' means, for many voters, 'an MP who comes from my area'. Nor is this just a hypothetical preference: having local roots can pay real dividends for candidates standing for election. Other things being equal, voters are more likely to support a candidate who lives close to them than a candidate who lives further away. This is not just a linear function of increasing distance. Where the candidate lives matters too: voters prefer candidates who live in their constituency or in an immediately neighbouring seat to one who lives in a constituency that is not contiguous with their own.[31] And there is evidence that local candidates' relative electoral advantage comes about in part because voters tend to use information on evidence of local ties as a 'short cut' way of evaluating how well they might represent local interests. As voters gain more information on just how well candidates really do on local issues, the advantage a candidate might get from being a local diminishes. But it does not entirely disappear.[32] Other things being equal, being local really does help.

It is not too surprising, then, that candidates often make much of their local ties, or of their work in and for the constituency. There is some evidence that a growing number of MPs have local connections with their constituency. In 1979 only around a quarter of MPs had 'direct local connections' with their seat, but by 2010 around 46 per cent did so. Almost 40 per cent of newly elected Conservative MPs in 2010 had some direct connection with their constituency, as did three-quarters of newly elected Labour MPs, and 70 per cent of the new Liberal Democrat intake.[33]

Of course, MPs don't have to hail from within the exact boundaries of their seat to have a reasonable claim to be a local candidate. Coming from the same general area is also a credible basis for such a claim. Over recent UK elections, the proportion of MPs representing seats in the region in which they were born has risen, from 44 per cent in 2010 to 49 per cent in 2017.[34] But localism in this sense was more prevalent in some regions than in others. In 2017, for instance, 100 per cent of Northern Ireland MPs, over 90 per cent of Welsh and around three-quarters of Scottish MPs were born in the respective region. Among north of England MPs, the percentage born in the region varied from about 50 per cent in Yorkshire and the Humber to around two-thirds in the North West. Further south, the proportions of MPs born in the region tended to be lower – and in the East of England, only 15 per cent could claim regional roots. And this followed party lines too: 83 per cent of MPs representing parties other than Labour or the Conservatives were born in the same region as their constituency (hardly surprising in 2017 given the extent to which Northern Ireland and nationalist – especially Scottish Nationalist – MPs dominated the 'other parties' group). Labour MPs were also relatively 'local': 54 per cent were born in the same region as their seat. But Conservative MPs were more likely to have been born in a different part of the country to that where their constituency was located: only 37 per cent in 2017 hailed from the same region. And intriguingly, younger MPs were much more likely to represent a seat in their home region than were older MPs: while just over 40 per cent of MPs born in the 1930s and 1940s did so, this rose to 73 per cent of MPs born in the 1980s and 1990s – further evidence that local ties are becoming more important for MPs.

Nor is that sense of 'community interest' and place representation restricted to a debate over whether MPs should themselves be locals. Whether from conviction or calculation, most MPs (whether they have personal ties to the constituency or not) make much of their links with their constituents, and of their interest in the place they represent. By tradition, their first, 'maiden', speech in the Commons is devoted in part to extolling the virtues and charms of their constituency (though it is very unlikely that many constituents notice or care about maiden speeches).

More importantly, the days when MPs rarely visited their constituencies or talked to their constituents outside election campaigns are in the past. As recently as the early 1960s, under a third of MPs had a home in their constituency, and a substantial minority held constituency surgeries only rarely.[35] Now most MPs maintain a constituency home (though this can also be the source of political difficulties, as numerous MPs found out in 2009, when many were revealed to be making dubious expenses claims to cover their domestic arrangements).[36] And all contemporary MPs undertake very substantial (and growing) amounts of constituency work, holding surgeries for local people to consult them, dealing with ever-expanding amounts of constituency correspondence, taking up constituents' cases with the authorities, and so on – and most see it as one of their most important roles.[37] Voters now expect their MP to be responsive.

One consequence is that many MPs now spend substantial amounts of time not only on constituency business but actually physically in their constituency. Commenting on how the UK Parliament is changing, Chris Mullin (a former Labour MP and junior minister) observed:

> The other day, after lunch in the Palace of Westminster, I made my way to the atrium of Portcullis House, where hundreds of MPs have their offices … I was struck by the absence of recognisable faces. There were many staffers and officials, but scarcely any MPs. A sad truth dawned on me: for many of the present generation of MPs, the business of

Parliament occupies only two days a week. Most out of town MPs travel down on a Monday morning and leave soon after Prime Minister's Questions on Wednesday ... It's not that MPs are lazy: on the contrary, many work long hours ... Many MPs have young families ... and constituents and constituency parties expect a great deal more from their elected representative than they used to ... Nowadays, an MP is expected to live, or at least have a base in their constituency, and to be highly visible ... MPs have become increasingly constituency-focused and some, especially those who represent poorer areas, have become glorified advice workers ... Some MPs in marginal seats actually prefer to devote their time to acting as fairy godmothers to their constituents.[38]

Mullin's anecdotal observations are borne out by the systematic evidence. The further MPs' constituencies are from London, the less likely they are to attend parliamentary debates on Thursdays and Fridays.[39] And MPs in marginal seats not only prefer to be seen in their constituency, they are often actively encouraged to do so by their party, which calculates that MPs who cultivate a visible constituency profile might help the party retain the seat at the next election.[40]

Those calculations are rational. MPs' constituency service does pay electoral dividends, especially for new MPs establishing their local credentials.[41] By working hard (and visibly) on their constituents' behalf, MPs can build a personal vote, over and above general levels of support for their party. When locally popular MPs retire (or die in office), their party's vote share in their constituency often drops at the next election, when their place is taken by a new candidate, who has not yet had time to build a personal reputation in the seat.[42]

Constituency service undoubtedly stands behind the tendency for voters to rate their own constituency MP more favourably than they rate MPs in general. Just before the 2015 general election, for instance, the BES asked respondents how much trust they had in MPs in general, and how much they had in their own constituency MP (Figure 2.1), On average, respondents placed greater trust in their constituency MP (most responses were to the right-hand, higher-trust end of the scale) than in MPs in general (here, most responses were bunched at the lower-trust end of the scale). It is the constituency link which seems to make the difference: voters trust what they experience first-hand but distrust the abstract. A slightly different twist on this was revealed during the 2009 UK MPs' expenses scandal, which was the occasion of an outpouring of (often visceral) public anger with

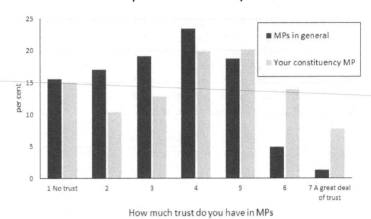

Representative democracy?

How much trust do you have in MPs

Figure 2.1 Trust in MPs, 2015

MPs. Almost every voter in the country was aware of the scandal, and almost 90 per cent, according to the 2010 BES, were angry or very angry about it. Yet only 17 per cent of Britons thought their constituency MP had been caught up in the scandal, and nearly 58 per cent didn't know: scandal, it seems, is something other MPs indulge in![43]

The relationship between MPs and their constituencies can also affect how MPs act in Parliament. A range of parliamentary devices, such as Early Day Motions, private members' bills, and parliamentary questions are available to (and extensively used by) backbench MPs wishing to push particular concerns which may fall outside the ambit of normal government business. The primary purposes of such measures are to hold the executive to account, and to raise important issues deserving of debate. But they can also serve as devices for signalling an MP's diligence and activities to his or her constituents. There is evidence, for instance, that MPs from more marginal constituencies table more written questions in Parliament than do MPs representing safer seats (the former group clearly has more of an incentive to demonstrate to their voters that they are hard at work).[44] And while MPs living in more far-flung constituencies may be less likely to attend parliamentary debates at the end of the week, they are more likely to sign Early Day Motions (a means of flagging issues of concern) than are their peers representing less remote constituencies.

The constituency link is clearly important to, and valued by, British voters. But it is also clearly important to their MPs, and not just in the pragmatic sense of being the only route to becoming an MP. Political representation is complex. Place and locality matter, both to the represented and to their representatives.

Moving on ...

This chapter raises a number of issues and challenges affecting the roles political representatives perform, and what it is that they are meant to represent – political parties and beliefs, particular social or demographic groups and so on. But a common thread runs through the history of political representation in the UK: the representation of particular places. Much has changed in British politics since Burke's time. The franchise is now many times wider and more inclusive, political parties are much more organised and powerful; and so on. Even so, constituency representation remains a central concern. In so far as they think about the electoral system, many voters seem to value the close link between a particular MP and a particular geographical community.

That said, the relationship between MPs and geographical communities enshrined in the constituency link is also a problematic one. No MP has the total support of all his or her constituents – and in many seats a majority of voters routinely plump for candidates other than the winner. As the franchise has widened, the personal link between voters and MPs has become ever more attenuated and notional. Edmund Burke had a good chance of knowing most of his Bristol electors. In a modern constituency, with on average some 72,000 registered voters, that is an impossibility (and many voters will struggle to even name their MP). What is more, as we explore in later chapters, there is a tension between the organic and arithmetic principles when it comes to defining constituencies. In a first-past-the-post system, the principle that every vote should carry equal weight increases pressure for all constituencies to contain more or less similar numbers of electors. But achieving this may necessitate riding roughshod over the 'organic' representation of communities, as the electoral arithmetic will seldom map neatly onto the geography of communities.

Yet too close an adherence to the organic principle raises its own problems. It may necessitate substantial variations in constituency electorates (as some communities are smaller than others). And community itself is a notoriously flexible and hard-to-define entity.

Even within the same area, different residents may have very different views of the extent, strength and viability of their local community, and very different degrees of attachment to it. There is no consensus on just what constitutes a community for the purposes of parliamentary representation – as becomes clear during boundary reviews, when rival proposals for the same area can come up with very different community maps, all justified with apparently impeccable 'community' credentials![45] What is more, as populations, and communities themselves, change over time, there is always pressure to redraw and redefine the constituency map. The difficulties and challenges are chronic.

So how has the representation of place in UK politics changed over time, and how have those responsible for redrawing the constituency map responded? In the following chapters, we look at some of the challenges raised by the representation of place in greater detail.

3
Creating an electoral system: 1832–1918

The years after the French and American revolutions witnessed growing demands for electoral reform in what was soon to become the United Kingdom of Great Britain and Ireland. The main demand was for the franchise to be widened from a very small proportion of the male population, almost all of them property owners; a working-class mass demonstration in Manchester demanding the right to vote resulted in the Peterloo 'massacre' of 1819, when a crowd of some 70,000 protesters was charged by cavalry, with several hundreds injured and fifteen killed.[1]

Two decades later the Chartist movement was launched. By then the first reform in 1832, responding to earlier unrest, had standardised the franchise across the country to middle-class male property owners. Previously, it had been determined separately in each county or borough, some of which granted it to a small number of 'working class' residents, who were now all disenfranchised. The working-class Chartists sought more extensive changes, several of them not achieved for many decades. Their People's Charter, presented in petitions to Parliament in 1839, 1842 and 1848, included calls for: universal adult male franchise; equal-sized constituencies according to their number of electors; and a secret ballot. The third was achieved in 1883, and the second in 1918 – with universal adult franchise a decade later. But it was not until 2011 that legislation to ensure (more or less) equal-sized constituencies was put in place.[2] The next three chapters tell the story of the move towards that end.[3]

Pre-reform parliaments

Though other parliaments can claim earlier origins (Iceland's Althingi and the Isle of Man's Tynwald both date from the tenth century while

UNESCO identifies the Decreta of Leon of 1188 as the oldest documentary manifestation of the European parliamentary system), the history of parliaments in the British Isles is nevertheless one of the longest, extending over 800 years. Beginning with the signing of the Magna Carta in 1215, the right of barons to be consulted on matters of national governance was established. The first representatives to attend Parliament were the county members, two knights from each English shire summoned in 1254 'in place of each and all in their counties'. They were joined in 1265 by their urban counterparts, two burgesses 'of each city and town', together forming what is generally accepted as the first forerunner of the modern Parliament. In the early years, parliaments were both irregular and without fixed composition, but by 1327 knights and burgesses were always summoned together forming, from 1332, the House of Commons.

Over the first century of the Commons' existence the list of counties remained constant but that of boroughs responding to the royal writ varied. Just over a hundred boroughs initially sent representatives but then later lapsed, but a core of fifty of the most important towns and cities were typically present alongside a smaller number of small towns whose leaders felt that the expense of representation was worth maintaining their seats in Parliament. A few additions came in the fifteenth century, but it was when the Tudor monarchs began enfranchising boroughs to increase royal influence that Parliament entered a stage of significant growth. Accompanied by the incorporation of Wales in 1542 and succeeded by further additions in the seventeenth century, the House of Commons had doubled from its original size when the last English borough was admitted in 1673. For the next 160 years, indeed, throughout the Industrial Revolution with its associated changes in population distribution, English and Welsh representation in Parliament was largely fossilised. It was only by the Acts of Union with Scotland (1707) and Ireland (1800) that the grand total of MPs in the unreformed House of Commons rose to 658.

The process of election by which these representatives were returned to Parliament varied considerably by place and time, but none would be described as vaguely democratic today. In the counties, the first limitation was the franchise, which from 1430 was restricted to those who held property or land bringing in an annual rent of at least 40 shillings. Interpretation varied from county to county but less than 20 per cent of adult males met the test. The right to vote in the boroughs was far more variable, but there were two main groups.

The smaller, and with a particularly restrictive franchise, consisted of those where the right of selection rested in the borough corporation or via the ownership of specific properties. All the Scottish burghs fell into this category, as did many in Ireland. The remaining boroughs offered the vote to freeholders, freemen or male inhabitants, or a combination of the same. The interpretation of these franchises varied between boroughs, but again most adult males were excluded.

A more significant barrier to participation came in the form of uncontested returns. Between 1696, when legislation first required a written return of poll, and 1831 fewer than 10 per cent of county elections were contested. County members were typically the product of informal agreements between the most influential local landowning families. Borough elections were more frequent, but over the same period little over 20 per cent of the possible contests took place. Again, and despite the borough appellation, those returned to Parliament were overwhelmingly members or nominees of the aristocratic landowning class.

And if franchise restrictions and lack of competition were not enough, corrupt practices of various sorts, be it treating (the provision of food and drink) or intimidation (the secret ballot was still many years away), were widespread. The terms pocket borough (controllable by a candidate whose capacity as landlord ensured the loyalty of his tenants) and rotten borough (a borough whose electorate had declined so much that support could be easily bought) both have their origins in Georgian Britain. Government at this time was not immune from the pressure of public opinion, but if that pressure was to be exerted it could not be through the ballot box.

The beginnings of reform: 1832–67

The extent to which the British population was disenfranchised before reform began is difficult to establish. Definitive figures are hard to come by in an era when registration was not compulsory, but of an 1831 census population of some 24 million adults, little over 500,000 had the right to vote, almost all of them male property owners. Agitation for reform ebbed and flowed. But the demand never went away and when Wellington's Tory government imploded in 1830 momentum for change grew again. Reform was not achieved straightforwardly; many resisted any change, Wellington, for example, still maintaining that the 'current representational arrangements were beyond improvement'.[4] The first attempt at a reform bill failed in 1830; the second was rejected by the Lords in 1831; the third was passed when Tory peers gave way and the Reform Act of 1832 became law. When it finally came the change was somewhat underwhelming – Seymour estimated that those entitled to vote in England and Wales only increased from 435,391 to 652,777[5] – and one of the measures introduced for the first time was a prohibition against women voting (few if any had exercised the right before, but the explicit prohibition was indeed one of the reforms!). According to Cannadine the franchise 'remained in many ways anomalous, inconsistent, restricted and oligarchic'.[6] But change it was, ushering in what several historians have labelled the 'decade of reform', and the Great Reform Act of 1832 became one of the landmarks of British history.[7]

As with all the franchise reforms of the nineteenth century, the legislation included provision for changes to the pattern of geographic representation across the UK. As previously noted, aside from the incorporation of Scotland and Ireland, this pattern had remained more or less unchanged for over 150 years. The expansion of the electorate was of the order of 50 per cent in both the counties and the boroughs, but the latter included the most egregious examples of the need for reform (36 had fewer than 25 electors and another 115 fewer than 200). As a consequence, 143 borough seats were removed, with 65 new ones created along with another 62 new county divisions.

Size was not the sole determinant of whether a borough should lose one or both of its MPs, however, since the government wanted to ensure that the newly enfranchised electors were men of 'property and intelligence, who will exercise it with honesty and discrimination'.[8] They assumed that people with relatively valuable properties were most likely to fit that description so the decision as to which boroughs to disenfranchise rested on not only their populations but also their relative wealth. Commissioners were asked to explore whether extension of some borough boundaries would encapsulate more 'desirable' voters so that those places retained at least one if not both of their MPs. They visited 120 boroughs and in 34 cases produced plans which showed that the built-up area extended beyond the borough boundaries; those extended areas were used in calculations of the number of properties whose owners would be enfranchised. Using these extended boundaries Thomas Drummond (the Commission chair) developed a formula to determine which of 110 boroughs considered should be wholly or partially disenfranchised;

the 56 with the smallest values were recommended to lose both of their MPs and the next 30 to lose one.[9]

Parliament agreed that all 56 should lose all representation. But the Commissioners were asked to consider whether further expansion of some boroughs' boundaries could create an entity with sufficient potential voters to warrant the retention of one seat. Some very extensive extensions were proposed, averaging 112 times the area of the pre-existing borough – Westbury's area, in Wiltshire, was extended 1648-fold; Woodstock's in Oxfordshire 482-fold. Balancing those withdrawals, 22 towns previously without separate representation were allocated two MPs and a further 21 received one MP each; all had their boundaries either drawn or redrawn by Commissioners.

Other Commissioners were given the task of dividing counties into electoral divisions – one reporting that he wished to divide those entitled to two MPs into 'two parts, equal in extent, equal in population, and equal in number of voters' but found that was impossible without splitting county administrative divisions; all that could be achieved was that 'I have endeavoured to approach towards each of these equalities'. This detailed work of boundary delimitation was undertaken after the Act was passed; which places were to be represented was decided before their boundaries were determined. It not only resulted in some of the most impressive examples of Georgian urban mapping, but also for the first time gave formal spatial definition to the areas which were to be represented in Parliament. With that new formality, a new term became ever more popular in the political lexicon, that of the constituency. The concept of a constituent, as somebody who appoints or elects a representative, has seventeenth-century origins and phrases such as the 'Irish constituency' had become quite common as a description of groups of electors. But the constituency as a geographic entity with defined boundaries dates from this time and by the end of the decade its use in official documents was well established.

The resulting redistribution had a clear geography. The vast majority of the abolished boroughs were located in southern England, a part of the country particularly well treated by previous monarchs when granting parliamentary representation. The five counties of the South West alone lost 57 MPs, a total exactly matched by the new seats created in the industrial areas of the Midlands and the North. Leeds, Bradford, Birmingham, Manchester and Sheffield were each allocated two seats; smaller industrial centres such as Huddersfield,

Rochdale and Salford received one each. These changes, though sub-stantial, in no way resulted in anything like equality of representation. Market towns remained over-represented: Harwich and Totnes, for example, had 214 and 217 registered voters respectively; Westminster had 11,600 and Liverpool 11,300. In terms of its political impact, there is little doubt that the bill was designed to promote Whig patronage, though the one successful Tory amendment – the Chandos amend-ment, granting the vote to the more substantial tenant farmers – operated to their disadvantage. Perhaps the more important point is that Tory and Whig both shared a class interest – that of preserving landowner influence – which the 1832 Act went a long way to main-taining. This was to be the first in a long line of electoral reforms where the interest of the elected came first and that of the elector a rather poor second.

Moving on: 1867

The reforms of 1832 were far from universally popular – to some Tories the destruction of most of the Houses of Parliament by fire in 1834 was divine retribution for its passage, and they were roundly condemned in 1835 by Disraeli. To many others the reforms were far too little, hence the foundation of the Chartist movement in 1838 and the growing belief – later shared by Gladstone – that the franchise should be further widened to incorporate 'respectable working-class men'. The anomalies of the geography of the 1832 settlement were becoming ever more apparent by the 1860s, Cannadine noting that the five boroughs of Honiton, Knaresborough, Marlborough, Totnes and Wells, with a total population of under 23,000, returned as many MPs as the 1.5 million inhabitants of Birmingham, Leeds, Liverpool, Manchester and Sheffield combined. This was also apparent to politi-cians: in 1851 Prime Minister Russell announced that he would pub-lish plans for a further expansion of the franchise in the following year, but this was opposed within his party (notably by Palmerston) and Russell resigned.[10]

A further franchise extension was proposed in an 1866 Bill by the Liberals, which also included a further redistribution of seats away from the small boroughs, without any expansion of the House. Total disenfranchisement of places was not part of the scheme, how-ever; instead small boroughs were to be combined, even if they were some distance apart – such as Honiton in Devon with Bridport in

Dorset some 21 miles away, and Cirencester in Gloucestershire with Evesham in Worcestershire (these were 25 miles apart but it took over four hours by rail to travel from one to the other). That bill was defeated and the government was replaced by a Conservative administration, led by Disraeli in the Commons. Believing that some form of reform was inevitable, Disraeli was determined that he should be its author. Facing down internal opposition, the Second Reform Act of 1867 almost doubled the electorate, from 1.4 to 2.5 million – one adult male in three now had the vote. The increase was concentrated in the boroughs – not obviously to Conservative advantage – but Disraeli felt that the enfranchisement of the 'respectable' was in the long-term interests of his party and hoped to mitigate any shorter-term downside by careful manipulation of the new constituency boundaries.

The task of determining those boundaries was again delegated to a Commission, 'packed with Conservatives',[11] who reported to a secret government sub-committee which consulted party agents regarding the proposals. Assistant Commissioners (ACs) conducted 265 local inquiries and their recommendations included some 'blatantly one-sided' recommendations with many borough boundaries extended into not only suburban areas but also rural tracts that might become suburbs in the future.[12] Liberal voters were thus concentrated into the borough seats, leaving a Conservative hegemony in the counties.

The system continued to favour the smaller boroughs, plus the large, rapidly growing boroughs, and the counties containing them continued to be disadvantaged; Buckinghamshire in 1884 had one MP for every 39,724 residents whereas South Lancashire had one to every 193,277. Many smaller boroughs had an MP for every 6–7,000 residents; in Sheffield it was one per 142,205. As one analyst noted, 'the upper classes profited greatly by the number of small boroughs and by the electoral disadvantages of the industrial constituencies'.[13]

Towards the current system: 1885

Governments moved on some of the Chartists' other concerns, even though the movement had been wound up two decades earlier. The Ballot Act 1872 required secret ballots for general and local government elections, and the Corrupt and Illegal Practices Act 1883 limited candidate expenditure during election campaigns (a provision little changed nearly 140 years later!) and criminalised any bribing of electors. Gladstone's Liberal government then produced a further reform bill – the first covering the entire UK in one piece of legislation – aimed at a common franchise for all boroughs and counties based on that introduced for the English boroughs in 1867. Facing rejection in the Conservative-dominated Lords without an accompanying redistribution Gladstone compromised, offering 'friendly communication with leaders of the Opposition' regarding the redrawing of boundaries. The Representation of the People Act 1884 duly passed, increasing the electorate from 3.2 million to 5.7 million. For the first time a majority of men had the vote (an amendment extending the franchise to similarly qualified women was defeated by 271:135) but fully one-third were still excluded as a consequence of not occupying land or tenements worth at least £10 a year.

The Redistribution of Seats Act 1885 went way beyond its predecessors in transforming the electoral geography of the UK. Rather than piecemeal change, it produced approximately equal representation, across countries, across regions and between town and country. To achieve this required the removal of all separate representation from 72 boroughs with 15,000 or fewer residents and the loss of one MP (of two) in a further 36. In the other direction, London's metropolitan boroughs received a further 39 seats and 18 went to the large manufacturing centres (from three to six each for Birmingham, Liverpool, Manchester and Sheffield, for example, with Liverpool's total being expanded to nine single-member constituencies). Of the counties, Lancashire was allocated a further 15 new seats and the West Riding of Yorkshire 13.

A major feature of this change was that most newly created constituencies were to return a single member. Until 1880 most MPs were returned as pairs, elected by a constituency's voters, each of whom could cast two votes. Of the 652 MPs elected then only 194 represented single-member seats; 418 were returned from two-member seats, 36 from those returning three, and one from a four-member seat. The change to single-member seats – in effect creating the electoral system that remains substantially unchanged 140 years later – resulted from secret meetings involving senior politicians (notably Lord Salisbury for the Tories and Charles Dilke for the Liberals). Salisbury had calculated that if the existing constituencies were used following the franchise extension his party could lose as many as twenty-seven seats.[14] Several authors, notably Roy Jenkins, credit Dilke as the author of the re-drawn map,[15] but Jones suggests that he was 'bamboozled' by Salisbury who got most of what he wanted.[16] Having failed to persuade Gladstone of the merits of proportional representation (the irony of a Conservative failing to persuade a Liberal in this respect is noteworthy) or of cumulative voting (in which electors in a two-member seat could give both their votes to the same candidate), Salisbury settled on single-member seats.[17] His aim was to ensure that these new constituencies were drawn in such a way as to separate town from country and, within the former, middle- from working class. With Gladstone as prime minister he did not have the licence afforded to Disraeli in selecting the Boundary Commissioners (in fact the Commissions were ostensibly neutral, chaired for the first time by civil servants) so Salisbury concentrated on ensuring that the remit they were given satisfied his needs.

In counties in England and Wales the Commissioners were to include all parts of populous urban localities within the same constituency unless, according to their instructions, this could not be done 'without producing grave inconvenience, and involving boundaries of a very irregular and objectionable character'; each constituency should be 'as compact as possible' and based on a grouping of 'well-known existing areas' such as parishes. Borough constituencies should include all areas whose populations had a 'community of interest' with the borough, again using 'well-established units, such as parochial or other similar boundaries'. And for both county and borough seats, constituency boundaries should be 'adjusted so that the population may be proximately equalised' and additionally 'special regard shall be had to the pursuits of the population' (i.e. segregate different classes into separate constituencies, as Salisbury wished).[18]

The Commissions and their ACs worked very fast – that for England and Wales held 81 local inquiries between its appointment on 29 October 1884 and reporting on 10 February 1885. They met the 'proximate equality' requirement in a number of areas; Cambridgeshire's three constituency divisions had populations of 48,650, 48,958 and 47,108, for example, and the two for Perth had populations of 46,933 and 48,111, In most boroughs, in line with popular demand, they kept local government electoral wards intact.

The 1884–85 Acts involved a revolution in the UK's electoral landscape, therefore. Not only was the franchise further extended but additionally the principles were established that each constituency should have a single MP, that constituencies should be as proximately equal in their size as the underlying local government units allowed, and that boundaries should be drawn to separate groups with different 'communities of interest'. That revolution occurred with little debate or murmur; a messy compromise between the two main parties, carried out without the likely consequences being appreciated, meant that the UK's electoral democracy was set on a very different road from that emerging among its continental neighbours. The UK's particular form of democracy was largely conceived behind closed doors to promote partisan interests – with unrealised implications not only for how that electoral system would operate but also for the nature of the country's political economy for the next 135 years – and probably much longer.[19]

That redistribution, in both general principle and detailed implementation, was not only achieved to promote one party's electoral interests rather than any wider principle but also in apparent opposition to much 'informed opinion' that had developed over several decades. Many in the country's intellectual elite were concerned that extending the franchise would eventually result in a Parliament (in effect, a House of Commons) in which the country's majority working class dominated, thus eroding the landowning classes' control of government – producing 'illiberal class rule' that muffled 'the polyphony of British society'. As Conti shows, there had been much debate in the decades leading up to 1885 over systems of electoral reform of which the most popular was what was then termed proportional representation, the system now generally known as the Single Transferable Vote (STV). This was not advanced, as it is now (see Chapter 7), to produce proportional representation for parties – indeed most of its advocates were opposed to their growing dominance over political life. Instead, it was promoted to ensure that all opinions with considerable support within the country were represented in the Commons, as the basis for debate leading to an agreed majority decision. This was, according to a major study of those debates, 'a major theme of Victorian and Edwardian political-intellectual life'.[20] Most of the would-be reformers opposed the use of territorially based constituencies as representing 'all that was bad about the United States political system, which used such constituencies – wire-pulling, gerrymandering, bribery and intimidation';[21] others defended the geographical basis of an electoral system, however, claiming that it was at the core of the country's robust civic culture' characterised by a 'back-and-forth of instruction, argument, and criticism' between MPs and their constituents. At the time of the reform, 184 MPs were members of the Proportional Representation Society, but only 31 supported its introduction when the Redistribution Bill was voted on. Those who favoured territorial constituencies as 'the natural context for political activity' prevailed, not because of principle but because their deployment best suited one party's electoral prospects – and that decision became the core of the UK's electoral system to the present day.[22]

Towards universal franchise and a further redistribution: 1917–18

The 1885 redistribution was the most extensive of the three undertaken in the nineteenth century, establishing principles – single-member constituencies, proximate equality (although the largest constituency still had a population eight times that of the smallest, compared to twenty-three times after the 1867 Act), and respecting local government boundaries, including those of wards – most of which were later formalised in the mid-twentieth-century legislation.[23] It completed a major shift in the geography of representation implemented by the three acts. A net increase of 78 seats for northern England and of 56 for what is now Greater London came at the direct expense of southern England, concentrated particularly in the South West and, more generally, among what had now become former parliamentary boroughs.

Despite the emphasis on proximate equality of electorates, however, within twenty years there was concern that growing disparities in constituency sizes required a further redistribution; additionally, 1888 legislation reforming local government substantially altered the pattern of counties, boroughs and urban districts. The Conservative government produced an internal paper in 1905, not disclosed to Parliament, proposing a not very radical change to the 'rules' for redistributions to reflect differential population growth. A resolution presented to Parliament recommended the appointment of a commission to implement the changes and draw new constituency boundaries but it was withdrawn for lack of parliamentary time. An independent committee was established to consider the issues raised; its report listed the boroughs where boundary changes were needed and produced six variants on the original scheme. But the government fell in 1906 before a formal redistribution – the first that would have been produced with little political involvement – could be tabled, and the incoming Liberal government abandoned the work.

Had these proposals been implemented, Ireland would have lost 22

Figure 3.1 A *Punch* cartoon showing Clive Morrison-Bell's
three-dimensional model with which he promoted his campaign for
electoral reform

seats, with England gaining 17, Scotland 4 and Wales 1.[24] This would
have had substantial political consequences a few years later because
with a reduction in the number of Irish seats the Liberals could have
lost their working majority after the 1910 elections when they could
only govern with Irish support, which generated Conservative fears
that to sustain themselves in power the government would yield
Irish Home Rule – an issue that created much concern for the main
political parties (and split the Liberals) for several decades. This argument was made by Clive Morrison-Bell, an army officer elected as
Conservative MP for Honiton in 1910, who made great use of maps
in his political and other propaganda.[25] He built a three-dimensional
model showing constituency-size variations to sustain his argument
for a redistribution that would bring fairness to England (Figure 3.1);
and in 1911 erected a large display board in The Strand which showed
the two largest and smallest constituencies in each of the four UK

Figure 3.2 Clive Morrison-Bell's exhibit in The Strand

countries, asking 'Is this fair?' (Figure 3.2). England's largest constituency was shown as having nearly 21 times more voters than the
smallest, for example

As the end of the First World War approached the organisation of the delayed next general election was raised and in 1916
a Speaker's Conference (chaired by the Speaker and normally

only used for major constitutional issues) was convened with a Conservative majority, with the driving force behind its work being the President of the Local Government Board W.H. Long, a strong proponent of electoral reform.[26] Most of its recommendations were uncontroversial – including universal male suffrage – and a Representation of the People Bill was formulated to give them effect; partial women's suffrage was also included after a free vote – those aged over 30 who owned property with a rateable value of at least £5 – or whose husbands did – were enfranchised, substantially increasing the electorate (from 5.2 to 12 million males plus 8.5 million females). This expansion, together with the inequalities identified by Morrison-Bell, justified an accompanying redistribution, to be undertaken by three Commissions (England and Wales were combined). The instructions for two of them (excluding Ireland) required the number of MPs from Great Britain to remain substantially unchanged. Each county and (county) borough (save the City of London which would continue to return two MPs) with a population of less than 50,000 would cease to have separate representation; those with two members should retain that number if their population was not less than 120,000. Municipal boroughs and urban districts with populations not less than 70,000 would have separate representation and they, along with the counties and county boroughs, should have one constituency for every multiple of 70,000 plus one for any remainder exceeding 50,000. Constituency boundaries should, 'as far as practicable', coincide with administrative area boundaries; the English and Welsh Commission decided to use the rural and urban districts (i.e. those with populations of less than 70,000) as their building blocks, finding it necessary to subdivide only 78 of 662 rural districts.

The instructions were later amended – as a consequence of parliamentary debate after they had been published the Secretary of State wrote to the Commissions altering the rules to give them greater flexibility. The Commissions could depart from strict application of the rules where otherwise constituencies might be created that were 'inconvenient in size or character' or the variations from the arithmetical requirements were slight; they could also 'have regard to electorate rather than population where it appears that the proportion of electorate to population is abnormal' – that is, where there was, for example, a relatively large number of non-enfranchised residents, such as young people, women without the vote and non-UK citizens (the Commission for England and Wales found no such cases that would require it to apply this instruction).

Reflecting the difficult Irish political situation at the time (as pressure for independence grew) – and so not producing the outcome promoted by Morrison-Bell and his colleagues – the Irish Commissioners were told that the number of seats should not be changed and constituency boundaries should only be altered if they thought it 'necessary or desirable' in the light of the instruction that 'regard shall be had to the population and size of the constituencies'.

The Commissions recommended increasing the House of Commons by 34 MPs, with Parliament adding a further three university seats. The main change was in the balance between boroughs and counties with the main gainers being the large boroughs: Birmingham's complement of MPs was increased from seven to twelve, Manchester's from six to ten, and Sheffield's from five to seven. Smaller cities also gained – Bradford, Hull and Nottingham each had their number of MPs increased from three to four – but many smaller places lost separate representation: Canterbury, Colchester, Peterborough, Shrewsbury and Warwick, for example. Constituencies across Great Britain became more equal in size, on average, but considerable variation remained.

The 1918 Act built on the four main principles established for redistributions in 1885. They were to be undertaken by independent Commissions; the map of local governments provided the template within which constituencies were to be allocated; population equality between constituencies was an important goal; and separate communities should be placed, where feasible, in separate constituencies.

Conclusions

The four reforms of 1832, 1867, 1885 and 1918 not only moved the UK towards a universal adult electoral franchise (completed with the Equal Franchise Act 1928, which granted all adult females the right to vote), therefore, but also very significantly changed the country's electoral map. The major imbalance of representation between rural and urban areas was substantially reduced with many small boroughs having their separate parliamentary status removed to allow more seats to be allocated to industrial Britain's burgeoning large towns and cities – plus London – which also removed the North–South imbalance in parliamentary representation that characterised much of the nineteenth century. There was also some movement towards the Chartists' goal of equal-sized constituencies. By 1920 the average constituency population was approximately the same in three of the four constituent countries (Northern Ireland having been treated differently after 1922 because of the creation of a devolved assembly there). But there was considerable variation around those averages because, despite the move towards an arithmetic basis to representation, place remained the dominant criterion deployed in the allocation of seats. The country's local government structure provided the matrix of places within which seats were distributed so that an MP was elected – and always referred to in House of Commons debates – as the member for a named place.

Although the move towards equal-sized constituencies met to some extent the Chartists' demand for 'one person, one vote; one vote, one value' this did not tackle what had become an increasingly important issue in British politics – equal representation for political parties, which by the early twentieth century predominated in political affairs. For almost the entire period, one party – the Tories, later renamed the Conservatives – was advantaged over the others as demonstrated by calculating, for each major party at each election, its ratio of percentage of seats gained to percentage of votes won.[27] If those ratios were 1.0, or close to it, then parties were equally represented in the House of Commons; if they were above 1.0, the parties concerned were over-represented; if below 1.0, they were under-represented.

Figure 3.3 shows those ratios for each of the three parties contesting a substantial number of constituencies at every election from 1830 to 1935. Near equality characterised the first few contests – serendipitously – but from then on, with very few exceptions, the ratios diverged, with the Tories at most elections being over-represented and the Whigs/Liberals under-represented. After 1900 Labour, too, was more likely to be under- than over-represented whereas Tory over-representation became more pronounced. The reasons for these trends are several. Throughout the nineteenth century the main source of Tory over-representation was the party's strength in the rural areas and small towns which, as shown here, had small constituencies compared with the boroughs where – as with Salisbury's careful manipulation of constituency boundaries – the Liberal votes were concentrated; additionally, as the century proceeded, the party widened its electoral appeal in response to the franchise extensions. After

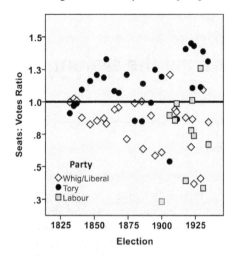

Creating an electoral system: 1832–1918

Figure 3.3 The ratio of seats to vote (percentage share of each) won by the major parties at UK general elections 1832–1935

the First World War, it benefited from Labour and the Liberals splitting the anti-Conservative vote as well as, in the case of the Liberals, being split among themselves. Despite the reforms, Parliament did not represent the electorate equally: some electors, in some places, had much more influence than others.

4

Consolidating the system: 1930–2010

Over just under a century, the United Kingdom moved from a democracy in which very few individuals, all male, had the right to vote to one with universal adult franchise. That expansion, confined to just four major legislative events, was accompanied by major changes to the country's electoral map, not least by the shift to single-member constituencies and the rules devised for alterations to their location and boundaries – what became known as redistributions.

Each of those four redistributions was an ad hoc exercise with Commissioners employed to undertake the cartography according to guidelines and rules laid down by the incumbent government, which sought to benefit electorally from the changes. A common set of procedures emerged – using the country's local government map as the template within which constituencies were placed, for example, and aiming for 'proximate equality' in constituency size. These were not enshrined in legislation, however; each redistribution started afresh. That changed in the mid-twentieth century, with a sequence of legislation that initiated a new period in creating British electoral landscapes.

Setting the agenda

With a universal adult franchise in place some of the impetus for redistributions associated with expansion of the electorate was removed. But changes in population distribution – between countries, between regions, between cities, towns and countryside, and within cities – meant that growing variation in constituency electorates eroded the 'principle' of proximate equality.

In 1934 (later Sir) Herbert Williams, a Conservative backbencher and former minister, introduced a private member's bill promoting a redistribution which failed because the government allocated insufficient time for its consideration. Williams's fully worked-through draft bill built on and extended the 1918 procedures. It would have established an independent Electoral Commission empowered to conduct a redistribution immediately and then every ten years. Draft schemes would be subject to public consultation, with a final scheme published within a further six months and then implemented. Its principles for redistributions are shown in Table 4.1.

If enacted these 'guidelines' would have crystallised previous practices and made regular, independent redistributions a legal requirement, although Parliament was not required to implement any recommended scheme. Regarding the tension between the organic and arithmetic conceptions of representation, the balance was clearly towards the former; the constituency map was to be created within the local government template, and only within that framework was equality of constituency electorates to be a consideration. Although no legislation was forthcoming, this detailed proposal became the blueprint for later developments (in which Williams participated).

Two years later Sir John Train, a Scottish Unionist (Conservative) MP, proposed a redistribution because constituency electorates varied between 30,000 and 150,000. In response, a Home Office undersecretary noted that the average constituency had 50,000 voters and only 38 in England and Wales deviated by more than 50 per cent from that figure. The government could not agree to a redistribution while it was reviewing some local government boundaries; a redistribution before that was completed could break a tenet of previous redistributions – 'to preserve local communities and not to interfere with administrative boundaries'. The government at least was clear that place still trumped arithmetic and hence nothing happened in the 1930s.

Preparing for peace

A general election was scheduled to be held by 25 November 1940, and in August 1939 the Prime Minister was asked if it would be postponed should war break out. War was declared later that month but it was a year before a Prolongation of Parliament Bill was presented in the House of Lords and quickly passed; local elections and the annual process of electoral registration had been postponed for a year in 1939, a decision renewed annually until 1945. The 1940 Act was renewed in 1944 by which time the government had taken significant

Table 4.1 Sir Herbert Williams's principles for redistributions

---

- A common 'quantum' (i.e. average constituency electorate) for the entire UK, calculated as the total registered electorate (excluding the City of London and the universities) divided by 650 – the fixed number of constituencies (again excluding the City of London and the universities);
- One constituency would be allocated to each administrative county and county borough[A] if its electorate exceeded one-half of the quantum;
- The total number of members for each administrative county and county borough would be determined as its electorate divided by the quantum, with an additional member allocated if the remainder from that division exceeded one-half of the quantum;
- In determining constituency boundaries within county boroughs 'regard shall be had' to local government ward boundaries;
- In determining constituency boundaries within an administrative county 'regard shall be had' to the boundaries of (non-county) boroughs and districts 'and to geographical and administrative considerations' (county districts were not then divided into wards, only parishes);
- If the electorate of a county or county borough is less than half of the quantum, it should be grouped with the whole or part of an adjacent county or borough;
- 'So far as is reasonably practicable' constituency boundaries should be defined 'so as to provide that the number of electors shall be as near as may be the same, save in thinly populated areas where on geographical and administrative grounds the number may be less, always provided that the population is not less than half of the quantum';
- Draft schemes should be published, inviting written objections to and suggested modifications of the scheme, that must be considered; and
- If considered desirable a local inquiry should be held to consider the objections and suggested modifications, before a final scheme is produced.

[A] These were the main units of local government at the time – with different terminology in Scotland. Counties were divided into municipal boroughs, urban districts, and rural districts.

steps towards creating a new electoral system as part of its preparations for the post-war period.

A committee, chaired by the Registrar-General, Sir Sylvanus Vivian, was charged with examining 'the technical problems involved in any scheme of redistribution of parliamentary seats by way of preparation for consideration of the principles on which any scheme should be based'. Its report stressed that 'the main representative body of the legislature should consist of persons elected under conditions which confer upon them an *equal representative status'*, immediately followed by: 'It is also a fundamental principle of our Parliamentary system that representation (with the exception of University constituencies) should be *territorial*.' Since 'both these features appear to us to be of the greatest importance' it followed that 'seats must be assigned to a series of local areas or communities each of which contains as equal as may be a share of the total number of persons to be represented'. Once again, the organic took precedence over the arithmetic.

Five key issues were to be addressed in determining the rules for future redistributions:

- The need for a *quota*, an 'average number of persons to be represented per member';
- The need to identify acceptable *tolerance limits* around that quota, so that any 'trifling' departures would not stimulate a change;
- The need for *continuity of constituencies*, with change only proposed when necessary, and even then continuity should be maintained by minor adjustments only to a constituency's boundaries so as not to have ripple effects on neighbouring seats;
- The need to *conform to local government boundaries* because 'these are the only defined, ascertained and recognised local boundaries' that could be deployed – changes to those boundaries would stimulate a redistribution;
- The *assignment of seats* to the four constituent parts of the UK should follow the quota and tolerance limits. With a universal adult franchise the question of whether 'the total of the persons to be represented' referred to population or electorate was unlikely to be significant because the difference would be slight save where there were relatively large proportions of the population aged under 21, but the choice between the two definitions 'may have some small effect upon the allocation of seats as between England and Wales and Scotland'.

Having argued that a machinery for redistributions should be established in legislation, including rules and procedures (including Local Inquiries) to be applied and undertaken by an independent commission, the committee recommended that 'a review of the state of constituencies coupled with redistribution proposals, where necessary ... [should] be forthcoming during the life of every

Parliament' (i.e. at least every five years). Using the latest available data, for 1939, it noted that 119 of the country's 615 constituencies had electorates either less than 30 per cent below or more than 70 per cent above the four-country average; the former group returned thirty MPs to every million voters the latter returned only nine. It doubted that a redistribution could be undertaken before the first post-war election, but suggested that a partial redistribution might be undertaken; the committee's three Labour MPs argued that this would mainly affect London (where Labour was electorally strong in 1935), which had experienced massive war-time population changes and where local government boundaries were obsolete.

The wartime government made repeated promises to introduce legislation on redistribution but, faced with growing parliamentary pressure, eventually plumped for a Speaker's Conference instead. Comprising 29 MPs (including Sir Herbert Williams) and three peers, it was asked to consider and, if possible, make recommendations on four issues: redistributions, franchise reform, electoral conduct and candidates' expenses, and voting systems. The Conference addressed the fourth issue first, since the nature of redistributions would depend on the electoral system it recommended; by votes of 25–4 and 20–5 it rejected both the Single Transferable Vote and the Alternative Vote respectively (on those systems see Chapter 7).[1]

The Committee's recommended rules and the machinery for their implementation built on previous practice and Williams's proposal. The organic continued to take precedence over the arithmetic. The registered electorate rather than the enumerated population should be the basis for calculating a national quota with a tolerance limit set relatively wide at +/–25 per cent of the quota.

The proposed machinery was a separate independent Boundary Commission for each country, with Scotland, Wales and Northern Ireland seeing no reduction in their number of MPs, and Northern Ireland having no increase from the current twelve. With no substantial increase in the total number of MPs for Great Britain, this implicitly determined the number for England. The reasoning behind separate Commissions for Scotland and Wales was that strict application of a UK quota could lead to a reduction in the number of seats there because of their sparsely populated areas; any reduction in the number of Scottish and Welsh MPs would be politically unwelcome there and 'would lend support to the separatist movements in both countries'.[2] Commissions could depart from strict application of the rules if special geographical considerations (including the area, shape and accessibility of a constituency) made that desirable.

The government then introduced a House of Commons (Redistribution of Seats) Bill in 1944, which was quickly enacted with little debate; most concern was expressed not over the main recommendations but on representation for the City of London and the universities – the former was to remain as a two-seat constituency (a Labour motion to end this was defeated by 163–31; a motion to retain the university seats, some of them also two-member, was accepted by 152–16). The four Commissions were given an immediate task, to create new constituencies to replace those identified as abnormally large – all of them in England – using a quota of 50,000. The Boundary Commission for England reported within six months, recommending 25 new seats, most of them on London's suburban fringes where population growth had been substantial.

One, presumably unforeseen, consequence of setting a minimum number of seats for both Scotland and Wales but limiting England's number through a suggested upper limit for Great Britain as a whole was that future population changes meant that England became under-represented at successive redistributions relative to Scotland and Wales. From 1951 on, England's population increased at a faster rate than either of the other two countries – save in Wales during the century's final decade (Table 4.2) but this differential growth was not represented in the four countries' complement of MPs.[3] Instead, the gap in their average constituency electorates widened so that by the end of the century the average English constituency was some 26 per cent larger than those in Scotland and Wales; England's 529 constituencies averaged 69,955 electors, Scotland's 72 averaged 55,262, and for the 40 Welsh constituencies it was 55,695.

The first statutory redistribution

The Commissions' first review of all constituencies had to be completed within 3–7 years of the Act's passage in 1944. They were required to publish provisional recommendations and invite representations; where desirable Local Inquiries should then be held, chaired by an Assistant Commissioner. (The Speaker's Conference had only recommended consultation with the political parties' national officers, but the Act widened the scope to the general public.)

Table 4.2 Electorates and electorate percentage change in Great Britain, 1951–2001

	England	Scotland	Wales
1951	38,669,000	5,096,000	2,597,000
1961	41,159,000	5,179,000	2,644,000
1951–61	+6.4 per cent	+1.6 per cent	+1.8 per cent
1971	43,461,000	5,229,000	2,731,000
1961–71	+5.6 per cent	+1.0 per cent	+3.3 per cent
1981	45,978,000	5,035,000	2,791,000
1971–81	+5.8 per cent	−3.7 per cent	+2.2 per cent
1991	48,198,000	5,083,000	2,812,000
1981–91	+4.8 per cent	+1.0 per cent	+0.8 per cent
2001	49,139,000	5,062,011	2,910,000
1991–2001	+2.0 per cent	−0.4 per cent	+3.5 per cent

The first substantive rule in the sequence set out in the Act employed an arithmetic requirement: 'so far as is practicable' each constituency's electorate should be within +/–25 per cent of the electoral quota (the British electorate divided by the existing number of constituencies – i.e. the number in place before the redistribution was undertaken). The next rule was that 'so far as is practicable having regard to the foregoing rules' constituency boundaries should be contained within those of local governments – clearly placing the organic conception of representation secondary to the arithmetic. The Commissions could deviate from those rules if special geographical considerations (size, shape and accessibility) indicated that it was desirable.

The Commissions found the conflict between the arithmetic and organic rules very constraining; it was not practicable to apply the arithmetic rule 'without disturbing the unity of local government areas'. Through the Speaker – each Commission's nominal chairman – they asked the Home Secretary to revise the 1944 Act. He informed the Commons in November 1946 that this was necessary because otherwise many 'unified communities' would have to be dismembered and a bill was enacted in 1947 giving the organic rule precedence over the arithmetic conceptions – which Churchill, as leader of the opposition, claimed amounted to gerrymandering because the government was doing it for party political (i.e. Labour) gain. After the rule regarding local government boundaries a new arithmetic rule significantly diluted the tolerance limit (removing its maximum and minimum of +/–25 per cent), stating only that 'the electorate of any constituency shall be as near the electoral quota as is practicable having regard to the foregoing rules' but giving the Commissions discretion to depart from that if the consequence would be 'excessive disparity' between either a constituency electorate and the quota or the electorates of neighbouring constituencies.

The Commissions then addressed an issue not covered in the rules – what spatial units to employ when dividing a local government area between constituencies. Williams's bill had specified wards as the only available, legally recognised units in all urban authorities and the Commissions decided to use these, and civil parishes in rural districts; rural districts were later warded and the Commissions used them for the next sixty years, defending the practice whenever it was challenged as the only feasible option.

The Commissions received few representations to their provisional proposals – none in a substantial number of areas. There were only three Local Inquiries in Scotland and one in Wales, and the twenty-one held in England covered just 70 of the country's 489 constituencies. The final proposals were tabled in early 1948 and some of the Commons debate focused on constituency electorate variations – Churchill declaring that 'one person, one vote' had not been achieved.

Much more controversial was a modification to the report introduced by the government. The Boundary Commission for England had written to the Home Secretary just before submitting its report indicating concern regarding its proposals for seats with more than 80,000 electors in eight boroughs (Battersea, East Ham, Hammersmith and Paddington in London; plus Blackburn, Gateshead, Norwich and Reading). The government responded by modifying the report and splitting those constituencies, adding seventeen seats to the Commission's recommendations – which again was challenged by the Opposition as favouring the Labour party. In subsequent debates some members proposed changes to their own constituencies and twelve of the forty-one proposed were accepted.

The 1948 recommendations were accepted by a large majority, despite Churchill's claims that they were pro-Labour in their likely impact. The government then enacted a new House of Commons (Redistribution of Seats) Bill 1949, alongside an extensive and wide-ranging Representation of the People Act. The latter abolished both the university seats and a separate seat for the City of London (the Act stating that there shall be a constituency containing the whole of the City and its name shall refer to the City of London), and plural voting (the business vote) was substantially reduced. The recommended number of seats for Great Britain was increased from 591 to 613 – allowing for expansion in the number of English MPs – and the rules were reordered to reflect the 1947 decision to place the organic before the arithmetic conception of representation.

Half-a-century of redistributions; organic predominance but greater arithmetic outcomes

The 1949 Act required the Commissions to conduct a further review and redistribution within 3–7 years. All reported in November 1954 and their recommendations were implemented before the general election on 26 May 1955.

1955: little change but further legislation – organic triumphant

Given the short period since the previous redistribution, much of the Commissions' work was uncontentious yet, although many constituencies were unchanged (including all of Northern Ireland's), over a quarter of all constituencies were proposed for significant change. Accordingly, when the final recommendations were debated in the House of Commons some MPs contested the amount, frequency and nature of the changes, using phrases such as 'constant chopping and changing', 'we do not want redistributions very often' and voters were being moved around 'merely to fit a mathematical equation'. Those views echoed the English Commission's report, which noted that many representations indicated that proposed changes 'were not wholly welcome because of the disturbance they would inevitably cause both to the electorate and to their representatives'. It suggested that 'consideration should be given to lengthening the minimum and maximum periods between reviews' and 'it would ease [its] ... future labours ... and remove much local irritation if Rule 5 [the 'arithmetic rule'] were to be so amended so as to allow us to make recommendations preserving the status quo in any area where such a course seemed to be desirable and not inconsistent with the broad intention of the Rules'. MPs clearly agreed: one pointed out that a ward in Kent had been placed in four different constituencies over a period of just nine years; and a Liverpool MP claimed that a redistribution broke links with 'ordinary people who live in the streets and villages of our constituencies', 'hiving off [an individual voter] to what is to her a foreign land where there are a lot of people who do not speak her language'!

Despite that 'hiving off' there were many examples of inequality of representation. The Walthamstow West seat had 41,298 electors, for example, whereas neighbouring Leyton had 76,457 and Edmonton 72,894; on the other hand, Reading South, with 41,624 electors before the redistribution, had been abolished. Against arguments favouring the arithmetic conception, largely made by Labour MPs, others promoted the organic view; a Conservative MP claimed that the rules 'gave the mathematical factor more importance than the House had wished' so that the Commissions 'paid insufficient attention to the factor of local organic unity'. Such opposing feelings meant that when MPs debated the specific recommendations – separate Orders were laid before the House for each major administrative area – some detailed changes were proposed, with a vote demanded in fifteen cases (all were defeated). Without any change to the law and presumably reflecting a cross-party consensus, such debates and votes over individual cases were not allowed by the House when subsequent redistributions were considered.

One final issue reflected the difficulty presented by the limitation on the total number of permitted constituencies in Great Britain. The Conservative Lord Mayor of Manchester and a city councillor sought a court decision preventing the Order for Manchester, Oldham and Ashton under Lyne being voted on, claiming that the Commission had not applied the rules correctly. It had aimed to recommend 506 constituencies for England but in applying all the rules found it necessary to increase that to 511. The plaintiffs claimed that a correct interpretation of the rules should have resulted in 519 (with probably one more seat for their group of boroughs). Their claim was initially upheld but overturned by the Court of Appeal, which ruled that the Commission's role was to advise Parliament and so it was outwith the jurisdiction of the courts to constrain how Parliament responded to that advice. It did consider the merits of the case, however, and ruled against the plaintiffs, finding that the Commission's recommendations were not at variance with the 1949 Act: 'it seems impossible to suggest that the Boundary Commissions have done anything ... to which anybody could take the slightest exception' (a judgment with which some scholars disagreed).[4]

Many of the views expressed in these debates, in line with those of the Boundary Commission for England, were recognised in the Conservative government's 1958 House of Commons (Redistribution of Seats) Bill. This made four main changes to the 1949 Act:

- The length of time between redistributions was extended to between ten and fifteen years.
- A separate electoral quota was to be calculated for each country.
- Criteria were established for the decision whether to conduct a Local Inquiry.
- The importance of continuity was stressed by adding the clause that: 'It shall not be the duty of a Boundary Commission ... to aim at giving full effect in all circumstances to the [organic and arithmetic] rules ... but they shall take account, so far as they reasonably can, of the inconveniences attendant on alterations of constituencies other than alterations made for the purpose of rule 4 of those rules [the organic rule: if local government boundaries were changed this would have to be reflected in constituency boundaries], and of any local ties which would be broken by such alterations.'

As the Home Secretary, R. A. Butler, observed, that final change introduced a 'presumption against making changes unless there is a very strong case for them' – according further importance to the organic conception of representation.

1969: the Callaghmander[5]

The Commissions next reported in 1969, having conducted their reviews in the middle of a major period of local government reorganisation – although only the creation of Greater London in 1962 and its 32 Metropolitan Boroughs was completed in time to influence their deliberations. The provisional proposals stimulated many more representations, and the English Commission held 70 Local Inquiries. Because MPs wanted the Commissions to justify their recommendations, especially proposed changes, the Boundary Commission for England stated that:

> The Rules embrace two principles of representative government, equal representation (Rule 5) and territorial representation (Rule 4), which are often difficult to reconcile. The more equality in constituency electorates is sought, the greater the likelihood of disrupting local government units. Conversely, the more the preservation of local government units is pursued, the greater is disparity in electorates.[6]

MPs had made it clear that any changes were likely to generate local inconvenience and had shown 'a broad measure of agreement that local ties were of greater importance than strict mathematical equality'. The Commission thus began its review

> with the intention of avoiding, where possible, proposals that would change constituency boundaries for the sake of adjustments in the size of electorates. We also considered it reasonable to assume that each existing constituency normally represents a community with its own distinct character, problems and traditions. Ties of many sorts may exist within this local community and we believe it proper for these ties, whatever they may be, to be taken fully into account before a constituency is disturbed. We were, however, not inclined to accept the argument put forward at some inquiries that 'local ties' could refer only to the specific ties of political life that would be broken by redistribution.

The implication, paralleled by those made by the other Commissions, was that the recommendations would make only minimal changes in many parts of the UK – excepting London.

The general belief then – which continued to be held as the conventional wisdom by many for several more decades when it was far less true – was that a redistribution would probably disadvantage Labour which would lose seats because many of its constituencies in inner cities were losing population as a consequence of slum clearance programmes whereas many outer suburban – Conservative-leaning – areas were growing rapidly. The electorate of Liverpool Scotland constituency fell from 56,176 in 1955 to 29,239 by 1970, for example, while over the same period that of South East Essex rose from 47,132 to 100,167. Thirteen constituencies lost more than 20,000 (five of them in Glasgow) and 92 had increases of 20,000 electors or more. By 1970 two seats had electorates below 20,000 and 48 had less than 40,000, compared to a national average of 62,000; 13 had more than 100,000 registered electors and 83 had more than 80,000.

Equalisation of electorates would reduce the number of inner-city seats and damage Labour's electoral prospects, therefore; indeed, the party calculated that if the Commissions' 1969 recommendations were fully implemented up to thirty seats could be lost (although some, including the Prime Minister, Harold Wilson, believed it might be as few as six). Labour's government thus delayed presenting the reports to Parliament, arguing that it would be inappropriate to change constituencies, other than in London, immediately before a major restructuring of local governments was completed. This did not receive a favourable reaction so an alternative bill was presented by which the reports, apart from that section dealing with London, would be shelved and the Commissions would do no further work until the due date for their next review (presumably in the 1980s) unless directed to by the Secretary of State (presumably after local government reforms were complete). This too drew opposition objections and it was feared that the proposal would be lost in the Lords, where the Conservatives had a majority. So the Home Secretary, James Callaghan, laid the Orders before the House, with the government whips directing Labour members to vote them down – which they did.[7] A general election was held in 1970; Labour lost and the replacement Conservative government then re-laid the Orders, which were passed and the new constituencies were in place for the next election in February 1974; the local government reforms – very different from those that might have been enacted under Labour – were not completed until 1974 and provided the template for the next redistribution.

1983: the rules are 'clarified'

There were two changes to the legislation prior to the next redistribution. The number of seats for Northern Ireland was increased from 12 to 'not greater than 18 and not less than 16', with the denominator for determining the quota set at 17. This was the outcome of a Speaker's Conference established at Prime Minister Callaghan's request, following lobbying by Democratic Unionist Party MPs, including Enoch Powell, to consider the issue of Northern Ireland's representation in the light of the reintroduction of direct rule following the suspension of the Stormont Parliament in 1972, and ensure that it had relative parity with Wales in the ratio of population to MPs.

The major local government reforms removed the separate status of borough and county (with the latter divided into urban and rural districts) and instituted a single system of counties (regions in Scotland) – including six new metropolitan counties in England – internally divided into districts. The organic rule was thus simplified to state that 'so far as is practicable': in England and Wales, no county or London borough should be placed in a constituency containing part of another such area; in Scotland regard should be had to local government boundaries; and in Northern Ireland no ward should be divided between constituencies. Why the Commissions' practice of not splitting wards should be commended for Northern Ireland only is not clear. These new rules removed the legal constraint of not dividing county districts but in correspondence with the Home Office the Commissions were advised to take district (including metropolitan borough) boundaries into account; the Boundary Commission for England recognised the 'emerging sense of identity of the new districts and of the resentment that disruption of that identity could create' but was nevertheless convinced that it should not 'leave unaltered constituencies of high electorates solely because each was contained in one district'. The arithmetic conception of representation was thus given slightly greater prominence relative to the organic than at the previous redistribution.

The redistribution proceeded somewhat slowly because the English Commission was constrained by the pace of re-warding being undertaken by the Local Government Boundary Commission. The reports were ready for submission to Parliament in late 1982 but this was delayed by a legal case brought on behalf of four leading Labour Party members (including Michael Foot, then party leader), though not explicitly supported by the party.

During the review, two Labour members – Edmund Marshall, MP for Goole and a former university lecturer in mathematics, and Gerry Bermingham, a Sheffield solicitor and adopted candidate for St Helens South – worked with local party members and councillors in some areas to promote modifications to the English Commission's provisional proposals that should be electorally favourable to Labour. Labour would probably lose seats again when the new constituencies were introduced so to prevent that they argued that in preparing its recommendations the Boundary Commission for England had misdirected itself because it was possible to produce constituencies more equal in their electorates than it had done – a case partly sustained by citing work using computer simulations of the range of possible constituency configurations within local authorities.[8] In Greater London variation in the proposed electorates was from 46,483 to 84,401 – with two adjacent constituencies having a disparity of 28,280.

The plaintiffs lost before both the Queen's Bench and the Court of Appeal on a number of grounds, of which two were important to the Commissions' work. The first was Justice Oliver's Queen's Bench opinion that the successive Acts from 1944 on had given the Commissions increasingly wide discretion such that 'it is unlikely in the extreme that a court will feel able to hold either that the rules ('guidelines') have been misconstrued such as to justify judicial intervention, or that the discretionary powers have been used unreasonably'. Sir John Donaldson sustained this opinion in his Court of Appeal judgment:

> It is important to realise that Parliament did not tell the Boundary Commission to do an exercise in accountancy – to count heads, divide by a number and then draw a series of lines around each resulting group. It told it to engage in a more far-reaching and sophisticated undertaking, involving striking a balance between many factors which can point in different directions. This calls for judgment not scientific precision. That being so, strict compliance with Parliament's instructions could result in several different answers ... all of which would be sensible ... Parliament has asked the Commission to advise on which, in their judgment, should be adopted.[9]

The second of the grounds concerned the relative importance of the criteria in the rules. The general interpretation had been that implementing Rule 4 (the 'organic' rule) took precedence over Rule 5 (the 'arithmetic') – which the Labour Party plaintiffs were seeking to reverse. But Donaldson argued that the new rule added in 1958 regarding continuity and inconveniences took precedence over both. It stated: 'It shall not be the duty of a Boundary Commission to aim at giving full effect in all circumstances to the above rules [i.e. 4 and 5], but they shall take account, so far as they reasonably can, of inconveniences generated by constituency alterations and the breaking of local ties.' The key words were *but* and *shall*: those new criteria *must* be taken into account, and they relieve the Commissions of their duty in all circumstances to apply rules 4 and 5 – therefore reducing them to guidelines only.[10]

The case was lost, therefore, and the proposed new constituencies were in place for the 1983 general election. Although Donaldson's judgment clearly indicated that the Commissions were not required to give precedence to electorate equality, nevertheless the Commissions were aware – well before the Foot et al. case was launched – of general concerns about that. In their reports on their Third Periodic Reviews all four included data to show how, while exercising the judgment that Oliver and Donaldson stressed was their prerogative, they had met the arithmetic criterion. Using 1976 electoral data (the latest available when the review started, and on which all of the deliberations were based even though the report was not submitted until 1982), the Boundary Commission for England showed that 75 per cent of its recommended constituencies had electorates within 10 per cent of the English quota and 97 per cent within 20 per cent, concluding that this represented 'a very much closer approach to electoral equality than exists at present'; the comparable figures for Scotland were 57 and 90 per cent. In Wales, 33 of the 38 recommended constituencies were within 15 per cent of the quota; two of the exceptions (both with small electorates) reflected use of the 'special geographical considerations' rule in sparsely populated areas. (That rule was also deployed in parts of Scotland.)

Alongside the concern about the variability of electorates came a growing sense of unease at the continuing increase in the number of MPs. Following the distribution of seats in the 1944 Act the initial review, which reported in 1947, allocated 506 seats to England, 71 to Scotland and 36 to Wales. The next review – known officially as the First Periodical Review – saw the English contingent of MPs increased to 511, and it grew again to 516 after the Second Periodical Review that reported in 1969. The Third Periodic Review[11] in 1983 saw increases for all three countries, to 523 seats for England, 72 for Scotland and 38 for Wales, giving a total of 633 – 20 more than the desideratum set out in the 1958 Act for Great Britain as a whole. (As noted, Northern Ireland's number had been increased from 12 to 17 in 1978.)

This creeping growth in the size of the House of Commons was the subject of an inquiry by the Home Affairs Committee which concluded that it was 'almost inevitable', following academic analyses of a 'fundamental defect' in the 1949 Act that had not been subsequently removed. There were four reasons: the denominator in the calculation of electoral quotas is the pre-existing number of constituencies so that, if the geographical distribution of the electorate changed between redistributions, even without any expansion of its number, an increase in the number of constituencies is probable; seats with small electorates created under the special geographical considerations dispensation are included in the denominator for the next redistribution, thereby reducing the quota; as constituencies are allocated to counties and boroughs the rounding-up on non-integer remainder entitlements is likely to result in an increase in the number of seats; and the presumption of no change introduced in 1958 could lead to small seats being retained, again increasing the total number.[12] The Committee recommended that this creeping expansion be ended by using fixed divisors in calculating the electoral quotas – 515 for England, 66 for Scotland, 36 for Wales and 17 for

Northern Ireland – but the government declined to amend the Act; although sympathetic to the Committee's goal, it felt that fixed divisors had disadvantages that outweighed the advantages.

1995: Labour triumphant

The Conservative government did legislate, however, introducing a Parliamentary Constituencies Bill in 1986 which consolidated the evolving provisions of, and repealed, the 1949–79 House of Commons (Redistribution of Seats) Acts, with the 'continuity, inconveniences and ties' criteria becoming Rule 7. This involved no changes to the basic procedures and it readily passed, forming the template within which the Commissions commenced their next reviews in the early 1990s, whose conduct was clearly influenced by their appreciation of Parliament's concerns about both electoral equality and expansion of the House of Commons.

The Boundary Commission for England did not set a target number of constituencies but concentrated 'upon recommending constituencies with electorates as close to the electoral quota as practicable whilst at the same time keeping in mind' the requirement regarding the total number of seats. It had already increased the number of seats by one, after an interim review created an extra constituency in Buckinghamshire in response to the rapid expansion of Milton Keynes new town, whose constituency had 103,239 electors by 1988. This increased the number to 524, and the Fourth Periodic Review, reported in 1995, increased that to 529. The Welsh Commission increased the number of seats there from 38 to 40, saying it had identified 'no viable alternative'. The Scottish Commission, on the other hand, set itself and met the target of 72 constituencies, which meant no increase in Scotland's complement of MPs.

Not long after the reviews started the Conservative party intervened by changing their timetable. It won only a small majority of 21 seats over all other parties in 1992 and was preparing for the next election. In line with conventional wisdom, and sustained by calculations undertaken by a former MP, Rob (now Lord) Hayward, it believed the next redistribution could deliver it a further 20 seats (he later reduced that to 10) and so wanted the Commissions to report in time for the new constituencies to be in place for that next election, to be held at the latest in 1997. Their timetable meant that they might not report until 1998, however, so the Conservatives passed a Boundary Commissions Act in 1992 requiring the Commissions to report by

December 1994 and changing the period between redistributions from 10–15 to 8–12 years. The Commissions indicated that this would be difficult – they were again constrained by local government reorganisations and re-warding and the necessarily lengthy consultation procedure, and despite being allocated additional resources only the Scottish Commission reported on time;[13] all were adopted by October 1995.

Building on Marshall and Bermingham's work during the previous review, the Labour Party realised it could influence the outcome of future elections if it could convince the Commissions, through both written representations and presentations at the Local Inquiries – including cross-examination of those representing other parties – to alter their proposals to constituency configurations that favoured Labour electorally. Those considerations could not be deployed in arguments before the ACs, so they had to be constructed using the local ties and inconveniences rule. To that end, a party official, David Gardner, prepared a desirable set of constituencies for each county and borough and then – supported by a group of senior MPs – convinced local party officials, councillors and, where relevant, MPs to support that alternative in representations and presentations to the Commission. That was an relatively successful exercise, in part because it took the Conservatives by surprise; they assumed the redistribution would yield them a considerable gain of seats and responded too late to the Labour party's preparations, which almost certainly denied the Conservatives their expected advantage.[14] The Commissions' provisional recommendations would have given the Conservatives a net gain of 31 seats; after the public consultation this was reduced – largely as a result of Labour's counter-arguments – to 22.

2005 and 2007: the last hurrah

Once again, the next Periodic Review (the Fifth) was preceded by a legislative change. A Scottish Parliament was created in 1998. By then, as a consequence of both the greater use of the special geographical considerations provision to create smaller constituencies in north-western parts of Scotland than elsewhere (indeed, its Commission was the only one to use that provision in the Fourth Review) and the slower growth of the electorate there than in England, Scotland was 'over-represented' in the House of Commons; its mean constituency electorate was 54,569 according to the Fourth Review, compared with England's 68,626. As a consequence of the extensive powers devolved to the Scottish Parliament it was decided to reduce Scotland's representation in the House of Commons. The Scotland Act 1998 thus amended the clause in the 1986 Parliamentary Constituencies Act that allocated not less than 71 seats to Scotland, replacing it by a requirement that at the next redistribution the number of seats there should be determined by dividing the country's electorate by the quota used for England at the previous review. The Boundary Commission for Scotland thus undertook an early review, reported in 2005, reducing the country's MPs from 72 to 59 – although, as commentators noted, since the new clause only referred to that first redistribution after devolution, if the Scottish Commission continued to deploy the special geographical considerations provision to justify small constituencies in the Highlands and Islands Region, the number of Scottish MPs was likely to increase at future reviews. No similar provision was introduced following Welsh devolution, which granted fewer powers to the National Assembly of Wales than to the Scottish Parliament, even though the mean Welsh constituency electorate after the Fourth Review was 55,559. (The Northern Ireland mean was 64,082.)

Conduct of the review was very similar to the previous exercise, except that the Conservative Party had learned the lesson of its 'defeat' by Labour at the Fourth Review. If it was to gain the expected net advantage for the redistribution it had to be better prepared for the Local Inquiries and it was (thanks in large measure to the work of Roger Platt, Rob Hayward and their team at party headquarters). The two parties contested the recommendations on almost equal terms.

The three other Commissions reported in 2007, with England's complement of MPs increasing again to 533; the Welsh complement was kept at 40, but Northern Ireland's was increased to the maximum allowed of 18. Each Commission again pointed to its success in narrowing the range of constituency electorates. In London, for example, the English Commission noted that in its Fourth Review 47 of the 74 recommended constituencies had electorates within 10 per cent of the electoral quota, whereas that was the case with 57 of the 73 recommended in the Fifth Review – in part because it adopted a policy of pairing boroughs and creating seats crossing their boundaries, reducing the need to create constituencies either much larger or smaller than the quota within individual boroughs.

The Commissions also sought to minimise change. To assess the extent to which this was achieved, we use a percentage index of

Table 4.3 Indices of change to constituencies in Great Britain at the Fourth and Fifth Periodic Reviews

Review	England		Scotland		Wales	
	4th	5th	4th	5th	4th	5th
No change	128	55	9	3	27	18
<5 per cent	61	139	10	1	2	10
5–10 per cent	43	89	6	1	2	8
10–25 per cent	120	105	19	11	2	1
25–50 per cent	82	70	14	20	2	1
>50 per cent	95	75	14	23	5	2
TOTAL	529	533	72	59	40	40
Mean per cent	24.2	20.6	27.8	45.8	12.5	7.8

Source: C. Rallings and M. Thrasher, Media Guide to the New Parliamentary Constituencies, BBC/ITN/PANews/Sky, 1995; C. Rallings and M. Thrasher, Media Guide to the New Parliamentary Constituencies, BBC/ITN/PANews/Sky, 2007.

change developed by Colin Rallings and Michael Thrasher as part of their work for the broadcast media estimating the result of the previous election if it had been held in the new constituencies – the larger the index, as a percentage, the greater the change.[15] At both redistributions a substantial proportion of both English and Welsh constituencies were either unchanged or only slightly changed (Table 4.3), though more experienced some change on the second occasion – mainly reflecting new ward boundaries in many areas. Against, this, however, in a considerable number of cases the boundaries of the new constituency were very different from those of the old (defined as the constituency with the largest proportion of the new). Most occurred where the number of constituencies in the county or borough was either increased or decreased because of electorate growth or decline; Cornwall, for example, had retained five constituencies in the Fourth Review, and none were changed from the previous redistribution. It was allocated six seats in the next review, which called for very considerable change: one of the new seats had an index of 95.5 and another 80.2. Substantial changes were thus generally only recommended if required where the number of MPs was altered – which is why very large percentage change figures characterise Scotland's fifth review, when the number of constituencies was reduced from 72 to 59.

Representative democracy?

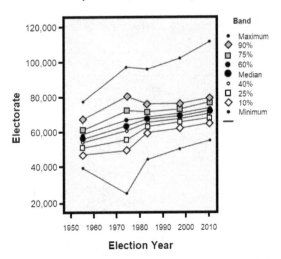

Figure 4.1 The distribution of electorate sizes at each general election in England after the post-1950 redistributions

Throughout much of this period, the legal emphasis within the rules/guidelines the Boundary Commissions had to follow stressed organic over arithmetic criteria. In their application, however, as made clear in their 2013 Review reports, the Commissions strove – while never downplaying the organic criteria – to produce constituencies as close to the quotas as possible. In that they were very successful. Figure 4.1 shows the distribution of constituency electorates in England at the first general election after each redistribution (i.e. 1955, February 1974, 1983, 1997 and 2010). There is a general upward trend in the median electorate, but the spread around that value becomes increasingly narrow, especially at the three most recent elections. The inter-quartile spread (containing one half of all constituencies – between the 25 per cent and 75 per cent bands) is compressed by 2010 to around half of its extent in 1974, and the wider spread (between the 10 per cent and 90 per cent bands) is also very substantially narrowed. The maximum electorate remains very large because of the special case of the Isle of Wight, which has over 100,000 electors (despite which, no Commission has been prepared to divide the island), but the minimum is much increased. By the end of the period, therefore, in the other three countries as well, there was a very considerable shift towards equal electorates; the Commissions achieved that while still giving the representation of communities and the minimisation of change the precedence that Parliament required.

Who makes the recommendations? Staffing the Commissions

Who were the Commissioners who made these recommendations? Each Commission has the Speaker of the House of Commons as its nominal chairperson, though he or she may have played no part in its deliberations. This provided the Commissions with a route to make representations to Parliament where considered necessary, as in 1946. Each Commission's work was overseen by its deputy chair, almost invariably a High Court judge, and two other commissioners, using selection criteria to ensure they were politically non-partisan. The Commissions varied somewhat in the desirable qualifications for those individuals: the English Commission preferred to appoint one with experience as a local government officer and another with a legal background; the Scottish Commission has frequently included an academic among its commissioners (a planner, a geographer and a political scientist, for example). They oversaw the work of a professional staff, career civil servants in most cases, many of whom would have had little if any experience of mapping or the detailed geography of various parts of the country; although a small permanent senior staff was retained between reviews many of those appointed – especially in England – were not retained once a review was completed.[16]

The Local Inquiries were conducted by ACs appointed specifically for that task; they chaired the Inquiries, assembled written and other evidence and delivered a report which, where they considered it desirable, recommended changes from the Commission's proposals. For this task the Commissions for England, Wales and Northern Ireland preferred to appoint senior practising lawyers, having ensured that they had no political affiliations and, in the English case, no detailed knowledge of the area concerned. In Scotland, the Commission used the Sheriffs Principal, senior law officers in the areas covered by an Inquiry. The reliance on lawyers reflected their experience in assessing evidence fairly and openly, and their ability to summarise it and reach conclusions on the basis of what they had heard and seen – including cross-examination of those making oral representations by representatives of the political parties seeking to promote their electoral interests.[17]

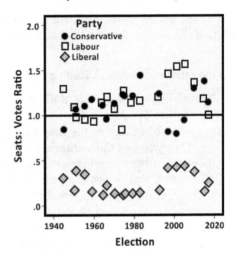

Representative democracy?

Figure 4.2 The ratio of seats to votes (percentage share of each) won by the major parties at UK general elections 1945–2017

Conclusions

As with the pre-1944 redistributions, equal treatment of the political parties was not among the goals set for the Boundary Commissions, although they were consulted at the start of each of the more recent exercises regarding the procedures to be adopted. At later reviews under the 1944 legislation and its successors, the parties became more involved in not only seeking to influence the Commissions' recommendations to promote their electoral interests but also varying the legislation – and, indeed, challenging its interpretation by the Commissions in the Courts – to gain partisan advantage. Did the Commissions produce sets of constituencies that were neutral in their impact on the parties?

Figure 4.2 replicates Figure 3.3 by showing the seats:votes ratios for each of the three main British parties (Conservative, Labour and Liberal) at every election from 1945 onwards. Three features stand out. The first is that the Liberals were significantly under-represented at every election, rarely getting even half the percentage share of MPs as of the votes cast. Complementing this, the two other parties usually obtained a larger percentage share of seats than votes; the Conservatives had a ratio below 1.0 at only five of the seventeen elections and Labour at just four. Most of the ratios were fairly close to

1.0, though not at Labour's landslide victory in 1945 (when constituencies were very unequal in size) or the Conservative's 1983 landslide victory. The two Labour landslides in 1997 and 2001 and its substantial victory in 2005 produced much greater inequality, however. Its share of the seats was approximately half as much again as its share of the votes, with the Conservatives getting ratios of less than one.

Detailed analysis of these patterns is undertaken in Chapter 6. But the outcomes at those three elections stimulated Conservative determination to change how the constituency-building procedure operated – without, of course, going as far as electoral reform. The Commissions had moved considerably towards meeting the arithmetic criterion over the preceding fifty years, while respecting the organic, but, as Figure 4.2 shows, this had resulted in one party gaining a very significant advantage over its opponents at several general elections – notably in 1997, 2001 and 2005. And so, as detailed in the next chapter, major change was to be imposed.

5
The 2011 legislation: major changes?

Labour won the 1997 general election by a widely expected land-slide. There was relatively little public discussion of the operation of the electoral system then. With 30.7 per cent of the votes the Conservatives had won one seat for every 58,199 votes, compared to Labour's 43.2 per cent and one seat for every 32,336 votes; the Liberal Democrats won more seats (46) than at any other previous post-Second World War general election, but each cost it 113,976 votes. The Conservatives won no seats at all in Scotland and Wales, despite winning 483,059 and 317,127 votes there respectively. The outcome in 2001 was very similar: Labour's seats:votes ratio was much more favourable than the Conservatives' and the Liberal Democrats' ratio was considerably worse than either of its rivals'.

Size matters

After 2001 members of the Conservative Party publicly acknowledged their concern that the electoral system was operating against them. Few were prepared to promote alternatives closer to proportional representation, believing this would almost certainly preclude them winning a House of Commons majority and forming a single-party government. So they focused on how the current system could be reformed to remove some of the party's disadvantage, and in particular on removing differences in constituency electorates; in 2001, for example, the seats they won averaged 72,138 registered electors compared to 67,544 in Labour-won seats.

The case was argued by Andrew Tyrie MP,[1] who realised that 'if we are to have disruptive boundary changes [a reference to the Fifth Periodic Review, then in progress], we should at least move towards the benefits of a smaller, more efficient House and fairer representation'.

There were currently not only great disparities across the four parts of the United Kingdom in average constituency electorates – 69,928 in England in 2001, for example, compared to 55,904 in Wales – but also within each part. The English Boundary Commission was currently proposing constituencies varying (excluding the particular case of the Isle of Wight with 103,480 electors) from 57,204 in Hackney South and Shoreditch to 78,817 in Banbury; that variation resulted from what Tyrie described as a 'decision not to allow parliamentary seats to cross county boundaries' which would have to be relaxed to create more equally sized constituencies.

Greater fairness would also be achieved by more frequent reviews. Banbury's electorate was initially close to the 'desired size' (i.e. the quota) when its boundaries were determined using 1991 data. At the 1997 election it was 8,000 voters above that 'target' and by 2001 it had a further 7,000. Sheffield Brightside's 1991 electorate was also close to the quota at 64,000; by 1997 it was under 59,000 and in 2001 'it was the smallest in England, scraping in at just over 51,000'. Such inequality was unfair to both electors and parties: 'Labour benefits from the over-representation of Wales (and, until the next election, Scotland) and from urban areas of declining population.'

Tyrie also argued there were too many MPs relative to their workload and proposed reducing their number by 20 per cent and fixing the number of constituencies – reducing it to around 600 at the next review and below 550 at the next. A single UK Boundary Commission would lose much of the discretion under the current rules; its overriding goal would be creating equal-sized constituencies, with a review every ten years, even if that meant constituencies crossing county and borough boundaries and, where necessary, splitting wards, notably in boroughs where they are large. (As he expressed it 'wards are designed for the convenience of local authorities, not parliamentary constituencies'.)

Tyrie's proposals were followed up when former Home and Education Secretary, Kenneth Baker, introduced the Parliamentary Constituencies (Amendment) Bill 2007 in the House of Lords; it limited the number of constituencies to 'not greater than or substantially less than 581', with a UK-wide electoral quota to allocate seats to each of the four constituent parts. Each constituency should have an electorate neither greater than 105 nor less than 95 per cent of that quota. The bill was sent to the Commons but never debated there.[2] Three years later, senior Conservative MPs tabled an unadopted amendment to the Labour Government's Constitutional Reform and Governance Bill which proposed reducing the number of MPs by 10 per cent and that no constituency should have an electorate greater than 103.5 or less than 96.5 per cent of the national quota. Electorate equality was to become even more exact.

Within a few months the party had regained power and was ready to legislate, its chairman having held a meeting to consult academics and other interested groups about the proposals. That meeting reached general agreement that the then-current rules were contradictory and not fit for purpose and should be replaced by a consistent set in which electoral equality was the dominant criterion, though its degree of dominance was disputed;[3] there was also agreement that Local Inquiries were probably not necessary. Anticipating the legislation, the British Academy commissioned research to address issues involved in implementing the anticipated new rules; the resulting booklet was provided to all MPs and peers,[4] as well as the media, and widely cited during the lengthy debates in the House of Lords.

Reform

The Conservatives' 2010 general election manifesto stated that:

> Labour have meddled shamelessly with the electoral system to try to gain political advantage. A Conservative government will ensure every vote will have equal value by introducing 'fair vote' reforms to equalise the size of constituency electorates, and conduct a boundary review to implement these changes within five years.

It also proposed cutting the cost of Parliament by reducing the number of MPs.

The 2010 election resulted in a Conservative-Liberal Democrat coalition government and to gain support for their proposals the Conservatives agreed to accommodate the Liberal Democrats' desire for electoral reform by holding a referendum on changing to the AV system, which retained single-member constituencies.[5] The two were combined in a Parliamentary Voting System and Constituencies Bill which amended the Parliamentary Constituencies Act 1986. It required the Commissions to report on their next review before 1 October 2013 and every five years thereafter.

The bill replaced the Rules for Redistributions by the following sequence:

1. There would be 600 constituencies.
2. The electorate of every constituency would be no less than 95 per cent and no more than 105 per cent of the electoral quota,[6] defined as the electorate of the UK defined by 598.
3. No constituency would cross the England–Scotland and England–Wales boundaries.
4. Each constituency should have an area of no more than 13,000 square kilometres, although a Commission could propose one with an area of more than 12,000 square kilometres if it believed it was 'not reasonably possible' to meet the +/−5 per cent constraint.
5. Subject to the size constraint (2), a Boundary Commission could take into account, to the extent that it sought fit: special geographical considerations (size, shape and accessibility); local government boundaries; any local ties that would be broken by changes in constituencies; and the inconveniences attendant on such changes – although the last of those would not apply in the first review undertaken under these new rule.;
6. Subject also to the size constraint, the Boundary Commission for England could, if it saw fit, take into account the boundaries of the electoral regions used as the constituencies for elections to the European Parliament (which were the same as the 'standard regions' used in much reporting of government statistics).
7. There should be two named constituencies – Orkney and Shetland, and Na h-Eileanan an Iar (commonly known as the Western Isles) – where the size constraint would not apply,[7] hence the divisor for calculating the electoral quota being 598.
8. The Boundary Commission for Northern Ireland could deviate slightly from Rule 2 in very particular circumstances: if it found difficulty creating viable seats within the UK tolerance limits it could adopt a slightly wider tolerance.[8]
9. The allocation of seats to England, Northern Ireland, Scotland and Wales should follow a particular formula (generally known as the St Lagüe formula).[9]

The Commissions were required to publish their provisional recommendations and allow twelve weeks for written representations to be made; if they then revised any of their recommendations these must be published and a twelve-week period allowed for further written representations. The bill was specific, however, that 'A Boundary

Commission may not cause a public inquiry to be held for the purposes of a report under this Act.'

The bill closely followed Tyrie's proposals and Lord Baker's Bill.
The dominant criterion in determining constituency boundaries was
electorate size, and – apart from two special cases in thinly populated parts of Scotland – only within the extremely tight tolerance of
+/–5 per cent of that quota could other considerations be taken into
account. (The bill was amended at the House of Commons committee stage to define the local government boundaries that could
be taken into account: in England, the boundaries of each county
for which there is a county council, of each authority not in such a
county, and each London borough; in Wales, the boundaries of counties and county boroughs; in Scotland, the boundaries of the councils
established in 1994; and in Northern Ireland, ward boundaries.)

A bill covering two major areas of constitutional reform attracted
considerable attention. Many amendments were put down by MPs,
but most were neither debated nor voted on. The debates were lengthy
and somewhat confused; they were time-limited and the bill passed
through the Commons virtually unchanged. The House of Lords has
no procedure for limiting debate and, alongside much discussion of
the AV referendum, Labour peers contested most of its provisions
regarding redistributions and tabled many amendments – whilst all
the time claiming they favoured greater electoral equality, though not
to the extent proposed (10 per cent rather than 5 per cent variation
around the quota was more acceptable).[10] Debates were spread over
seventeen days, with 15 divisions on amendments which applied to
the constituencies part of the bill or procedural motions – one of the
longest periods that any bill had been considered in the Lords.

Labour peers clearly understood that their party could lose part of
their current advantage over the Conservatives in the number of seats
won relative to their vote total by the equalisation of electorates and
greater frequency of reviews,[11] to which they added a concern that the
large number of eligible people not on the electoral roll (the Electoral
Commission's research suggested that as many as 15 per cent of those
eligible were not registered) could further disadvantage the party as a
consequence of the equalisation. They also challenged the reduction
in the number of MPs, arguing that no convincing rationale had been
provided (in response to one question as to why 600 was chosen, the
reply was that it was 'a good round number'!). But they lost on all
occasions.

Not all of the amendments were introduced by Labour peers. One moved by a Conservative peer creating two constituencies for the Isle of Wight was carried; if that had not been done, part of the isle would have to be hived off and included within a Hampshire constituency on the mainland. A Liberal Democrat amendment that no constituency should cross the Cornwall–Devon boundary (an issue of much local concern) was lost; other special geographical considerations, such as for the Isle of Anglesey, were promoted but not accepted. The result was that four rather than two protected constituencies were included in the amended rules, and the denominator for calculating the electoral quota changed to 596.

Although not yielding on the basic principles – 600 constituencies, a national electoral quota and a tolerance around that of +/–5 per cent – the government amended the bill in response to some issues raised. For example, it inserted another rule allowing the Commissions to take 'boundaries of existing constituencies' into account and expanded the range of local government boundaries that should be considered.

Labour peers also pressed very hard for changes to the public consultation procedures, opposing the prohibition on Public Inquiries, with support from several cross-benchers, notably Lord Woolf, a former Lord Chief Justice of England and Wales. He argued that abolishing Inquiries might generate procedural problems and provide grounds for judicial review by persons who considered their concerns had not been properly considered. The government was unwilling to yield, fearing that Inquiries could lengthen the process and make it impossible for the Commissions to recommend new constituencies in time for the 2015 general election. But it also feared the bill might not be passed in time for the AV referendum to be held on the already scheduled date and so, with the assistance of the convenor of the cross-bench peers, introduced amendments to the consultation procedure: which required:

- the Commissions to publish their provisional recommendations and allow twelve weeks for written representations to be made (the 'initial consultation period')
- that during that twelve-week period Public Hearings should be held beginning in the fifth week and ending in the tenth
- the publication of all written representations received plus transcripts of the Public Hearings, and for written representations to

be invited from the constituencies affected, during a four-week period (the 'secondary consultation period)
- that if after receiving those representations, they modified their proposals, they should publish them and invite written representations within an eight-week period.

They would then consider those further representations and make final recommendations to Parliament.

A new Schedule gave instructions regarding that revised consultation procedure:

- The Boundary Commission for England would schedule at least two and no more than five hearings in each region; the Boundary Commissions for Scotland, Northern Ireland and Wales would each schedule between two and five hearings.
- The hearings held in England would consider only issues concerning proposed constituencies in the particular region whereas those in the other three countries should cover any constituencies within their borders.
- The Commissions would appoint persons to chair the hearings.
- All hearings should be completed within two days.
- The chairs would determine the procedure to be deployed, and allow representations to be made by 'qualifying parties' (i.e. the political parties) as well as any other persons; they would determine the length of representations; and they could both put themselves and allow questions to be put 'to a person present at a hearing' and 'may regulate the manner of questioning or restrict the number of questions a person may ask'.

Conservative party officials and members worked with ministers and civil servants in formulating these rules, which reflect their desire that the Hearings not take on the confrontational features that were increasingly common at Local Inquiries under the previous legislation, where representatives (including specially briefed barristers) defended their party's proposals by challenging its opponents. Labour peers introduced an amendment reintroducing Local Inquiries as under the previous legislation but this was lost by five votes – 60 cross-benchers voted for it and 20 against. The government's proposals were then accepted without a division.

At a late stage in the Lords debate a cross-bencher, Lord Pannick, introduced an amendment that the tolerance around the quota be extended to +/−7.5 per cent 'if it is necessary to do so in order to achieve a viable constituency' because of 'special geographical considerations or local ties ... of an exceptionally compelling nature'. This attracted considerable cross-bench support (they voted 75:10 in its favour) and was carried by 275 votes to 257. It was removed from the bill by the House of Commons before it was returned to the upper house. Lord Pannick then moved to reinsert it during the 'ping-pong' stage when the two Houses seek to agree a final version but it was lost by 242 to 241 (it had the support of 50 of the 68 cross-benchers who voted at that late stage). The agreed bill was then enacted and received Royal Assent. The AV referendum was held on 2 May 2011 (AV was heavily defeated) by when the four Boundary Commissions had begun their first review under the new rules that prioritised arithmetic over organic criteria.

Implementing the new rules

In February 2011 the four Boundary Commissions commenced devising a new set of 600 constituencies. Using the December 2010 electoral roll the quota was 76,641, so all 596 constituency electorates had to fall within the range 72,809–80,473. Wales's complement of MPs was cut from 40 to 30, Scotland's from 59 to 52, Northern Ireland's from 18 to 16, and England's from 533 to 502.

Two important decisions were then made. The first was whether to continue using wards or their equivalents (electoral divisions in Wales) as constituency building blocks. The Boundary Commission for Wales decided that 'it would normally be desirable, once again, to use whole electoral divisions to create constituencies where it is feasible to do so'; in its initial proposals it split just four. The Northern Ireland Commission's initial proposals split just one – which had been split in the previous review.

The Boundary Commission for England's *Guide to the 2013 Review* stated that 'The BCE uses wards (in district and borough council areas) and electoral divisions (in areas of unitary authorities that have county status) as the basic building block', expanding on this in a *Newsletter* with three reasons:

- Wards are clearly defined in Statutory Instruments and the number of registered electors is reported for them and their boundaries are mapped by the Ordnance Survey; no other areas smaller than constituencies (e.g. the polling districts into which many wards are divided for the conduct of elections) have such a status.

- Wards 'are generally indicative of areas which have a broad community of interest', they 'have an identity that is generally known to the local electorate who understand how they are organised and where they may vote in them', and 'local party organisations are usually based on wards or groups of wards'.

- '... wards usually have an established and well run administrative machinery in place for organising elections within them' and 'the Commission's experience from previous reviews also confirmed that any division of a ward between constituencies would be likely to break local ties, disrupt party political organisations, cause difficulties for Electoral Registration and Returning Officers and, possibly, cause confusion to the electorate'.

The Commission concluded that 'in the absence of exceptional and compelling circumstances ... it would not be proportionate or appropriate to divide wards in circumstances where it is possible to construct constituencies that meet the 5 per cent statutory requirement without doing so'; at an early meeting with political party representatives the deputy chairman stated that 'the Commission would only split a ward if there was felt to be no realistic alternative in order to create a viable constituency. Counter-proposals could be submitted that included split wards, but reasons to split the ward would need to be compelling, and the representations would need to include robust data for the sub-ward level.' This reluctance was reflected in its actions: no wards were split in its provisional proposals.

In Scotland the Commission had already split a number of wards in its 2010 proposals for new Scottish Parliament constituencies because a change in the electoral system for Scottish local government to STV in multi-member wards (most returning 3–4 members) meant they had relatively large electorates (ranging from c.6,000 to c.24,000 electors). The split-ward constituencies raised very few concerns with either the political parties or the electorate and the Commission noted when it commenced its new review of Westminster constituencies that it was 'impracticable ... to create constituencies by simply aggregating electoral wards ... [especially given the] desire to fit [constituencies] within council area boundaries'. Its initial proposals for 50 constituencies split 29 wards.

The Commissions warned that there would be much more disruption of the existing map than at previous redistributions because of both the +/–5 per cent tolerance limit and the reduction in the number of seats. They sought to retain as many of the existing constituencies as possible – or at least their main parts – and minimise the number that crossed county and/or borough boundaries, but frequently found this very difficult. Only one of the current Welsh constituencies – Cardiff North – had an electorate within the +/–5 per cent tolerance, for example, but it proved impossible to retain it.

The Commissions' initial proposals formed a very different map in many parts of the country from that currently in place. Boundary-crossing and the dismemberment of existing constituencies was particularly common in urban areas. Although twenty of London's seventy-three existing constituency electorates were within the tolerance limits, for example, only four were retained unchanged among the proposed 68 new constituencies, 37 containing wards from two boroughs. Indeed, 11 London boroughs had no constituencies all comprising wards drawn from that borough alone and only 3 had no wards allocated to a constituency that included wards from another borough.[12] Outside the metropolitan areas, such dismemberment was less common. Ten of the 19 East Midlands constituencies with 2010 electorates within the tolerance limits were retained unchanged, for example, as were 13 of the 23 in the South West. (If only very minor changes are included 17 of the former group and 19 of the latter remained intact.)

The Commissions' deliberations resulted in some proposals that looked decidedly 'odd'. Several Leeds wards, for example, were combined with rural wards in North Yorkshire extending to the edge of the Yorkshire Dales National Park. Other constituencies contained a single 'orphan ward' with which they had few apparent community links and travel between the parts was difficult. Radley, in Oxfordshire, was placed in the Thame constituency even though it is separated from all of the other wards in the proposed seat by an unbridged stretch of the River Thames; and a proposed constituency of Mersey Banks included two wards from the borough of Halton which were separated from the remainder of the wards (in Cheshire) by unbridged sections of both the River Mersey and the Manchester Ship Canal. Probably the oddest 'orphan ward' proposal was for the former Forest of Dean seat (held by the minister – Mark Harper – who piloted the 2011 legislation through Parliament!). Four of Gloucestershire's six existing seats had electorates within the tolerance; one – Gloucester – was slightly too large and the other – Forest

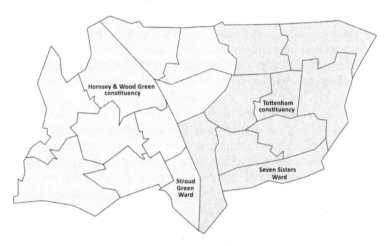

Figure 5.1 Haringey's two constituencies after the 2007 redistribution,
showing their constituency wards in 2011

of Dean – some 4,000 electors too small. The Commission claimed
that the only 'viable' option, retaining the other four seats unchanged,
was to move one ward from Gloucester to the Forest of Dean, to create
a new seat called Gloucestershire West. That ward covered the centre
of the city of Gloucester (including several important civic buildings
and the cathedral) and was separated from the Forest of Dean constituency by the unbridged River Severn.

The problem the Commissions faced is illustrated by the London
Borough of Haringey. Its electorate of 150,040 entitled it to 1.96
constituencies – or two with average electorates of 75,020, well
within the tolerance. But it was impossible to create two constituencies there using the borough's nineteen wards, shown in Figure 5.1,
currently split between two constituencies: Hornsey & Wood Green's
electorate of 79,878 was within the tolerance, but Tottenham's was
slightly small at 70,162. The simple answer would seem to be to
transfer one ward from Hornsey & Wood Green into Tottenham:
four lie on the border between the two but their electorates of 7,438,
7,866, 8,321 and 8,196 meant whichever was moved would result in
Hornsey & Wood Green's electorate falling below the lower limit of
72,809. The Commission, unwilling to split wards, had to cross the
borough's boundaries: it proposed one constituency based on the

current Hornsey & Wood Green with one of its wards (Stroud Green) removed and replaced by another from neighbouring Enfield to the north; Stroud Green was added to the current Tottenham seat, which lost the Seven Sisters ward to a constituency based in the neighbouring borough of Hackney to the south.

The Commissions' proposals generated many written representations and public hearing presentations. The consultation stage was dominated by the political parties' officials, MPs, councillors and supporters, many mobilised either to write or appear in person (or both) by party officials seeking changes to the proposals in its electoral interest. Some 70 per cent of the 1189 who spoke at the English Public Hearings were affiliated to a political party. Of 115 speakers at the Welsh hearings, 72 per cent had party backgrounds; only 65 spoke at the Scottish hearings, 78 per cent with a party background; and just twelve spoke at the three in Northern Ireland – 10 had party affiliations but neither of the two largest parties (DUP and Sinn Féin) provided a spokesperson from their central organisation. The Boundary Commission for England received over 22,000 written representations during the initial consultation stage and 1305 oral presentations were made at its Public Hearings.[13]

Although the Commissions encouraged positive submissions supporting the proposals, negative representations were much more common: MPs, for example, were much less likely to make representations if their assumed new seats (i.e. the one containing the largest part of their existing constituency) were likely to be won easily than if they were marginal; they were more likely to oppose a proposal if their seat was to be changed substantially than if it were largely unchanged.[14] There was very little concern about the proposals for South Yorkshire, for example, where all but one of the proposed constituencies was likely to be safe for Labour; much of the two days scheduled for the Hearing in Sheffield had nobody present wishing to speak – although one couple told the Assistant Commissioner that they had come in just to shelter from the rain! And yet some of those proposals clearly either split communities or grouped wards between which there were few local ties; one, for example, combined two wards in Sheffield with five in Rotherham, separated by a stretch of the M1 motorway, but there was no attempt to get a different configuration; whatever was done, Labour was certain to win the seats. Elsewhere the proposals stimulated considerable public disapproval – there was a protest march in Gloucester when the proposals were

Table 5.1 The estimated outcome of the Boundary Commissions' and the parties' 2011–12 proposals if the 2010 general election had been fought in those constituencies in Great Britain

Seats	Con	Lab	LD	Nat	Oth	Total
2010 result	306	258	57	9	2	632
Commissions' provisional	299	231	46	8	0	584
Party counter-proposals						
Conservative	312	219	45	8	0	584
Labour	289	242	45	8	0	584
Liberal Democrat	295	225	56	8	0	584
Commissions' revised	302	223	51	8	0	584

being considered at a Public Hearing in Bristol and a demonstration outside the Hearing in Birmingham over the proposed treatment of the town of Bilston.

Calculations suggested that if the 2010 general election had been fought in the 600 proposed constituencies the Conservatives would have won 299 (compared to 306 in the 650-member House elected then), Labour 231 (258) and the Liberal Democrats 46 (57: Table 5.1).[15] The Conservatives submitted counter-proposals covering 251 seats in Great Britain, Labour's covered 278 and the Liberal Democrats' 316, Labour contesting more seats in the urban areas and the Conservatives in the more rural areas. Labour submitted counter-proposals for 79 per cent of seats in the North West region and 70 per cent in the West Midlands, for example, but only 25 per cent in the South West, 27 per cent in the East of England and 36 per cent in the South East.[16] All three parties were more likely to propose alternatives to seats that were likely to be marginal. Labour submitted alternatives for 45 per cent of the seats, for example, but 75 per cent of those it was estimated to win by only 5 points or less.

Whereas most of those counter-proposals were designed to promote the parties' electoral prospects they had to use the criteria in the rules; they rarely mentioned the size constraint and focused on the issues that the Commissions were permitted to take into account. The Conservatives were very clear in this. At the first ('lead') hearing in each English region they summarised their counter-proposals, for example claiming in Greater London that under their proposals:

- A total of 178,921 fewer electors were moved from their current constituency than under the Commission's proposals.
- The number of unchanged constituencies increased from four to five.
- No constituency contained wards from more than two local authorities.
- 'We restore a number of community links and therefore break far fewer local ties than the Commission.'

Would the parties' counter-proposals have made a difference, assuming they were all accepted? The estimated outcome in 2010 in each party's alternative set of constituencies is shown in Table 5.1. The main differences were in England – indeed whatever the parties suggested in Scotland (and they made few) would not have changed the outcome, and in Wales the differences were no more than two seats either way from the Commission's initial proposals. If all the Conservatives' counter-proposals were accepted they would have won 12 more seats than in the Commission's proposals – with Labour and the Liberal Democrats losing 10 and 2 seats respectively. Labour's full set of proposals would have delivered it a further 10 seats – 9 from the Conservatives and one from the Liberal Democrats; the Liberal Democrats would have been even more successful in relative terms, gaining 8 more seats than in the Commission's proposals.

The Commissions considered the representations (written and oral) and published revised recommendations in late 2012. Of the 514 constituencies initially proposed in its revised recommendations the English Commission changed 331, over half in every region but many more in some – notably the North East, Yorkshire and the Humber, and London. Of the revised total, 103 were unchanged from the existing constituencies, but these were much more common in some regions than others: the maps for London and the North East were almost totally dismembered, whereas almost one-third of the seats in the South East and South West regions were unchanged from those contested in 2010, because population growth there offset the reduction in the number of constituencies, meaning less change than in other regions of relative decline.

In consideration of the representations the Commissions were, as under the previous legislation, provided with reports from their ACs – which they published. These ACs faced much more substantial tasks than their counterparts employed before 2011, each of whom only oversaw a single Local Inquiry relating, in nearly every case in England, to one county or borough. The 2011 legislation suggested that the English Commission use nine regions as the framework within which to conduct the public consultation. Three regions (London, North West and South East) had three ACs each, and the other six had two. ACs were responsible for conducting the Public Hearings and evaluating the written and oral representations before preparing a report (in each case extensive and involving working with Commission staff) and making recommendations; this had to be done for both the initial and the revised proposals (although there were no Hearings involved at that second stage). The ACs were appointed after public advertisement; twelve were lawyers but the other nine came from a range of backgrounds, mainly in the public sector.[17] The Boundary Commission for Scotland continued to employ Sheriffs Principal to conduct its Local Hearings.

Many of the changes in the Commissions' revised recommendations were extensive, and although they removed some of the more unusual elements in the initial proposals there was again widespread disruption to the current constituencies. The proposed seat linking parts of north Leeds with wards in North Yorkshire was removed, for example, but the revised proposals included just three constituencies comprising Leeds wards only (five in each case): three linked Leeds wards (1, 2 and 4 of them respectively) with Bradford wards; two linked Leeds wards (3 and 2) with wards from Wakefield; and one grouped two Leeds wards with three from Kirklees. The seat linking two east Sheffield wards with five in Rotherham was retained, the Commission noting that Sheffield City Council accepted that 'the proposals for South Yorkshire represent the only practicable division of the sub-region within the rules [...] and the presumption against splitting wards. [...] The [...] constituencies covering Sheffield, Barnsley and Rotherham are the only possible option available to the Boundary Commission within its rules and guidelines.'

Concerning the 'orphan wards', the proposal for Mersey Banks was replaced. In Oxfordshire, however, despite strong pressure to relocate Radley ward in an Oxford West and Abingdon constituency, where it was previously located, the original proposal was retained: the Commission noted that this was 'not popular with many local residents in Radley, and its more natural links clearly are with Abingdon. However, the more rural nature of the ward (electorate of 1,982) aligns it with Henley far better ... [It therefore concluded that] the

Commission's initial proposals do provide the best solution for the overall composition of constituencies in Oxfordshire and, within the statutory requirements, are the least disruptive and best that can be achieved when judged against the key criteria.' It similarly rejected counter-proposals that tried to contain as much of the University of Oxford in a single constituency as simply not practicable.

The other orphan ward discussed earlier provided the only case in which the Commission decided to split wards. Recognising the 'strength of feeling adverse to our initial proposals [...] and [...] of the arguments presented against them', it was 'persuaded by the evidence and reasoning set out by the ACs that there are exceptional and compelling circumstances that justify splitting two wards in Gloucester and Tewkesbury, in order to produce a solution that provides adequate recognition for very strong ties within Gloucester itself'. Gloucester's central ward would not be linked to the Forest of Dean across the unbridged Severn, therefore.

Compared to the provisional recommendations, the number of constituencies crossing London borough boundaries was reduced from 37 to 33, and 26 boroughs had at least one revised constituency containing wards from that borough alone – six had two such constituencies and one (Bromley) had three. One of the most contested of the initially proposed constituencies – joining wards in Waltham Forest and Edmonton which would have crossed the River Lee, with the current MPs from both sides claiming there were no links between the two areas – was replaced by one further down the river. The Commission noted that it 'received no counter-proposal that did not involve a constituency crossing the River Lee. Nor would the various statutory factors be satisfactorily balanced across the 68 constituencies in London without crossing the River Lee.' In this, as in other cases, the rigidity of the new rules operating within the geography of local government and other boundaries meant that many of the proposed constituencies had elements that previously would have been considered undesirable and would have been removed; the Commissions were tightly constrained by the arithmetic criterion's predominance.

Under the previous rules, it was rare for Commissions to receive many representations to their revised recommendations. Under the new rules, however, changes made to the initial proposals for a constituency could have substantial implications for neighbouring seats that were not initially much affected. For example, the initial proposals dismembered two existing seats near Hull: 46 per cent of the Beverley and Holderness constituency electorate were placed in a new Beverley constituency, with 40 per cent allocated to a new Bridlington seat and the remaining 15 per cent to Kingston upon Hull East; nearby East Yorkshire had 46 per cent of its electorate allocated to the new Beverley seat and the remaining 54 per cent to Bridlington. South of the Humber, the relatively small Great Grimsby seat was to remain intact, with 16,991 electors added to it from the existing Cleethorpes seat, the remainder of which was placed in a new Brigg and Humberston constituency. The proposals for change north of the Humber attracted strong arguments for retaining the two current seats, which both had electorates within +/−5 per cent of the quota.

South of the Humber, concern was expressed at splitting Cleethorpes but the Labour Party's representation recognised that 'any alternative would be likely to divide the town of Grimsby so we make no formal counter proposal in this area' which the ACs interpreted as saying that 'the Labour party does not endorse the division of Cleethorpes but might prefer that to dividing Grimsby'. However, to accommodate the changes they wished to make north of the river without creating constituencies that dismembered parts of Kingston upon Hull,[18] changes south of the river were needed. The ACs' report noted that this issue

> is a very clear illustration of the operation of the electoral quota in requiring decisions to be taken on a 'package' basis because of the consequential effects of relatively modest variations.

They proposed retaining the two north Humberside seats and not dismembering Hull which meant that they found it necessary to divide Grimsby, which would be balanced by reuniting Cleethorpes, creating two seats of Grimsby North and Barton, and Grimsby South and Cleethorpes; they argued that 'all wards within Grimsby and Cleethorpes are part of the same local authority and the two towns, despite different characteristics [one a declining fishing port, the other a seaside resort], are closely linked with each other and their surrounding hinterland ... This configuration takes account of local ties by allowing Cleethorpes not to be split. It also meets the concerns of the many submissions that attached weight to the retention of Cleethorpes in a constituency name.'

This angered Grimsby's MP, Austin Mitchell, who obtained a Westminster Hall debate on the issue. He called the decision to split

Grimsby 'political vandalism', stressing that it was currently 'one of the few parliamentary constituencies that is also a community' that would have been maintained as Labour and the Liberal Democrats had wished. The Commission's arguments for the changes were apparently only needed as responses to representations for changes in neighbouring areas. In response, a government minister upheld the Commission's independence and defended the reforms that 'are designed to restore equality and fairness in setting constituency boundaries'. The outcome of Mitchell's arguments is unknown (he later submitted alternative proposals with separate seats for both Grimsby and Cleethorpes, involving crossing the regional boundary into the East Midlands), because the review ended before the Commissions submitted their final reports.

The Boundary Commission for Wales received over 700 written representations with 100 oral presentations at its Public Hearings. It revised 21 of the 30 constituencies initially recommended – extensively in some cases – and changed 14 names. Although none of the existing constituencies was retained unchanged, 14 would be wholly contained within one of the new constituencies, and of the 26 local authorities, six were entirely within a single constituency. Of the 50 constituencies initially proposed by the Scottish Commission (other than the two island constituencies separately defined in the legislation), 32 were unchanged in its revised proposals (although six had a name change); 31 wards were divided between constituencies, and 38 of the constituencies contained at least one part-ward. Of the 50 'mainland constituencies' 35 were contained within a single local authority, 14 contained parts of two authorities and one contained parts of three.

Would ward-splitting have resulted in much less disruption overall? We conducted an experiment covering London and the six English metropolitan counties with the results compared with the situation in Scotland where wards were split in the provisional recommendations.[19] We classified as 'sub-optimally placed (SP)' electors those either: placed in a different constituency from the majority of electors in their existing constituency; or placed in a different constituency from the majority in their local authority; or placed in a different constituency from the majority in their ward. In Scotland, constituencies created in the experiment with no ward splitting would have seen 53 per cent of the country's electorate classified as SP, whereas in the Commission's provisional recommendations this was reduced to 41 per cent. In metropolitan England, 43 per cent of the electorate was classified as SP in the Commission's provisional proposals; in the experiment, 64 wards were split (21 of them in Greater London), which was less than one per local authority, and the percentage of SP voters reduced to 22 – clearly suggesting that while respecting the arithmetic criterion now dominating the rules, the organic criterion, as the Scottish Commission had shown, could be much better implemented with a small amount of ward splitting without harming application of the organic criteria – assuming, of course, that the pre-existing constituencies reflected local communities.

The Commissions didn't reach any final recommendations; their work was prematurely halted early in 2013 because of conflict within the coalition government over the Liberal Democrats' wish to replace the House of Lords by an elected chamber. A bill to that effect gained second reading support in the House of Commons despite some Conservative backbench opposition, but it was clear that the House would not support the proposed timetable for debate and the Prime Minister withdrew the bill. The Liberal Democrat leader indicated that his party considered that this violated the coalition agreement and the withdrawal could result in his party not voting for the Order implementing the new constituencies when the Commissions reported in 2013; as all of the opposition parties would likely vote against too, the new constituencies would have been rejected and the 2015 election fought in the existing seats. However, before that could happen Liberal Democrat and other peers attached an amendment to the Electoral Registration and Administration Bill altering the Parliamentary Constituencies Act 1986 (that had been amended by the Parliamentary Voting System and Constituencies Act, 2011) by changing the date for the Commissions to submit their reports on their first review under the new rules from 1 October 2013 to 1 October 2018. The government's attempt to remove that amendment when the bill returned to the Commons in January 2013 was defeated, so that when the bill was enacted the Commissions immediately halted work on their reviews.

Would those proposals have addressed the Conservatives' reason for changing the rules for redistribution – assuming that their final form was similar to that of the revised proposals published by the Commissions after the initial and secondary consultation periods? At one level, the answer is 'yes': under the revised recommendations the disparity would have been reversed – Labour would have won a seat for every 38,594 votes cast in 2010, compared to 35,518 votes for every Conservative elected. This is a much smaller disparity than that observed in 1997, 2001 and 2005, the elections that had focused Conservative minds on the problem. But (for reasons explored further in Chapter 6), the advantage Labour enjoyed over the Conservatives at those contests had already largely dissipated by 2010 anyway, even before the new boundary review rules were introduced: at the 2010 election, Labour won a seat for every 33,359 votes and the Conservatives for every 35,054. The Conservatives' problem with how they were treated by the electoral system was not primarily a function of how the seats were drawn. In some respects, they were aiming for the wrong target.

Changing the rules again?

After the reviews ended in 2013 several Liberal Democrat peers considered a change to the rules before the next redistribution began in spring 2016. They were particularly concerned about the degree of disruption to constituency boundaries in the Commissions' proposals, and commissioned research to determine which factor – the reduction in the number of MPs, the +/−5 per cent tolerance around the quota, and the English Commission's reluctance to split wards, individually or together – was most responsible for the extensive disruption, as well as the creation of many constituencies that either split communities or combined disparate places. That investigation concluded that the impact of changing the number of MPs on the Commissions' provisional and revised recommendations was only slight, that whatever the size of the House of Commons, including retaining 650 MPs, extensive disruption would result.[20] The causes of (and possible remedies to) the disruption lay elsewhere – in the single UK quota and the tight tolerance limit, plus the unwillingness (other than in Scotland) to split wards. The research divided Great Britain into 75 areas and explored whether, without ward-splitting, there were feasible solutions within each area involving constituencies all within a given tolerance ranging from +/−5 per cent to +/−12 per cent. With a +/−5 per cent tolerance few if any feasible solutions were identified, but the wider the tolerance the greater the number available: indeed with a +/−8 per cent tolerance feasible solutions were available for most areas. With a small amount of ward-splitting, however, there were feasible solutions involving greater continuity in the map of constituencies and much less boundary-crossing, especially in urban areas – especially if the tolerance limit was relaxed to +/–8 per cent.

The research report was presented at a meeting in Parliament attended by MPs and peers from all parties; there was general acceptance of the case for some ward-splitting but reluctance, especially among Conservatives, for relaxing the tolerance limit. The report stimulated the House of Commons Political and Constitutional Reform Committee to recommend in early 2015 that the government should legislate before the next review began to retain 650 MPs and alter the tolerance limit to +/–10 per cent.[21] The new – Conservative majority – government didn't respond until February 2016, reiterating the Conservatives' belief that 'equality and fairness must be paramount' in redistributions and its intention (in its 2015 election manifesto) 'to reduce the number of MPs to 600 to cut the cost of politics and make votes of more equal value; and to implement the boundary reforms that Parliament has already approved' (the meaning of the final clause is unclear, since no reforms had been approved).[22] Its 2017 manifesto made the same general commitment, to 'continue with the current boundary review, enshrining the principle of equal seats, while reducing the number of MPs to 600'.

The Labour Party remained determined to change the rules, however, and a former shadow minister, Pat Glass MP, who came high in the ballot for introducing private members' bills introduced a Parliamentary Constituencies (Amendment) Bill 2016–17, prepared by the party. It changed the 2011 legislation in three main ways: the number of MPs should be 650; the tolerance limit should be +/–10 per cent; and reviews should be held every ten years. It also called for reviews to be based on more recent data. It had a successful second reading and was remitted to a Public Bill Committee, which never met. Immediately after the 2017 general election, with the next review well underway, that, slightly altered, private member's bill was revived by another Labour MP, Afzal Khan. It too had a successful second reading (229 in favour and only 44 against), in December 2017, and was referred to a Public Bill Committee. This could not meet for procedural reasons until May 2018, when it still could not proceed for another procedural reason – no money had been granted, without which debate could not proceed; it met each Wednesday and adjourned to the following week.

Normal practice was for a money resolution to be passed when a bill was sent to committee but when this did not happen an emergency Commons debate was held (on 21 May 2018), Khan arguing that because the government feared it would lose a vote on the bill it was denying the money resolution as a delaying tactic.[23] The Leader of the House argued that it was not without precedent for the government not to bring forward a money resolution if it believed that it was 'not in the taxpayers' interest to do so at the time' and argued that it was best to wait until the Commissions had reported in September 2018 when, in the words of Mark Harper MP, 'the Government would then reflect further'. After three hours of debate the House resolved, without a division, that it had 'considered the expectation that the Government brings forward a Money resolution'. No such resolution was brought forward; the committee met and adjourned on eleven occasions between May and July 2018 without being able to debate the bill: its next sitting was scheduled for 5 September 2018, the day on which the four Boundary Commissions indicated that they would be delivering their reports. Nothing changed. The Commissions' recommendations were tabled but no Order was placed before Parliament that they be implemented.[24] The Public Bill Committee continued to meet and adjourn because it was prevented by the lack of a Money Resolution to proceed. When it met on 24 April 2019 – for the thirtieth time – the minister overseeing preparation of the Orders stated that this was a complex task requiring time (although after previous redistributions the Orders contained little more than a list of the new seats and their constituent wards, information that is all in the Commissions' reports). The Committee then voted to reconvene every month – but the dissolution of Parliament in November 2019 meant that the bill was lost. (It is clear that although – as the analyses reported below indicate – introduction of the new seats would benefit the Conservatives they were uncertain that they could get a majority in favour of an Order implementing the proposals.)

While Afzal Khan's bill was awaiting its arrival in the Public Bill Committee the House of Commons Public Administration and Constitutional Affairs Committee considered what would happen if the Commissions' proposals were not accepted by Parliament. A further review would presumably have to be undertaken, which might not be completed in time for new constituencies to be in place for the 2022 general election, which would have to be fought in very unequal constituencies designed using electoral data for 2000.[25] It therefore recommended, on 19 February 2018, that the government allow an early debate on the issue and decide whether to continue with the review.[26] The government's response, on 11 May 2018, was that the reviews should continue in order to deliver constituencies that, as agreed by Parliament in 2011, 'will make sure that everyone's vote carries more equal weight'.[27]

Starting all over again

These discussions were taking place while the four Commissions were undertaking a further review, due to report by October 2018. Although they could draw on the experience of the unfinished review, they basically had to start again from scratch because of changes in the size and distribution of the electorate. In addition, re-warding in parts of England and the whole of Northern Ireland had altered the building blocks in many areas. The size and distribution of the electorate was of particular concern, notably to the Labour Party. The Electoral Commission's research showed that only some 85 per cent of those eligible to be on the electoral roll were registered, and there were also concerns about the roll's accuracy – which the government tackled by introducing new registration procedures that removed many individuals from the roll each December if they did not personally register. The new review began in March 2016 using the register compiled in the preceding December and therefore did not include more than a million individuals who had enrolled in the first five months of 2016 so that they could vote in the 2016 referendum on the UK's continued membership of the EU. If they had been on the register in December 2015 the allocation of seats across the four countries and England's nine regions might have been different. As it was, with a quota of 74,769, nearly 2,000 fewer than that used for the previous, unfinished, review, England was allocated 499 seats (plus two 'protected constituencies'), Scotland, 51 (also plus two), Wales, 29, and Northern Ireland, 17. The range of permitted electorates was from 71,031 to 78,507.

The review proceeded as its predecessor, with the same issues arising though not always in the same places. One significant change was in the English Commission's attitude to ward-splitting, influenced by what it heard in the public consultations. As the 2014 research report noted earlier had established, if it had been prepared to split wards there could be less disruption to the existing constituency map, fewer communities need be split, and fewer seats need cross local government boundaries. At the Review's outset, however, the Boundary

Commission for England maintained its position that it would seek to avoid ward-splitting 'wherever possible', but continued:

> However, the BCE recognises that in a few cases there may be exceptional and compelling circumstances – having regard to the specific factors identified in Rule 5 – that may make it appropriate to divide a ward. Strong evidence and justification will need to be provided in any constituency scheme that proposes to split a ward, and the number of such split wards should be kept to an absolute minimum. Examples of such circumstances in which the BCE might propose splitting a ward could include: (a) where all the possible 'whole ward' options in an area would significantly cut across local ties; or (b) where splitting a single ward may prevent a significant 'domino effect' of otherwise unnecessary change to a chain of constituencies. Where the BCE does accept the need to split a ward, it will seek to do so along the boundaries of the polling districts that form part of the ward.[28]

The Boundary Commission for Wales included a similar, though shorter, statement in its *Guide*; the Boundary Commission for Northern Ireland's *Guide* stated that 'as far as practicable wards will not be split between constituencies'; the Boundary Commission for Scotland remained more willing than its counterparts to countenance splitting wards – its final proposals split 34 wards involving 41 constituencies.

In England, the Commission eventually agreed to split ten wards – a small number but setting an important precedent. There were none in its initial proposals; those eventually included were responses to pressure from political parties and individuals. The Commission and its ACs were clearly reluctant to accept counter-proposals including split wards, dismissing many because they lacked a compelling rationale. In every case where split wards were accepted the ACs visited the sites and some called for more evidence before reaching their final decision, as in East Sussex where with one split ward they avoided dividing Newhaven and could create three Brighton and Hove constituencies, all with 'direct access to the seafront'. In the London Borough of Enfield, the initial proposals split the existing Enfield Southgate constituency across five new seats; the ACs recommended splitting one ward to ameliorate this but because 'the splitting of wards is untested in the London region' the Commission invited further evidence before accepting that recommendation. One ward was also split in Gloucestershire as were three wards – at the Conservative Party's suggestion with evidence the Commission found 'exceptional and compelling' – in Dudley and Sandwell; the new constituencies were much closer to those they were replacing than in the Commission's initial proposals.

By far the major change involving split wards was in Sheffield. Noting that the city's large ward electorates there had 'proved challenging' (they averaged some 13,600 electors each) the Commission's initial proposals included just two constituencies wholly contained within Sheffield: two more combined five Sheffield wards with one from either Barnsley or Rotherham; another combined two Sheffield wards with five from Rotherham. These generated many objections, with several counter-proposals splitting wards. The ACs were most convinced by one from a Sheffield Labour MP, supported by not only three other Sheffield Labour MPs but also the Conservative Party (which had no prospects of winning a seat there, whatever the constituency configuration). It involved splitting three wards – a scheme supported by the Labour Party centrally at the secondary consultation stage. A major benefit was that whereas the Commission's initial proposals would involve only 55 per cent of Sheffield's electorate being located in constituencies containing Sheffield wards only, this was increased to 94 per cent – one ward was placed in a constituency containing eight Barnsley wards. After extensive consideration and site visits, this configuration was recommended to, and accepted by, the Commission which noted in its final report that, not only was there 'no significant opposition' to the ward-splitting, but also that its acceptance meant that there was much less disruption to constituencies in neighbouring Rotherham – it had avoided the 'domino effect' of otherwise unnecessary change to a chain of constituencies' – that it stated at the outset was one of the reasons why it might accept split-ward proposals. Overall few wards were split but the precedents were set for proponents to use that stratagem to create equal-sized constituencies that were less disruptive and fitting more closely to community geographies: the organic was gaining greater recognition within the determining arithmetic criterion.

Another important aspect of the rules highlighted by the 2018 Review was the change in national and regional entitlements. Compared with five years earlier, Scotland and Northern Ireland were each entitled to one additional seat (at the expense of Wales and England) and, within the last-named, three of the nine regions had an altered entitlement. Supporters of the new legislation could justifiably point out that these changes simply reflected the changing patterns of electoral registration, but the scale of the consequences seems rather less well appreciated.

The reduction in allocation to the North East region brings the point out rather well. At the 2013 Review, the North East was allocated 26 seats, but by 2018 its entitlement had fallen to 25. Most of the previously recommended seats were still within 5 per cent of the UK quota, but one would need to be abolished and its c.70,000 electors transferred elsewhere. In order to minimise disruption it is highly likely that a constituency towards the geographic centre of the region would face the axe,[29] but as each of its neighbours had little room for numeric expansion, electors would have to be 'passed on' in gradually decreasing numbers, much like the ripples which result when a stone is thrown into a pond. The net effect would be change, often significant, to a majority of that region's constituencies as recommended by the 2013 Review. And while this example almost certainly does reflect a real change in the regional balance of electors, the vagaries of the UK's system of electoral registration are well enough known that the possibility exists that a region's or a country's allocation could flip backwards and forwards at five-yearly intervals with constituencies successively abolished and re-created. Indeed, earlier research had shown that between 1989 and 2009 the number of constituencies allocated to Northern Ireland using the 2011 formula would have varied between 14 and 16, and England's between 498 and 503.[30] Disruption on this scale and with this regularity is the clearest demonstration yet of the changed priorities in British redistricting.

Another illustration of the potential difficulties of changing entitlements occurred in Northern Ireland, where the 2016 review involved a reduction in the province's allocation from 18 to 17 seats. The Northern Ireland Commission's initial proposals involved very considerable disruption to the existing map, with Sinn Féin possibly winning more seats than the DUP, as suggested by the press coverage when the provisional recommendations were published.[31] The very substantial concern over the amount of disruption encouraged the Commission to implement one of the new rules introduced in 2011 that applied to Northern Ireland only and gives its Commission greater flexibility because of the relatively small number of seats (see p. 79); if the difference between the total Northern Ireland electorate and the UK quota multiplied by the number of seats allocated to Northern Ireland exceeds one-third of the UK quota, it could employ a wider tolerance – which was calculated as 69,031–80,137 rather than the range of 71,031–78,507 applied in Great Britain. The Commission decided to apply this in its revised proposals which included three constituencies (two of them in Belfast) with fewer electors than the UK lower tolerance limit, with the Commission claiming that this greater flexibility allowed it to produce what it termed 'more compliant patterns'.

Unfortunately, this decision added fuel to the partisan fire. A major issue was whether there should be three or four seats focused on Belfast. The initial proposals for three angered the DUP. Its lengthy representation contained an alternative scheme that moved many fewer voters from their existing seats, in part by creating four Belfast constituencies. So when the Commission yielded to the pressure to apply the more flexible quota with revised proposals that appeared more favourable to the DUP than Sinn Féin, the latter was unimpressed.[32] Sinn Féin had broadly accepted the initial proposals as fair and equitable but was strongly opposed to the revised recommendations – which it claimed reflected the influence of a 'Unionist lobby' – and argued that, with minor changes, the initial proposals should be reinstated,[33] whereas the DUP, on the other hand, was largely satisfied and commended them, suggesting a few small changes only. The Commission made no significant changes to its revised proposals.

Some months after the four Commissions had delivered their final reports, a Belfast elector (initially granted anonymity but subsequently identified as Patrick Lynch) petitioned the Northern Ireland High Court for judicial review on the grounds that the Northern Ireland Boundary Commission 'erred in law procedurally and fettered its discretion' in adopting the approach that allowed a wider tolerance there than in Great Britain. Mr Lynch had mixed success – the High Court found in favour of the Commission in its interpretation of Rule 7 but that it had contravened 'aspects of the common law principles governing consultation' in its treatment of representations. Lynch appealed, the Commission cross-appealed, and, in June 2020, the Court of Appeal in Northern Ireland delivered its verdict. Finding in favour of Lynch on all counts,[34] the Appeal Court concluded that the Commission had misinterpreted the conditions which needed to be satisfied for the application of Rule 7; that it had 'failed to give adequate reasons for its conclusions'; and that its application of a 'consultation hierarchy' (wherein representations to initial proposals stood more chance of success than those to revised proposals) 'unlaw-

Table 5.2 The estimated outcome of the Boundary Commissions' 2016–18 proposals if the 2015 and 2017 general elections had been fought in those constituencies in Great Britain

Seats	Con	Lab	LD	Nat	Oth	Total
2015 Result	331	232	8	59	2	632
Commissions' provisional	319	203	4	55	2	583
2017 Result	317	262	12	39	2	632
Commissions' final	307	234	8	32	2	583

fully impugned' the Commission's final recommendations. Aside from the embarrassment for the Commission (whose Deputy Chair is herself a High Court judge), the Appeal Court judgment raises important questions regarding the process of public consultation and the difficulties all four Commissions face in balancing responses to initial and revised proposals.

Although the four Commissions' final proposals differed from their revised recommendations in detail, they had no effect on the likely electoral impact across Great Britain (Table 5.2). Their initial proposals were published after the 2015 general election, at which the Conservatives had gained a small majority overall but a 99-seat lead over Labour; the Liberal Democrats experienced a major decline in their number of MPs from the previous election (from 56 to just 8) and the SNP won all but three of Scotland's 59 seats (compared to six in 2010). The Commissions' initial recommendations – as at the previous, unfinished Review (Table 5.1) – favoured the Conservatives, increasing their majority over Labour to 116 seats in a smaller House of Commons, largely as a consequence of the equalisation of electorates.

Another general election was held, in June 2017, before the Commissions produced their revised and then final recommendations, both of which had the same electoral impact. The Conservatives lost ground at that election compared to 2015, lacking an overall majority and having a lead of 55 seats over Labour. But once again, if that election had been held in the new seats the Conservatives' advantages would have been significantly enhanced: they would have achieved a small majority in the smaller House, and their lead over Labour would have been stretched from 55 to 71 seats.

Naming constituencies

One aspect of both the 2013 and 2018 reviews is worthy of comment
- the length of constituency names. As discussed in Chapter 2,
constituency names reflect the importance of place to many. These
typically refer, in urban areas, to the main settlement and, where it
is subdivided into several seats, either its geographical location (e.g.
Glasgow East) or named sections (e.g. Ealing Acton and Central;
Ealing Southall); in more rural areas the name is commonly either
the county and some section of it (e.g. Mid Derbyshire; Derbyshire
Dales) or one or more of its main settlements (e.g. St Ives; Truro
and Falmouth). Residents and their representatives are keen to
have their place contained within the constituency name, which
can lead in some cases to names of considerable length. Two
Scottish examples were mentioned in Chapter 2: East Kilbride,
Strathaven and Lesmahagow; and Inverness, Nairn, Badenoch and
Strathspey; nine English constituencies have three places identified in their constituency names in the 2018 final proposals
(including Harborough, Oadby and Wigston); the longest in Wales
was Brecon, Radnor and Montgomery (Aberhonddu, Maesyfed a
Threfaldwyn).

In creating constituencies with longer names than previously the
Commissions were responding to representations from residents,
political parties and MPs who wanted those names to reflect local
identities in seats that covered several settlements; the then MP for
Plymouth Sutton and Devonport, for example, attended a public hearing in Bristol just to press that the current name be retained, rather
than replaced by Plymouth South (he succeeded). In urban areas, the
greater number of proposed constituencies containing wards from
more than one local authority saw names identifying their separate
parts, as with Ruislip, Northwood and Pinner for the recommended
seat (in 2018) covering parts of Harrow and Hillingdon in London;
and Isleworth, Brentford and Chiswick, which combined wards in
Ealing and Hounslow. In Scotland, however, although some names
were recommended with three separate components (e.g. Argyll,
Bute and Lochaber), in the least densely populated areas the decision was made to use the portmanteau names Highland North and
Highland South.

The trend to longer names has been studied by Philip Cowley and
Matthew Bailey. In 1950 a constituency name's mean length was 12.8

characters; by 2010 it was 15.1 characters; and in the Commissions' recommended new constituencies in 2018 it is 16.7 – a 30 per cent increase. Only 160 of the proposed names comprise a single word, compared to 272 in 1950; the number including the word 'and' will increase from 53 to 216. Scotland has always had the longest names on average: a mean of 19.9 characters in the 2018 recommended constituencies compared to 16.3 in both England and Northern Ireland; the Welsh mean is 18.4.[35]

Conclusions

The major change to the rules for creating new constituencies implemented in 2011 was introduced by the Conservatives because of the way in which the electoral system disadvantaged them at the 1997 and 2001 elections. What the incoming government failed to acknowledge, however, was that the general election which returned them to power had far less of the unfairness of its predecessors. Indeed, there was little difference between the number of votes required to elect a Conservative (34,980) and a Labour (33,370) candidate in 2010; it was their coalition partners, the Liberal Democrats (119,944) who had more reason to feel aggrieved. And while the Conservatives could not be expected to foresee the reversal of the advantage at each of the next three elections (all of which required fewer Conservative than Labour votes to elect an MP), they should have recognised that the proposed remedy could not on its own produce 'fair votes'.

There can be little objection to attempts to reduce inequalities in the size of constituencies, especially if those returning representatives of one party are systematically larger than those of its opponent(s). The difficulty arises when the rules designed to achieve that effect produce unintended consequences. The reduction in the size of Parliament was bound to cause a major one-off redrawing of the electoral map and in that context the introduction of national, and within England, regional entitlements, was unexceptionable. The insistence on a maximum deviation of 5 per cent from the national quota was a different matter, not least because there was no clear rationale for the figure. There was little partisan advantage to be gained from such a tight restriction (not least because the same legislation introduced reviews every five years) and it was well known that there were many areas where the Haringey dilemma (Figure 5.1) would have to be confronted. The resultant and widespread fracturing of long-standing electoral ties, especially in urban Britain with its larger wards, was an entirely avoidable consequence.

What seems to have been even less well appreciated is the redrawing of boundaries that will be required in subsequent reviews consequent upon quite small changes in national and/or regional entitlements. Had the 2013 review been implemented, each of the twelve subdivisions of the UK would have been awarded a number of seats based upon its theoretical entitlement. By the time of the 2018 review, half of those entitlements had changed – an extra seat each for Scotland, Northern Ireland and The East of England; one less for Wales, the West Midlands and North East England. The smaller the region, the bigger the proportionate disruption.

Under this new set of rules, as before, the parties and others sought to influence the Commissions' recommendations by using the organic criteria that were now subsidiary to the arithmetic criterion. In doing so, they could suggest – and in some places gain – changes to constituency boundaries that favoured their electoral prospects. But not all of their proposals were made for electoral gain, as some of the changes made to the Commissions' initial proposals during the second – as yet not implemented – review show. Organic criteria were used – as in the Sheffield example – to suggest alternative boundary configurations that would make no substantial difference to the electoral outcome, but which provided a better fit to the area's community structure. Some of those changes were achieved by convincing a reluctant English Commission to split wards in a small number of cases – setting a precedent that might be more widely used in future reviews.

This chapter is entitled 'The 2011 legislation: major changes?'. To date, the answer is no. Two reviews and three general elections later, we still have the same constituency boundaries, with all the implications that has for 'fair votes'. A coalition fall-out, followed by a minority government and backbench unease over reducing their numbers has resulted in Parliament failing to deliver the boundary changes which are needed in any FPTP electoral system. The Commissions have carried out their part of the bargain; the politicians have not.

Not so far, at least. One of the first pieces of legislation introduced by the incoming Conservative government has been the Parliamentary Constituencies Bill 2019-21. With cross-party support for the repeal of the Fixed-Term Parliaments Act 2011 highly likely,[36] the Bill follows the 2011 legislation in making equal electorates, with a 5 per cent margin either side of the UK quota, the primary requirement, but also proposes extending the interval between boundary reviews from five years to eight; cancelling the reduction in the size of parliament with a reversion to the existing 650 MPs; and making the implementation of new boundaries automatic rather than subject to parliamentary approval. By the autumn of 2020 the Bill had made its way through most of its stages with the government resisting calls for relaxation of the 5 per cent tolerance, while accepting a Conservative amendment which would make Ynys Mon a fifth 'protected' constituency, not subject to that arithmetic constraint. All four Commissions face a significant task in meeting the 2023 deadline for the submission of their reports, with the complications that COVID-19 brings to the process still to be fully understood. If, and it still must be an if, the legislation proceeds, the Commissions report, and judicial review does not intercede, the next general election will be fought on a set of constituencies which will bear little relation to those currently in place. The 2011 Act will finally have achieved its goal – though whether the public and MPs will be thankful in the long run will take far longer to establish.

6

How representative is our democracy?

The previous three chapters have outlined changes to the British electoral system over the last two centuries. Although occasionally challenged then and since, the decisions taken during the nineteenth century to have a plurality voting system in single-member constituencies have remained in place. What has changed, however, has been the relative importance placed on arithmetic and organic criteria in drawing constituency boundaries. Although the arithmetic criterion, with equal-sized electorates, was on occasions given precedence, either explicitly in the legislation or implicitly in the Boundary Commissions' internal guidelines, for most of the period organic criteria have dominated – MPs have been elected to represent communities, and many constituency boundaries have been changed as little as possible to ensure continuity of links between places and their representatives. Only since 2010 has that situation been significantly challenged, through legislation that insists upon arithmetic predominance in the redrawing of constituency maps – a change that has yet to be fully implemented let alone evaluated.

One consequence of that long sequence of decisions has been unequal treatment of political parties. Graphs of the seats:votes ratio for each major party at each election (Figures 3.3 and 4.2) show that one or more parties has been substantially either over-represented or under-represented at each election. That inequality has not permanently disadvantaged one of the two largest parties which have dominated UK politics since the 1920s but it has more frequently favoured the Conservatives than Labour[1] – in part because the Conservatives have more often been the largest party, although when it has gained a Commons majority Labour has generally been more substantially advantaged than its opponent. For smaller parties, the consequence has almost invariably been a disadvantage; they have won fewer seats

than their national vote shares would entitle them should proportionality be a criterion for evaluating the system's operation.

This chapter extends those findings using two methods for evaluating the extent of over-/under-representation, applied to both recent
election results and the estimated outcomes from different constituency configurations proposed by both the Boundary Commissions
and the political parties. The methods are closely linked and illustrate
the fundamental features of single-member electoral systems where
the winning candidates are those with a plurality of the votes cast
in each constituency, as established in Gudgin and Taylor's classic
study.[2] They showed, and we demonstrate here, that the number of
seats a party wins is a function of not only how many votes it wins as
a proportion of the total cast but also three aspects of the geography
of its support: the degree to which its voters are clustered in particular
areas; the degree to which those clusters are concentrated together
in larger areas; and the configuration of the constituency boundaries
superimposed on those cluster and concentration maps.

Disproportionality

The first measure is of disproportionality, a system-wide metric that
builds on the seats:votes ratios used earlier. If an election result was
entirely proportional, each party should get a percentage share of
the seats equivalent to its percentage share of the votes. Of several
measures proposed to assess the extent to which a result deviates
from that norm, the one used here is the Gallagher – or least squares
– index of disproportionality.[3] This ranges between 0, which indicates
complete proportionality (i.e. each party has a seats:votes ratio of 1.0),
to 100, which indicates complete disproportionality. The latter could
never happen, since it would imply – in a two-party system – that one
party wins all of the votes and no seats whereas the other wins no
votes and all of the seats; but the larger the index value the greater the
disproportionality. As a general rule, the index indicates that percentage of the seats that would have to be reallocated across the parties in
order to achieve proportional representation, although the nature of
the formula – which places greater emphasis on the larger deviations
– means that is not a precise quantity.[4]

The formula is

$$ID = \sqrt{0.5 \sum (V_i - S_i)^2}$$

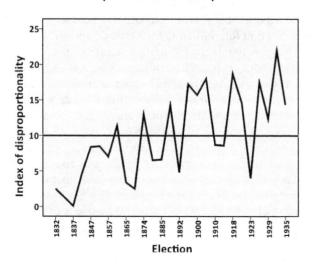

Figure 6.1 The Index of disproportionality for elections in the
United Kingdom from 1832 to 1935

where V_i is the percentage of the votes won by party i and S_i is its
percentage of the seats.

Thus in a three-party system, where parties a, b and c win 45, 35
and 20 per cent of the votes respectively and 55, 40 and 5 per cent of
the seats, the calculations are

$$[\{(45-55)^2 + (35-40)^2 + (20-5)^2\}/2] = \{[(-10^2) + (-5^2) + (15^2)]\}/2] =$$
$$[\{100 + 25 + 225\}/2] = [350/2] = 175$$

and the square root of 175 = 13.2, which is the ID value.

Figure 6.1 shows the index for each election from 1832 to 1935.
(There is some generalisation at a few of the elections – when, for
example, the Liberal Party was split after 1918 the votes and seats for
the separate parts have been combined for this purpose.) There is a
general upward trend, with election results on average more disproportional in the twentieth than in the nineteenth century, though
with considerable variation about that trend. Before the 1870s the UK
basically had a two-party system (in 1868, for example, the Tories and
the Liberals together won over 96 per cent of the votes cast), but the
emergence of new parties in Parliament (notably the Irish Party from
1884 and the Labour Party from 1900), together with the decline of

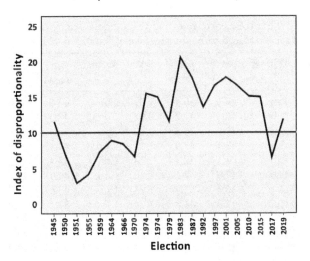

Figure 6.2 The Index of disproportionality for elections in the United Kingdom from 1950 to 2019

the Liberal Party from 1918 onwards, was largely responsible for the rise.

Figure 6.2 shows the index for elections from 1945 to 2019. Until 1970 the level of disproportionality was relatively low, exceeding 10.0 in 1945 only, reflecting the Conservative–Labour dominance throughout the country until then. From 1974 on it was on average much higher – over 15 at many of the contests – as more smaller parties began to win significant shares of the vote total, though rarely commensurate seat shares. There was, however, a notable fall in 2017 when Conservative and Labour predominance was reinstated (see Table 6.1 for the vote shares) but it increased to over 10.0 again in 2019 when the two-party hegemony was significantly reduced.

These index values suggest that at many elections party representation in the House of Commons was far from commensurate with the pattern of votes. Gallagher showed that indices for 23 countries using proportional systems between 1979 and 1989 averaged less than 10.0 whereas for those using single-member district systems (or FPTP) it was never less than 10.0, with the highest average being for the UK, at 16.6. Gallagher later reported average values of less than 2.0 for elections in West Germany, the Netherlands, Austria, Denmark and Sweden for the period 1979–89; a later compilation gave 1.95 for

Table 6.1 The percentage of votes and seats and the seats: votes ratio for the first- and second-placed parties at general elections 1950–2019

Election	Winner	per centV	per centS	S:V	Second	per centV	per centS	S:V
1950	Lab	46.1	50.4	1.09	Con	43.5	47.8	1.10
1951[A]	Lab	48.8	47.2	0.97	Con	48.0	51.4	1.07
1955	Con	49.7	54.8	1.10	Lab	46.4	44.0	0.95
1959	Con	49.4	57.9	1.17	Lab	43.8	40.9	0.93
1964	Lab	44.1	50.3	1.14	Con	43.4	48.2	1.11
1966	Lab	47.9	57.6	1.20	Con	41.9	40.2	0.96
1970	Con	46.4	52.4	1.13	Lab	43.0	45.7	1.06
1974F[B]	Con	37.8	46.8	1.24	Lab	37.1	47.4	1.28
1974O	Lab	39.2	50.2	1.28	Con	35.8	43.6	1.22
1979	Con	43.9	53.4	1.22	Lab	37.0	42.3	1.15
1983	Con	42.4	61.1	1.44	Lab	27.6	31.7	1.15
1987	Con	42.3	57.8	1.37	Lab	30.8	35.2	1.14
1992	Con	41.9	51.7	1.24	Lab	34.4	41.7	1.21
1997	Lab	43.2	63.4	1.47	Con	30.7	25.0	0.82
2001	Lab	40.7	62.5	1.53	Con	31.7	25.2	0.79
2005	Lab	35.2	55.1	1.57	Con	32.4	30.7	0.95
2010	Con	36.1	47.2	1.31	Lab	29.0	39.7	1.37
2015	Con	36.9	50.9	1.38	Lab	30.4	35.6	1.17
2017	Con	42.5	48.9	1.15	Lab	40.0	40.3	1.01
2019	Con	43.6	56.1	1.29	Lab	32.2	31.1	0.97

[A] Labour won most votes at the 1951 election but Conservatives won most seats.
[B] Conservatives won most votes at the February 1974 election but Labour won most seats.

Key: per centV – percentage of votes; per centS – percentage of seats; S:V – seats:votes ratio

Germany in 2017 and 0.96 for the Netherlands in the same year, plus 1.85 for Austria and 2.39 for Denmark in 2019, and 0.63 for Sweden in 2018.[5]

To illustrate how FPTP produces such disproportionality, we use a hypothetical set of seven constituencies, each comprising seven wards with 10,000 electors. Of those 49 wards, 25 are won by party A by 4,000 votes to 3,000; Party B wins the other 24 by the same margin. Remaining electors either abstain or vote for minor parties. Across all 49, therefore, the two main parties have very similar vote shares: A gets 172,000 and B 171,000. But how many seats will each win? In Figure 6.3 the 25 wards where A gets most votes are shown in

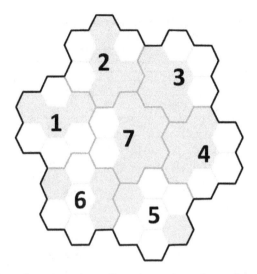

Figure 6.3 A hypothetical set of seven constituencies, each comprising
seven wards

grey and those where B prevails in white; as in the real world, support
for parties is not randomly distributed but tends to be clustered. In
any constituency where A wins four of the wards it gets 25,000 votes
to B's 24,000, and so wins the seat – as it does where it wins five or
more wards. Of the seven constituencies, A wins four, or 57 per cent
of the total – a disproportional result as a consequence of where its,
very slightly over, half of the votes were won within that constituency
configuration.

To account for this disproportionality we introduce the concepts
of wasted, surplus and effective votes.[6] In any constituency where
it loses, all of a party's votes are *wasted* – they do not contribute to it
winning any seats. Complementing that, any votes for the winning
party additional to those needed for victory there are *surplus* – they
too are not needed. Consider the victory of Party A in constituency
7 in Figure 6.3. It wins five wards to Party B's two, producing a total
constituency majority of 26,000 to 23,000. In this seat all of B's
votes are wasted, 2,999 (3,000 minus one) of A's are surplus, leaving
23,001 (the minimum number of votes Party A needs to win the seat)
as effective. Table 6.2 shows this breakdown for all seven seats and
for the city as a whole. Summed across all seven constituencies, both

Table 6.2 Introducing the concepts of wasted, surplus and effective votes for the constituencies shown in Figure 6.3

Seat	Total votes A	B	Wasted votes A	B	Surplus votes A	B	Effective votes A	B
1	24,000	25,000	24,000	0	0	999	0	24,001
2	25,000	24,000	0	24,000	999	0	24,001	0
3	25,000	24,000	0	24,000	999	0	24,001	0
4	25,000	24,000	0	24,000	999	0	24,001	0
5	23,000	26,000	23,000	0	0	2,999	0	23,001
6	24,000	25,000	24,000	0	0	999	0	24,001
7	26,000	23,000	0	23,000	2,999	0	23,001	0
Total	172,000	171,000	71,000	95,000	5,996	4,997	95,004	71,003

parties have a similar number of surplus votes, but whereas over half of A's votes are effective, over half of B's are wasted.[7]

A's relative success is a function of the geography of its support – of where its clusters of votes are concentrated within the constituency map (Figure 6.3). Of course, in any city with an odd number of constituencies contested by two major parties, one is going to come out on top; and if overall support is (more or less) equally split then a degree of disproportionality is inevitable. More troubling is the capricious nature of the potential bias. Consider Figures 6.4 and 6.5 for example. In both cases A wins 25 wards as before, but in Figure 6.4 it wins six of the seven seats compared with just one in Figure 6.5. While accepting that these are extreme cases, the fact that two more or less equally matched parties can win anything from 14 per cent to 86 per cent of an area's representation, *purely because of where their supporters are concentrated*, is more than a little disconcerting.

As Gudgin and Taylor point out, not only is the clustering and concentration of a party's support important in determining how well it is represented, consideration must also be given to the pattern of constituency boundaries that is superimposed upon those distributions. To illustrate this we return to the original example depicted in Figure 6.3. Through the creation of seven compact constituencies, the type most frequently favoured by impartial cartographers such as the UK Boundary Commissions, Party A secured a 4:3 advantage in terms of representation. Had Party A itself been able to draw the city's boundaries it might have come up with the proposal illustrated in Figure 6.6,

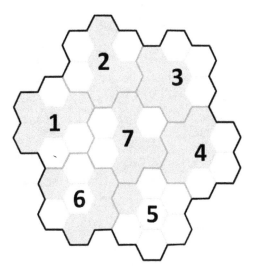

Figure 6.4 The same 49 wards as in Figure 6.3, aggregated into the same seven constituencies, but with a different pattern of support for the two parties

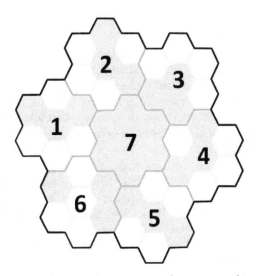

Figure 6.5 The same 49 wards as in Figure 6.3, aggregated into the same seven constituencies, but with a further different pattern of support for the two parties

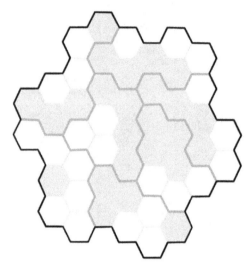

Figure 6.6 The same 49 wards and distribution of support for the two parties as in Figure 6.3, but with the boundaries of the seven constituencies drawn to favour party A

while its opponent would have much to gain from Figure 6.7 (in both cases the victorious party wins 6:1).

Neither of these configurations is overtly gerrymandered – Figure 6.8a shows the original 1812 gerrymander in Massachusetts and none of the constituencies outlined above is quite as peculiar in shape; neither is there any of the irregularity that was evident in the Liverpool Mossley Hill constituency, approved by the Boundary Commission for England in its Fourth Review (Figure 6.8b), or the Birmingham Yardley seat proposed in its 2018 Review (Figure 6.8c).[8]

Indeed, by elevating arithmetic considerations above the organic, as the most recent legislation has done, the 'shapeliness' of constituencies across the UK has suffered markedly. In itself, this may not matter, but in so far as it increases the scope for political parties to propose configurations which meet their electoral needs without demonstrably 'fiddling' the arrangement, it may be a legitimate cause for concern. Whether a party achieves its ends is, of course, another matter, but there can be no doubt that FPTP is far more susceptible to political manipulation than any of the more proportional alternatives.

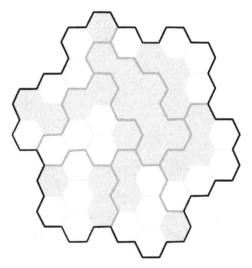

Figure 6.7 The same 49 wards and distribution of support for the two parties as in Figure 6.3, but with the boundaries of the seven constituencies drawn to favour party B

The geography of disproportionality

In international comparisons, UK general election outcomes are among the most disproportional. But that general conclusion at the national scale conceals considerable variation more locally; disproportionality may be even greater in some areas but less in others. To explore that, we look here at the results of the 2010, 2015, 2017 and 2019 general elections at three scales.

Table 6.3 shows indices of disproportionality for each of the UK's twelve government standard regions. These decline, in some regions considerably, between 2015 and 2017, reflecting the collapse in support for several smaller parties. (In 2010 and 2015 the Conservative and Labour parties together won 65.1 and 67.3 per cent of the votes; in 2017 this increased to 82.5 per cent but it fell back again in 2019 to 75.8 per cent. Fewer votes for smaller parties meant that, even though most were again under-represented, the differences between their vote and seat percentage shares were smaller, which was reflected in the smaller indices.) In some regions at the earlier elections, the index well exceeded 30: in 2010, for example, Labour won 43 per cent of the votes and 86 per cent of the seats in the North East; in the East

Figure 6.8a The original gerrymander: South Essex, Massachusetts (1812).
In 1811 the state governor of Massachusetts, Elbridge Gerry, approved a
redrawing of the state's electoral districts in such a way as to benefit his
own party. One of the resulting districts, that of South Essex, meandered
around the perimeter of Essex County, reminding some of the shape of a
salamander – hence the hybrid term 'gerrymander'.

Figure 6.8b The inquiry-led ice skater: Liverpool, Mossley Hill (1983).
The Mossley Hill constituency was recommended by the Boundary
Commission on the advice of the Assistant Commissioner who had
conducted the Local Inquiry in Liverpool. He in turn had been persuaded
by the evidence of local ties put forward by the local Liberal Party which
coincided with the greatest areas of Liberal support.

Figure 6.8c The rules-based mallard: Birmingham, Yardley (2018).
The Birmingham Yardley constituency proposed by the Boundary
Commission in 2018 also has an idiosyncratic shape, but in this case
political calculations are less relevant than are the rules on arithmetic
variability which severely constrained the Commissioners in the choice of
which four Birmingham wards to group together.

Table 6.3 Indices of disproportionality, by region, at the 2010, 2015, 2017
and 2019 UK general elections (number of constituencies in brackets)

Region	2010	2015	2017	2019	Region	2010	2015	2017	2019
North East (29)	35	35	30	18	South East (84)	33	34	27	28
North West (75)	19	20	14	9	South West (55)	18	37	28	29
Yorks/ Humber (54)	22	20	16	12	London (73)	15	15	10	16
West Midlands (59)	19	18	8	17	Scotland (59)	23	37	28	29
East Midlands (46)	24	22	14	23	Wales (40)	23	21	18	12
East (58)	35	33	27	27	N. Ireland (18)	18	16	20	19

of England, the Conservatives' vote share was 47 and their seat share 90 per cent. In each case supporters of the other large party were very substantially under-represented: the Conservatives won 23 per cent of the votes in the North East but only two (7 per cent) seats; in the East of England, Labour's 20 per cent of the votes yielded only two (4 per cent) seats. There, and to a lesser extent elsewhere, at all four elections, one of England's two largest parties wasted virtually all of its votes so that its supporters (considerable in number overall) achieved virtually no representation. In Scotland in 2015 when the SNP won 50 per cent of the votes and 56 of the 59 seats, the Conservatives, Labour and the Liberal Democrats won 14.9, 24.3 and 7.6 per cent of the votes respectively but each gained only one seat, wasting virtually all of the results of their campaigning for votes.

In 2017 disproportionality had declined in most regions, although only the West Midlands had an index less than 10, and in London it was 10.1. Even there, the disproportionality was much greater than in many other countries. The Conservatives won 49 per cent of the West Midlands votes and 59.3 per cent of the seats, for example; Labour's 54.5 per cent of London's votes brought it 67.1 per cent of the seats. And that relative proportionality was not sustained two years later: for the West Midlands the index value more than doubled, for example. In the North East and North West regions of England, and also in Wales, however, there was a substantial decline in the index between 2017 and 2019. This reflected Labour's loss of votes – and a substantial number of seats – there as the Conservatives won substantial support from former Labour voters who were disillusioned with that party's Brexit policy and its leadership. Elsewhere the indices changed little over the more recent elections, reflecting one party's predominance in each region.

At smaller scales, disproportionality was even greater as shown by indices for English and Welsh counties (Table 6.4).[9] Fourteen counties in 2010 and seven in 2015 had indices of 40 or greater, and a further thirteen and twelve respectively in the two years were between 30 and 39. The 2019 election saw a reduction in these high levels of disproportionality, with only four of 40 or more – in most cases reflecting Conservative gains in areas where Labour formerly dominated. Very high levels of disproportionality are recorded for very different areas. Among the seven metropolitan counties shown at the start of the table, both South Yorkshire and Tyne and Wear had indices greater than 40 in 2010, and above 30 in 2015 and 2017 (and also

Table 6.4 Indices of disproportionality, by county in England and Wales, at the 2010, 2015, 2017 and 2019 UK general elections (number of constituencies in brackets)

County	2010	2015	2017	2019	County	2010	2015	2017	2019
London (73)	15	16	11	16	Kent (17)	41	43	33	29
Greater Manchester (27)	34	29	24	16	Lancashire (16)	16	16	6	19
Merseyside (15)	28	27	19	23	Leicestershire (10)	27	22	17	14
South Yorkshire (14)	41	36	38	29	Lincolnshire (7)	41	40	20	28
Tyne and Wear (120)	43	39	35	44	Norfolk (9)	29	28	24	26
West Midlands (28)	25	27	17	9	North Yorkshire (8)	35	31	29	28
West Yorkshire (22)	19	19	21	12	Northumbria (4)	16	22	10	22
					Northampton (7)	44	41	41	36
					Nottinghamshire (11)	24	21	6	20
Avon (11)	15	28	10	12	Oxfordshire (6)	33	28	16	17
Bedfordshire (6)	22	18	7	13	Shropshire (5)	29	43	39	38
Berkshire (8)	32	27	18	23	Somerset (5)	30	43	39	38
Buckinghamshire (7)	35	34	35	40	Staffordshire (12)	23	20	17	34
Cambridgeshire (7)	33	32	19	31	Suffolk (7)	45	41	25	34
Cheshire (11)	28	18	14	11	Surrey (11)	39	32	35	40
Cleveland (6)	21	33	26	11	Warwickshire (6)	46	42	25	22
Cornwall (6)	12	46	44	39	West Sussex (8)	41	37	37	37
Cumbria (6)	16	19	6	30	Wiltshire (7)	31	38	37	36
Derbyshire (11)	22	21	5	25					
Devon (12)	21	36	26	24	Clwyd (7)	29	21	20	34
Durham (7)	45	43	41	15	Dyfed (5)	12	17	21	16
East Sussex (8)	22	27	8	18	Gwent (7)	35	35	28	35
Gloucestershire (6)	33	41	26	39	Gwynedd (3)	29	27	27	28
Hampshire (18)	25	34	27	27	Powys (2)	13	47	42	39
Hereford & Worcester (8)	44	39	37	33	Mid Glamorgan (6)	43	42	34	28
Hertfordshire (11)	42	39	40	33	South Glamorgan (5)	8	20	22	23
Humberside (10)	24	20	8	12	West Glamorgan (5)	45	29	36	43
Isle of Wight (1)	45	47	40	37					

in 2019 in Tyne and Wear): in 2010, for example, Labour won 40.9 per cent of South Yorkshire's votes and 92.9 per cent of the seats;[10] in 2017, 56.9 per cent of the votes won it 100 per cent of the seats. In Hertfordshire, 50–55 per cent of the votes gave the Conservatives victory in every seat apart from St Albans in 2019 at all four elections.[11]

Whereas substantial disproportionality favouring the largest party characterised many English and Welsh counties, it was even more extreme in the UK's cities – those (other than London) with three or more parliamentary constituencies (Table 6.5). None had an index less than 10 at any election; the majority had indices of 30 or more at all four. In most cases this reflects one party's predominance – usually Labour – and changes reflect where that is challenged: in Stoke-on-Trent, for example, Labour won all three seats in 2010 and 2015 with 40.7 and 47.9 per cent of the votes respectively, but in 2017 the Conservatives gained one of the three, hence the much lower index. Conservative candidates won the other two seats from Labour incumbents in 2019, hence the higher index again – a major switch in the beneficiaries of the disproportionality.

In many cities, therefore, one party is substantially, if not totally, under-represented. Labour won both of Swindon's two constituencies in 1997 with 47,972 of the 99,432 votes cast, winning both again in 2001 and 2005: both seats were lost to the Conservatives in 2010, 2015, 2017 and 2019. For thirteen years Labour provided both of Swindon's MPs with less than half of the votes, and then around 30 per cent of the votes meant no Labour representation. Disproportionality favouring one party at some elections was followed by disproportionality favouring another at the next. But such 'swings and roundabouts' did not characterise the situation everywhere: Barnsley, where Labour rarely wins as much as half of the votes cast, last elected a non-Labour MP in 1931; Salisbury has elected a Conservative at every election since 1924. National trends in support for the main parties are reflected in the allocation of seats in some places, but not others: the geography of party support makes the seats in some places safe for one of the parties almost whatever the national vote pattern so that changes in the distribution of House of Commons seats across the parties reflects voting trends in some parts of the country only. This became very clear in 2019 when the Conservatives extended their appeal to voters in constituencies in the north of England that had returned Labour MPs for several decades at least, winning a considerable number of seats outside

Table 6.5 Indices of disproportionality, by city, at the 2010, 2015, 2017 and 2019 UK general elections (number of constituencies in brackets)

City	2010	2015	2017	2019	City	2010	2015	2017	2019
Belfast (4)	13	22	30	24	Leeds (5)	34	31	34	38
Birmingham (9)	38	39	31	24	Leicester (3)	44	36	29	39
Bradford (3)	30	42	33	33	Liverpool (4)	32	22	15	18
Bristol (4)	15	31	36	39	Manchester (4)	23	34	23	27
Cardiff (4)	11	27	38	39	Newcastle upon Tyne (3)	47	41	33	39
Coventry (3)	46	46	39	48	Nottingham (3)	47	40	32	38
Edinburgh (5)	35	31	29	20	Sheffield (5)	33	27	35	41
Glasgow (7)	35	39	38	44	Stoke-on-Trent (3)	48	50	15	42
Kingston upon Hull (3)	47	40	36	48	Wolverhampton (3)	21	45	44	16

the major urban centres of Leeds, Liverpool, Manchester, Newcastle upon Tyne and Sheffield; those where the Conservatives unseated Labour incumbents had provided majority (in many cases substantial majority) support for Leave at the 2016 referendum and Labour had lost support there in 2017.

Bias

Disproportionality is a consistent feature of UK election results, therefore. Each party's share of seats after a general election is rarely commensurate with its vote share; some parties are over- and some under-represented. With the same vote share different patterns of clustering and concentration can produce different election outcomes within the same set of constituencies, whereas different sets of constituencies can also produce different outcomes even though the clusters and concentrations are unchanged.

This can be fair if each party is treated in the same way, so that if Party A got x percentage of the votes and y percentage of the seats at one election then if Party B had won x percentage of the votes instead it too would have gained y percentage of the seats. But that has not been the case at UK general elections since 1950. Table 6.1 showed the percentages of votes and seats for the winning and second-placed party then, plus the seats:votes ratios. With the exception of the 'unusual' election in 1951 when the party with the larger vote share did not also get the larger share of the seats, the winning party always had a seats:votes ratio in excess of 1.0, but those ratios varied substantially, from only 1.09 in 1950 to 1.57 in 2005.

Were the two parties treated equally? Compare the 1979 and 1997 elections. At the former, the Conservatives won 43.9 per cent of the votes and 53.4 per cent of the seats – a ratio of 1.22; at the latter, Labour won slightly fewer votes (43.2 per cent) but a much larger share of the seats (63.4 per cent), giving a ratio of 1.47. Or compare the Conservatives' experience in 1983 and 2017: at the former date 42.4 per cent of the votes returned 61.1 per cent of the seats (ratio 1.44) whereas at the latter virtually the same vote share (42.5 per cent) resulted in only 48.9 per cent of the seats, a ratio of 1.15. In addition, since 1974 at every election when it has come second Labour has always gained a greater share of the seats than votes whereas on three occasions when the Conservatives came second their ratio was less than 1.0, even though the Conservatives gained greater vote shares when they came second nationally than did Labour when it came second.

The process of translating votes into seats varies both between parties and within parties over time, therefore. This reflects what has been termed electoral bias since pioneering work by a New Zealand political scientist, Ralph Brookes, in the 1960s,[12] later taken up in both the UK and the United States – where it is more generally known as partisan asymmetry. The basis of this bias can be initially appreciated by an analogy with the two types of electoral manipulation/abuse that have characterised US elections: gerrymandering and malapportionment.

Gerrymandering involves the drawing of constituency boundaries to benefit one party over another – as illustrated in Figures 6.6 and 6.7; the same distribution of votes cast but a different set of constituency boundaries can produce a very different number of seats won. This can be achieved by one or, more usually, both of two strategies: packing by the gerrymandering party involves concentrating the opposition's votes in as few constituencies as possible, where it will win seats with very large majorities (Figure 6.7 exemplifies that); cracking involves distributing the opposition party's votes widely across constituencies where it loses by relatively small majorities (as in Figure 6. 6). In a cracked gerrymander, therefore, the losing party has a large number of wasted votes; in a packed gerrymander, it accumulates large numbers of surplus votes. For a successful gerrymander, therefore, the party wishing to maximise its number of seats should deploy a 'win small and lose big' strategy – where it wins it doesn't want very large majorities because that would mean too many surplus votes; where it loses it doesn't want large wasted vote totals.

Malapportionment refers to variations in electorates. In a constituency with 70,000 voters where none abstain and only two parties contest the seat, 35,001 votes are needed for victory, but in a similar seat with only 60,000 voters, the required total is only 30,001. If a party's support is concentrated in the seats with smaller electorates then it will need fewer votes overall to win there than a party whose support is concentrated in the larger seats. A party which wins smaller constituencies on average can get the same number of seats with a lower vote total than one which wins mainly in the larger seats.

Of course gerrymandering is not a characteristic of the UK electoral system as constituency boundaries are drawn up by non-partisan Boundary Commissions acting independently – although, as discussed in Chapters 4 and 5 the parties do try to influence where the boundaries are placed during the public consultation.[13] But gerrymander-like outcomes can result – what can be termed 'non-partisan or unintentional gerrymanders'. Have such unintentional gerrymanders characterised the election results summarised in Table 6.1? Similarly, although there have been constituency-size variations since 1944, there has been no explicit favouring of one party over others in the rules that the Boundary Commissions have applied so if one party has benefited from those size variations it would have been serendipitous.[14]

So, has there been bias in UK election results over recent decades, and which party was favoured? To answer that question quantitatively we use Brookes's method, adapted for the UK situation.[15] The calculation is based on a simple premise; if a system is unbiased then if two parties obtain the same share of the votes they should also get the same share of the seats – the process of translating votes into seats should favour neither. At any one election the vote totals are almost never equal so the method proceeds by constructing a notional election with a different result. Take the 2017 election, where the Conservatives and Labour won 42.5 and 40.0 per cent of the votes respectively. The notional election allocates 41.25 per cent to each party by simply taking 1.25 per cent of the total votes cast in each constituency from the Conservatives and adding them to Labour's total there. This gives them equal vote shares overall, and if the system is unbiased with the revised vote totals each should win the same number of seats; any variation from that indicates bias favouring one party over the other – and the difference in numbers of seats won by the parties provides a measure of its extent.

Figure 6.9 shows that measure for the relative bias between Labour and Conservatives for all general elections from 1950 to 2019, ignoring the situation of the smaller parties; in this, and all other bias calculations, a positive figure indicates bias favouring Labour and a negative figure indicates pro-Conservative bias. Four main phases with separate bias patterns can be identified. In the first two decades, there is a fairly large pro-Conservative bias initially at around 50 seats (i.e. if the two parties had obtained equal vote shares at the 1950 and 1951 elections the Conservatives would have won approximately 50 more seats than Labour). Its extent then declined and by 1966 there was a small pro-Labour bias. The 1970s and 1980s saw relatively little bias – never more than 26 seats and in three cases less than 10 – with

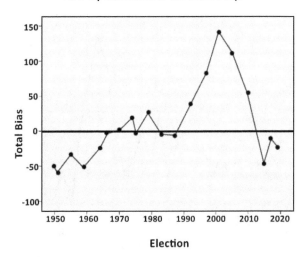

How representative is our democracy?

Figure 6.9 The net bias in general election results, 1950–2019
(a positive bias is pro-Labour, a negative bias pro-Conservative)

Labour the more likely beneficiary. The third period (1992–2010) saw Labour benefit very substantially, notably at the three elections it won: biases of 82, 141 and 111 seats respectively at those three contests were very much greater than in the previous period and exceeded by a substantial margin the Conservatives' advantages in the early 1950s. Even when Labour lost the election in 2010 it nevertheless enjoyed a bias towards it of 54 seats, but then in the final period – the 2015, 2017 and 2019 elections – there were pro-Conservative biases of 47, 11 and 23 seats respectively.

For much of the 70-year period, therefore, the translation of votes into seats produced outcomes that were far from even-handed in treatment of the two largest parties: at the extreme in 2001, if instead of winning 40.7 and 31.7 per cent of the votes respectively Labour and the Conservatives had each won 36.2 per cent, Labour would have gained 141 more seats than its opponent. To what extent was this a consequence of either or both of malapportionment and the distribution of each party's votes (the equivalent of an unintentional gerrymander)? One strength of Brookes's algebra is that the bias can be decomposed into its various sources, and Figure 6.10 shows the relative importance of those two. From the mid-1950s the malapportionment component favoured Labour, by an average of 20–25 seats. Offsetting that, the

Representative democracy?

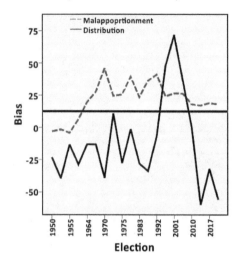

Figure 6.10 The malapportionment and distribution bias components in general election results, 1950–2019 (a positive bias is pro-Labour, a negative bias pro-Conservative)

distributional (or efficiency or unintentional gerrymander) component generally favoured the Conservatives by about the same number of seats, excepting the 1997–2010 period.

Why was that short period, covering the three elections won by Labour under Blair's leadership, so different? At most of the preceding elections Labour suffered from the equivalent of a pro-Conservative unintentional gerrymander – the constituency map meant that the Conservatives tended to lose large in seats that Labour won with relatively large majorities (equivalent to an anti-Labour packed gerrymander) and won relatively small in those where it succeeded in electing the MP (equivalent to an anti-Labour cracked gerrymander).[16] Labour's votes were both more clustered and more concentrated than the Conservatives'. It was different in the Blair years. Support in Labour's heartlands had been eroded by the impact of Thatcherism, the decline of many heavy industries and the decimation of the coalfields, allied with the neutering of the trade union movement, plus the increasing number of former Labour supporters who abstained from 2001 on.[17]

Reduction in the size of the working-class vote that was Labour's traditional strength meant that victory could only be achieved by appealing to a substantial proportion of the middle class in seats, many in southern England, outside the areas where it had been successful at previous contests – and these were the focus of New Labour's winning electoral strategy. Additionally, there was an increase in tactical voting by Labour and Liberal Democrat supporters. In seats where Labour appeared most likely to defeat the incumbent Conservatives in 1997, for example, some Liberal Democrat supporters voted Labour, which won a number of formerly Conservative-held seats by small majorities, and thus with few surplus votes. Complementing that, in seats where the Liberal Democrats had the better chance of defeating the Conservatives, some Labour supporters voted to achieve that end.[18] The Liberal Democrats got their largest share of the seats at any election since 1950 and Labour, because of the tactical voting, had a reduced number of wasted votes there – and also in seats where the Liberal Democrats came second. As the Blair government's popularity declined after 2001 so did the impetus for anti-Conservative tactical voting: Labour's vote distribution advantage dissipated and that component favoured the Conservatives again. That pro-Conservative advantage was particularly large in 2015 when the SNP won 56 of the 59 Scottish seats, many of them previously held by Labour and whose wasted vote total there soared as a consequence.

Malapportionment comes about in the UK for two reasons, and that element of the bias calculations can be decomposed accordingly. The first relates to the different electoral quotas for the separate countries. As described earlier, when seats were allocated in 1944 there was a relatively equitable share for each of England, Scotland and Wales but over time England's electorate grew more rapidly than in the other two countries, which meant that the latter become increasingly over-represented (a situation partly rectified in Scotland after the 1998 devolution settlement). Scottish and, especially, Welsh constituencies had on average fewer voters than their English counterparts and, as Labour was particularly strong there (only until 2015 in Scotland) this meant that it won a substantial number of seats with relatively small vote totals. This is shown in Figure 6.11 by the National Electoral Quotas segment of the malapportionment component. Labour was always the strongest party in Wales and by the 1980s it was the strongest in Scotland too; together that advantage was worth around 10 seats to Labour in notional elections with equal vote shares for much of the period.

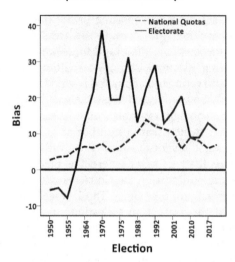

Representative democracy?

Figure 6.11 The separate malapportionment bias components in general election results, 1950–2019 (a positive bias is pro-Labour, a negative bias pro-Conservative)

The second segment of the malapportionment component relates to variations in constituency size within each country. Labour's strongholds are almost entirely in the country's urban areas. In the first two redistributions the Boundary Commissions, especially the English, argued that it was harder for MPs to service relatively low-density rural areas and so they created constituencies there, many of which had smaller electorates than urban areas. That practice ended after the First Periodical Review and from then on the advantage has been with Labour which represented many inner city areas with small constituencies. Furthermore, those inner cities were areas of significant depopulation for several decades, so over time after a redistribution Labour-held seats tended to experience electoral decline – relatively if not absolutely – while Conservative-held seats in the outer suburbs and beyond grew. As that disparity increased, so Labour's malapportionment advantage grew, as shown by the jagged line in Figure 6.11. After each redistribution, that bias component fell, only to rise again gradually – with the greatest rise leading up to the 1970 election, which was fought in the constituencies defined in 1955 because of the Callaghmander discussed earlier (p. 62). More recently, as depopulation of the inner cities ended – with a few exceptions – and redevelop-

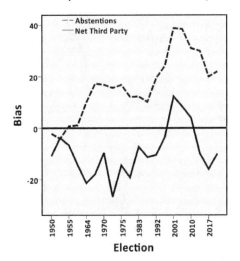

How representative is our democracy?

Figure 6.12 The separate abstentions and third-party bias components in general election results, 1950–2019 (a positive bias is pro-Labour, a negative bias pro-Conservative)

ment there saw populations grow again, so the increase in that bias component between redistributions became less.

There are two other bias components not yet discussed, which operate similarly to malapportionment. The first is abstentions. The lower the turnout in a constituency, the fewer votes needed to win there: with an electorate of 70,000 and an 80 per cent turnout 28,001 votes would be needed for victory in a two-party contest; a 60 per cent turnout needs only 21,001 votes. Labour-held seats have traditionally had higher abstention rates than Conservative-held, especially at the start of the twenty-first century when turnout rates fell nationally, especially among the working class.[19] Before then, higher abstention rates in Labour-held constituencies were worth about 20 seats to the party in a notional election with equal vote shares (Figure 6.12); more recently they have given the party an advantage of up to 40 seats.

Finally, there is the impact of third parties – that is all those except the two largest. Their impact is the same as that for abstentions; the more votes they win in a constituency the fewer each of the two largest parties – on whom the bias estimates focus – need for victory there. For most of the period the largest third party was the Liberal

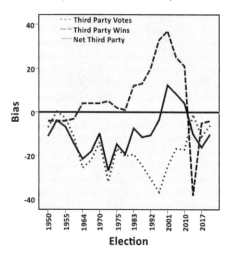

Representative democracy?

Figure 6.13 The third-party vote and win bias components in general election results, 1950–2019 (a positive bias is pro-Labour, a negative bias pro-Conservative)

Democrats (and their predecessors) who tended to perform better in Conservative- rather than Labour-held seats, reflecting their greater support among middle-class voters. Thus Figure 6.12 shows a pro-Conservative bias component of around 20 seats until the 1990s. In 2005 and 2010 the Liberal Democrats attracted considerable support in some Labour strongholds, replacing the Conservatives as the second-placed party in local government as well as at national elections, and this is reflected in the trend. At the end of the period the component showed a Conservative advantage again, largely because of the decline in Liberal Democrat support and the rise of the SNP, the latter having a major effect on Labour's performance in Scotland and becoming the third largest party in the House of Commons after 2015.

Of course, third parties may win seats – the Liberal Democrats won 52 in 2001, 62 in 2005 and 57 in 2010; the SNP won 56 in 2015, 35 in 2017 and 48 two years later. When this happens they deny one of the largest parties victory there. There are thus two separate bias effects – of third-party vote totals and third-party seat victories – and these are separately isolated in Figure 6.13. Throughout the period third party votes have favoured the Conservative Party overall, making its seats easier to win; this advantage was least at the earliest and latest elections when the Liberals won few votes and seats. Until 2015, however, third party wins have favoured Labour – most of the Liberal Democrat victories were in seats that the Conservatives would other-wise have won, benefiting Labour by as many as 37 seats at a notional equal-shares election. But in 2015, 2017 and 2019, when the Liberal Democrats won only 8, 12 and 11 seats respectively, the SNP's success – Labour's share of the Scottish seats fell from 41 in 2010 to just one in 2015, recovering only slightly to 7 in 2017 and then falling to just one again in 2019 – meant that the overall third-party advantage went to the Conservatives.

Redistributions, disproportionality and bias, 2011–

At each redistribution since 1970 the Boundary Commissions sought to reduce the variation in constituency electorates. The 2011 legis-lation made that an explicit requirement. What was its impact on disproportionality and bias? Further, during the public consultation exercise each party sought to redraw parts of the proposed constitu-ency map to its electoral advantage: did those efforts also have a substantial impact on the various measures? To answer those ques-tions, we compared the Commission's proposals with the outcome of the previous general election. In addition, for the aborted review begun in 2011 we collated all three main parties' counter-proposals for the whole of Great Britain, to assess the extent to which they were able to change the outcomes, should the Commissions accept their suggestions.

Table 6.6 compares the distribution of seats across the three larg-est British parties (Conservative, Labour and Liberal Democrat) at the 2010 general election in Great Britain, when there were 632 constitu-encies (i.e. excluding Northern Ireland with its different party system), with the Commissions' initial proposals (for the reduced number of 584 seats), each party's counter-proposals, and the Commissions' revised proposals,[20] showing the percentage of each party's votes that were effective (i.e. 100 minus the percentages that were either wasted or surplus) and the index of disproportionality. The initial proposals made little difference to the effective vote percentages from the preced-ing election and slightly increased the disproportionality index. The parties' counter-proposals altered the allocation of seats somewhat, and so changed the effective vote percentages and the index. Thus, for example, if the Conservatives' alternative configuration of con-

Table 6.6 The 2011 redistribution in Great Britain: seat allocations, effective vote percentages and indices of disproportionality

	Seats won			Effective votes (%)			
	Con	Lab	LD	Con	Lab	LD	IDisp
2010 general election (632)	306	258	57	41	34	13	15.7
Commission initial proposals (584)	299	231	46	42	34	12	16.8
Party counter-proposals							
Conservative	312	219	45	45	31	11	17.3
Labour	289	242	45	41	36	12	16.9
Liberal Democrat	295	225	56	42	33	14	14.7
Commission revised proposals	302	223	51				12.8

Key: Con – Conservative; Lab – Labour; LD – Liberal Democrat; IDisp – Index of Disproportionality.

stituencies had been entirely accepted by the Commissions, it would have given them thirteen more seats compared to the Commissions' initial proposals and reduced Labour's total by twelve; in doing so, the Conservatives would have increased their effective vote percentage by three points compared to the Commissions' proposals and reduced Labour's by three. (These numbers seem small, but the Conservatives won over 10.7 million votes in 2010: three per cent of 10.7 million meant that over 320,000 more Conservative votes would have been effective if that alternative configuration had been implemented.) Countering that, Labour's alternative configuration would have increased its effective percentage and reduced the Conservatives'.

The Liberal Democrats' alternative would have been even more successful. The Commissions' initial proposals would have reduced their seat total from 57 at the 2010 election to 46 if that contest had been fought in the new constituencies; the party's counter-proposals would have increased that by ten and its effective vote percentage from 12 to 14 – a 16.7 percentage increase, relatively much more successful than either of their larger competitors. Of course, the Commissions did not accept the entirety of any party's counter-proposals, but the Conservatives and Liberal Democrats benefited from the revised proposals by three and five seats respectively, whereas Labour's total was down by eight compared to what the Commissions had originally proposed.

Table 6.7 The 2011 redistribution in Great Britain: bias components

	Mal	Dist	Abst	TP	Net[21]
2010 general election	+18	0	+31	+4	+54
Commission initial proposals	0	−13	+29	+8	+27
Party counter-proposals					
Conservative	0	−41	+29	+4	−5
Labour	0	−6	+31	+4	+31
Liberal Democrat	0	−16	+30	+4	+21
Commission revised proposals	0	−18	+29	−3	+16

Key: Mal – Malapportionment; Dist – Distribution; Abst – Abstentions; TP – Third Parties.

Table 6.7 looks at the impact of these five alternative configurations for the new 584 British constituencies on the bias components, compared with the 2010 election: in this, we have combined the two malapportionment components – since national quotas disappear under the 2011 legislation – and also just shown the net third-party impact. The prime purpose of the new rules was to remove Labour's advantage from winning in constituencies that had smaller electorates on average – and it was successful. In 2010, with equal vote shares Labour would have won 18 more seats than the Conservatives because of malapportionment – nine because of differences in national electoral quotas and nine because of within-country variations in constituency electorates; the equalisation of electorates removed these entirely. The abstentions component was hardly altered – whatever configuration was deployed Labour would have an advantage of some 30 seats over the Conservatives; nor was the third-party component, from which Labour gained a small advantage. The big change was in the distribution component. At the 2010 election this was zero, with neither Labour nor the Conservatives gaining an advantage over the other as a result of their vote distribution, but the Commissions' initial proposals gave the Conservatives an advantage of 13 seats. If the Conservatives' alternative configuration had been accepted in full this would have more than tripled to 41 seats; the Conservatives' proposals 'gerrymandered' the map very considerably. They didn't get everything they asked for, of course, but the revised proposals did increase their advantage by five more seats compared to the initial proposals – three times more than Labour's alternative configuration would have produced. Because, as discussed in Chapter 5, the exercise was

Table 6.8 The 2016 redistribution in Great Britain: seat allocations and indices of disproportionality

	Con	Lab	LD	Other	Total	IDisp
2015 general election	331	232	8	61	632	15.5
Commission initial proposals	319	203	4	57	583	16.5
2017 general election	317	262	12	41	632	6.7
Commission final proposals	307	234	8	34	583	8.2
2019 general election	365	202	11	54	632	11.8
Commission final proposals	352	174	7	50	583	13.6

Key: Con – Conservative; Lab – Labour; LD – Liberal Democrat; IDisp –
Index of Disproportionality.

stopped prior to its completion, we do not know what the outcome would have been.

The Commissions started their next redistribution after the 2015 election and published their initial proposals in late 2016; they were working on revised recommendations through 2017 and published them some three months after the 2017 general election. The analyses for this redistribution in Tables 6.8 and 6.9 thus compare the initial proposals with the 2015 election outcome and the revised proposals with the 2017. Because the final proposals did not differ from the revised proposals in the allocation of seats if the 2017 election had been held in the proposed constituencies, only the final proposals are considered. Information was not compiled to make a full evaluation of the parties' counter-proposals.

At both stages of that redistribution the main beneficiary was again the Conservative party. The initial proposals would have reduced in its number of MPs in the smaller house (583 seats in Great Britain as against 632) by twelve, compared to a reduction of 29 for Labour, with the Liberal Democrats suffering a halving of their seats. The index of disproportionality was slightly increased. After the 2017 election, the Commissions' final proposals reduced Labour's MPs by 28 compared to ten for the Conservatives – again, the anticipated consequence of an equalisation of electorates across the entire country – and it was the same in 2019, when Labour's complement of MPs would have been reduced by 29 compared to only 13 for the Conservatives (Table 6.8).[22] The index of disproportionality was much smaller in 2017 than in 2015 or 2019, reflecting those two parties' substantially increased share of the vote total in 2017; it was increased slightly by the redis-

Table 6.9 The 2016 redistribution: bias components

	Mal	Dist	Abst	TP	Net[23]
2015 general election	+17	−60	+24	−39	−47
Commission initial proposals	0	−65	+20	−31	−67
2017 general election	+19	−32	+20	−16	−11
Commission final proposals	0	−55	+18	−23	−41

Key: Mal – Malapportionment; Dist – Distribution; Abst – Abstentions; TP – Third Parties.

tribution. The equalisation of electorates again eliminated Labour's advantage of 19 seats from the malapportionment bias component (Table 6.9).

The big change in the bias measure between the 2011 and the 2016 redistributions was in the size of the distribution and third-party components. These very substantially favoured the Conservatives at both the 2015 and 2017 general elections, largely because of the impact of the SNP's success in Scotland. Labour wasted a very large number of votes there at both contests: 667,854 out of its total of 707,147 in 2015 compared to the Conservatives' 413,338 out of 434,097; in 2017, when Labour gained six more Scottish seats compared to the Conservatives' twelve, Labour wasted 585,175 of its total of 717,007 and for the Conservatives the number was smaller at 476,337 out of a total of 757,949. Labour continued to waste too many votes where it came a relatively good second: the Conservatives gained ground in the seats that they won from the SNP but much less elsewhere.[24]

That the distribution component shifted so strongly towards the Conservatives in 2015 and 2017 compared to 2010 reflects the changing pattern of inter-party competition, therefore, and in particular Labour's collapse of support in Scotland. But why should that bias component be larger in the Commissions' initial proposals compared to the preceding election? The answer lies in the reduced number of constituencies and the relatively greater clustering and concentration of Labour votes in certain parts of the country compared to the Conservatives.

To illustrate this, we return to our 49 wards with the original distribution of party support as shown in Figure 6.3. If the overall reduction in the number of constituencies requires our area to lose a seat, then it will be the task of the independent Commission to propose

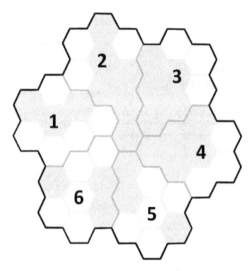

Figure 6.14 The same 49 wards and distribution of support for the two
parties as in Figure 6.3, but with six rather than seven constituencies,
thereby removing Party A's advantage

how that should be achieved. There will be a preference for minimis-
ing the level of disruption (not least because of the relevant legislation) and this is most easily achieved by abolishing constituency 7
and redistributing its wards to the remaining six seats. Figure 6.14
shows the configuration of constituencies which involves the least
possible disruption (the decision to transfer the eighth ward to seat 2
is arbitrary – it could have gone to any of the six retained seats – but
whichever seat inherited it, the effect would be the same). This new
configuration results in three victories for Party A and three for Party
B, a net loss of one for the former. The party with the more clustered
and concentrated distribution of support is the one to be penalised by
the reduction in the number of seats.

With one party's votes more clustered and concentrated than
the other's, therefore, the smaller the number of seats the greater
the potential for an unintentional gerrymander: the reduction in the
number of seats (on face value, uncontroversial and impartial) was
always going to be in the Conservatives' interests – a point almost
certainly appreciated by the party's strategists. And to the extent that
intentional gerrymandering is possible, by the parties seeking to

influence the Commissions to produce constituency configurations in their favour, that disadvantage can be exacerbated. Both are clearly shown in Tables 6.7 and 6.9. At each of the two redistributions the Commissions' initial proposals involved a greater distribution bias component favouring the Conservatives than at the preceding general election, clearly indicative of an unintentional gerrymander. At the first redistribution, the Conservatives' counter-proposals would have enhanced that bias very considerably (Table 6.7). Labour's counter-proposals, on the other hand, would have not only entirely nullified the effect of the Conservatives' but halved the impact of the Commissions' initial proposals. In responding to the parties' counter-proposals during the public consultation stage, therefore, the Commissions are faced with a range of party strategies (by the Liberal Democrats, the SNP and Plaid Cymru as well as Labour and the Conservatives) each seeking to maximise its vote effectiveness and minimise the others' – using the criteria set out in the rules which allow no reference to partisan advantage. If one party is more successful than its opponents it enhances the unintentional gerrymander.

Conclusions

In terms of party representation, British election results are both disproportional and biased, as a result of the interaction of the three geographical elements identified in Gudgin and Taylor's analyses – the degree to which each party's support is spatially both clustered and concentrated, and the location of the constituency boundaries overlain on those maps. As the placing of those boundaries is changed, so the degree of disproportionality and bias can be altered – illustrating why the parties place such importance on the rules for redistributions, how they are conducted and influencing their details through their contributions to the public consultation.

But could it be different? That is the subject of the next chapter.

7

Does it have to be this way?

As discussed in previous chapters, the first-past-the-post (FPTP) electoral system used for elections to the UK's Westminster Parliament has evolved considerably over the years. Compared to contests before the passage of the 1832 Great Reform Act (and even to elections in the later nineteenth and early twentieth centuries), Britain's elections are now much fairer, much more transparent, and much better run.

What has not really changed is the basic electoral system used for Westminster elections: contests are still fought on FPTP plurality rules. This system is very simple to operate and to understand. Most voters are willing to accept the candidate who gains most votes in their seat as their legitimate MP, even when (as happened in 27 per cent of seats at the 2017 election and 36 per cent in 2019) the winning candidate obtained less than 50 per cent of the constituency vote. It generally rewards the most popular party with a larger share of seats than its share of the vote, making one-party majority government more likely. And a cornerstone of the modern FPTP system is the single-member constituency, which guarantees the Burkean link between the voters of a distinct geographical area and their representative in Parliament – which British voters say they like.

But FPTP has perhaps more than its fair share of oddities and problems. Since 1950, no party has achieved the support of a majority (i.e. over 50 per cent) of British voters. Yet 17 of the 20 elections between 1950 and 2019 have produced parliaments in which just one party has had a majority of MPs (albeit sometimes only a very narrow majority): only the February 1974, 2010 and 2017 general elections failed to produce a one-party majority in Parliament. A problem or a benefit? Those who value strong single-party government might see this as a positive feature of the system. Those who dislike what Lord Hailsham once described as the 'elective dictatorship' aspects of the

UK's political system (between elections, there are few real checks or controls on what a government with a Westminster majority can do) might see things differently.

And, as shown in earlier chapters, FPTP election results are disproportional and biased. Not only does the most popular party tend to enjoy an exaggerated share of MPs, but smaller parties (especially those with support spread relatively evenly across the country) find it hard to win individual constituencies and so tend to be seriously under-represented.

What is more, as discussed in Chapter 6, there is a degree of arbitrariness in both how biased and how disproportional FPTP results can be. The translation from vote share to seat share is neither automatic nor regular. And it is even possible for the 'wrong' party to win an election – that is, for the party with the largest vote share to gain fewer MPs than the party with the second-largest vote share. In 1951, Labour took 49 per cent of the UK vote, and the Conservatives 48 per cent – but 321 Conservative MPs were elected to Labour's 295, giving the former party a clear majority. And in February 1974, Labour got 301 MPs for 37 per cent of the vote, compared to the Conservatives' 297 for 38 per cent, making Labour the largest party in the Commons (though short of an overall majority).

That said, FPTP is far from the only electoral system on offer. A divide is often drawn between plurality or majoritarian systems like FPTP on the one hand, and proportional systems on the other (reflecting Raymond Plant's distinction between 'Schumpeterian' and 'microscopic' electoral systems, discussed in Chapter 2).[1] Debates over which electoral system should be used for elections to Westminster have been a recurrent feature of British politics since the early nineteenth century (although, extensions to the franchise aside, these have seldom been the subject of much public interest). What is more, since the early 1990s the UK has experimented with a surprisingly wide range of different electoral systems for non-Westminster elections. Elections to the European Parliament, to the devolved administrations in Scotland, Wales and Northern Ireland, to local government in Scotland and Northern Ireland, for the London Assembly and for elected city mayors have all used a variety of different systems, all intended to be rather more proportional in their outcomes than Westminster's FPTP system. And in 2011, as we have seen, a proposal to change how Westminster elections took place from FPTP to the AV was put to a referendum.

That raises an obvious question: what difference would moving from FPTP to some other electoral system make to British general elections? We cannot simply project from election results under existing rules to how those elections might have turned out under different rules: if the election rules changed, both parties and voters would be faced with different strategic decisions to those they face at present. The incentives for tactical voting, for instance, are high in FPTP elections, but much lower under some other systems. However, we can learn from the experiences of voters in those parts of the UK where other electoral systems have already been put in place for other levels of government. And some studies have tried to replicate how Westminster contests might look under different rules. In this chapter, we look at the debate over electoral reform for Westminster elections. How has it evolved? What are some of the main alterative electoral systems on offer and how do they work? And, crucially, what effects do they have on representation?

The electoral reform debate

Though rarely if ever a major (or even a minor) priority for most voters, reformers have since relatively early in the nineteenth century argued for the replacement of FPTP by a more proportional electoral system.[2] John Stuart Mill was an early advocate, arguing in 1861 that:

> In a really equal democracy, every or any section (of society) would be represented, not disproportionately, but proportionately.[3]

Mill supported the Single Transferable Vote (STV) system, proposed by his friend Thomas Hare in 1859. During an 1867 parliamentary debate on the Second Reform Bill, Mill moved an amendment which would have introduced STV for Westminster elections. Other speakers in the debate were unwilling to support the proposal (Viscount Cranborne, for instance, felt it 'belonged to the class of impracticable things'[4] while for Serjeant Gaselee MP it was an example of 'philosophical eccentricities')[5] and the amendment was withdrawn without a vote: STV failed its first test in the British Parliament. A similar attempt to introduce electoral reform as part of the 1884 Reform Act also failed (discussed in Chapter 3).[6]

The 1916–17 Speaker's Conference (discussed in Chapter 3) considered a range of reforms to the electoral system, including the introduction of proportional representation.[7] A number of pressures at the time had revitalised interest in PR, not least the emergence of the Labour Party, and the growing number of countries which had already adopted proportional systems (in some European states PR was seen as a means of accommodating substantial religious, linguistic and ethnic divisions within the electorate; in others, as a means of protecting the interests of previously important parties facing new challenges from growing competitors).[8] The Conference's recommendation – that STV be introduced for borough constituencies and AV for rural seats – was included in the Representation of the People Bill 1917. But while the bill's most famous measures – expanding the franchise to most adult men and to women aged over 30 – made it into the subsequent 1918 Act, the proposal to introduce PR was lost, opposed by the main party leaders.

Those setbacks notwithstanding, STV has for many years been the 'front runner' among British electoral reformers. The Electoral Reform Society, founded in 1884, has consistently favoured STV. Since 1922 the Liberals (and, since 1988, their successor, the Liberal Democrats) have supported the introduction of a more proportional electoral system (the only mainstream party to do so) – and STV has been their preference too.

That said, STV has not been the only proposal for electoral reform. As noted, the 1916–17 Speaker's Conference suggested the adoption of the AV sysem in rural seats. AV was also proposed by a Royal Commission in 1910 and discussed by the 1930 Ullswater Committee[9] – though the latter could not come to a clear recommendation.

There the debate in Britain foundered for much of the twentieth century. Proportional representation remained a fringe cause, supported by parties which (like the Liberals from the 1920s onwards) did badly out of FPTP elections, and by a few enthusiasts. But the two largest parties (from the 1920s, Labour and the Conservatives) were opposed, not least as they benefited from FPTP and stood to lose out in a more proportional system. As all twentieth-century UK governments after 1918 were dominated by these larger parties (with one or the other winning a majority in most elections), and as the combined Labour and Conservative vote routinely exceeded 90 per cent for much of the middle part of the century (making the underrepresentation of smaller parties a point of academic interest only – in the bad sense), electoral reform for Westminster elections was effectively off the agenda.

But from the mid-1970s, it re-emerged as a topic of mainstream political discussion. One driver was the growth of minor party voting and the declining vote share going to Labour and the Conservatives. Suddenly, the under-representation of smaller parties in the Commons began to look rather more serious. The 1983 UK general election provided a particularly egregious example, with Labour and the Liberal-SDP Alliance almost tied on vote share (winning 27.6 per cent and 25.4 per cent respectively) but, thanks to FPTP, far apart in terms of MPs elected (209 versus 23).

Not surprisingly, the smaller parties (including the Liberals and their SDP partners) were most pro-reform. But, from the late 1980s on, some Labour politicians also showed interest, because of a growing concern within the party that – after a series of defeats at the hands of the Conservatives – Labour might risk being permanently locked out of government under existing electoral rules. Yet, as some in the party noted, each election from 1979 until 1987 produced large Conservative majorities even though a majority of voters supported other parties (a feat the Conservatives repeated with a similar vote share but a smaller majority in 1992). While their arithmetic was clear, their political logic was shaky. It could equally be said that a majority voted against Labour. And analysis of Liberal-SDP Alliance support suggested that while Labour was the alternative choice for many of its voters, a significant minority put the Conservatives in that position.[10]

Given these pressures, in 1990 Labour's National Executive initiated an inquiry into electoral reform, led by Raymond Plant, a Southampton University politics professor. The Plant Commission looked at some of the principles behind choosing an electoral system. It argued that the first decision was what sort of elected Parliament – Schumpeterian single party majority governments or microscopic, deliberative chambers containing a representative cross-section of views – was desired.[11] PR systems in general were more effective in producing the latter, but majoritarian and plurality systems – like FPTP – were more likely to achieve the former. But Plant did not recommend which particular electoral system to adopt.

Electoral reform for Westminster elections did not feature in Labour's 1992 manifesto. But, following the party's fourth consecutive election defeat, anxieties continued. For some, that year's election seemed to have been Labour's last chance – and the party had blown the opportunity.[12] Tony Blair's New Labour was a response.[13]

At least initially, senior New Labour strategists feared that (large and sustained opinion poll leads over the Conservatives throughout the most of the 1992–97 Major government notwithstanding) the party might once again fail to win a parliamentary majority at the next general election. Partly because of this fear, they considered the possibility of a 'radical realignment' of British politics in combination with the Liberal Democrats. Labour's 1997 manifesto therefore committed the party to establishing a Commission to look once again at electoral reform and to holding a referendum on the electoral system for the Commons. This, it was felt, would help 'tie in' Liberal Democrat support. In the event, Labour won the 1997 election by a landslide. In December 1997, it set up a Commission on Voting Systems under the chairmanship of Lord Roy Jenkins, which reported just under a year later.

The Commission argued that the constituency link was a much-valued part of the UK electoral system and should be maintained, though it worried about the number of MPs elected under FPTP with less than majority support in their seat, and felt that a greater degree of proportionality in election results was desirable. To meet all these concerns, it recommended that elections for Westminster should be carried out using a variant of the Alternative Member System (AMS; also known as Mixed Member Proportional – MMP – and claimed by some to be the 'best of both worlds').[14] Under the Commission's plans, voters would have two votes: one for a constituency MP, and one for a regional MP. The great majority of MPs (between 80 and 85 per cent) would be elected in single-member constituencies using AV, to maximise the number of constituency MPs with true majority support in their seats. The remaining 15–20 per cent of MPs were to be elected using a regional top-up scheme using an open list form of PR, in relatively small regions (Jenkins suggested 80 top-up regions based on counties and city-regions). As a result of both the low proportion of MPs to be elected via the regional top-up, and of the small district magnitudes of the proposed regions (no region would have more than two MPs drawn from the top-up vote, in addition to the constituency MPs elected there), the proposal (though an improvement on FPTP) would almost certainly still have fallen well short of complete proportionality. But Labour's political need to consider electoral reform for Westminster had largely evaporated in the light of its 1997 landslide. The Jenkins report was shelved: no referendum on electoral reform was forthcoming.[15]

Proportional representation was not entirely off the 1997 Labour government's agenda, however. It established devolved Parliaments in Scotland and Wales, both of which were to be elected using AMS. Of the 129 Members of the Scottish Parliament (MSPs), 73 are elected via FPTP contests in single-member constituencies, and 56 via closed-list PR in eight regions. In Wales, 40 of the 60 Assembly Members (AMs) are elected from single-member constituencies using FPTP, and 20 from closed list PR in five regions. (In closed list systems, voters opt for a party only; the party lists its candidates in rank order and the number of seats it gains determines which from that ordering are elected. In open list systems, voters not only opt for a party but can indicate which of its candidates they prefer.)[16] In both countries a relatively proportional system was employed to minimise the risk of hugely biased elections, in which one party might sweep up a substantial majority in the devolved body based on a mere plurality of votes. When the Parliaments were first set up, Labour was the most likely to achieve this in both countries under FPTP rules. But the Labour government's bigger fear was that local nationalist parties might be beneficiaries in the future. AMS was seen as a means of both ensuring a plurality of voices in the new parliaments, and of keeping the nationalist threat under control.

As part of the 1998 Good Friday Agreement seeking to bring an end to the long-running conflict in Northern Ireland, a devolved Assembly was also established there. This was not Northern Ireland's first devolved body. Between 1921 and 1973 it had its own parliament. That body, however, had been controlled by the Protestant Unionist majority population, with elections held under FPTP rules in what were seriously gerrymandered constituencies, designed to ensure Unionist control. The Good Friday Agreement sought to escape from that legacy and to build structures which would require cross-community working. As part of that enterprise, therefore, the new Northern Ireland Assembly, first elected in 1998, used STV to ensure more proportional representation of the province's main communities.

The New Labour constitutional shake-up also brought in other electoral systems for other new offices. For instance, a directly elected mayor for London was instituted in 2000: the mayor was elected using the Supplementary Vote (SV: a system similar to AV). In an SV election, voters can express a first and a second preference among a list of candidates. Any candidate getting over 50 per cent of first preferences is elected. If no candidate gets over this threshold, all candidates other than the two with the most first preference votes are eliminated, and the second preferences of those voters whose first preference was for an eliminated candidate are recounted, with second preferences for each of the top two candidates being added to their respective tallies. The candidate with the highest vote after this process is complete is then elected. However, the SV has short-comings.[17] For instance, it ignores the preferences of voters whose first and second preference votes are for eliminated candidates (quite possible, as voters will not know for sure before the election who the two most popular candidates might be). Because of this (and because voters do not have to cast a second preference vote) it is possible for candidates to win in SV contests even if they are not supported by a majority of voters. SV has also been adopted for the election of other city mayors – and, after 2012, for Police and Crime Commissioner elections.

Labour also legislated in 1999 to change how Britain's Members of the European Parliament (MEPs) were elected. Direct elections to that body had been held since 1979. In the first four Euro-elections, Britain's MEPs (78 in 1979, 1984 and 1989; 84 in 1994) were elected using FPTP in large single-member seats (STV was used to elect Northern Ireland's MEPs). That changed in 1999, when a regional list PR system was adopted for EU elections throughout Great Britain (STV was retained in Northern Ireland) in order to meet the EU requirement that all MEPs be elected by some form of proportional representation. During the passage of the legislation, there was debate over whether a closed or open list PR system should be intro-duced. There was also disagreement over which electoral formula – the d'Hondt or the Sainte-Laguë – should be used to allocate seats. The government favoured d'Hondt, and the Liberal Democrats in particular favoured Sainte-Laguë. In the event, closed list PR was adopted, using the d'Hondt method – which Jack Straw MP, the Home Secretary responsible for the legislation, misleadingly pre-sented to the Commons as the more proportional of the two formulae (he was wrong, and had to apologise to the House). Over the course of a very few years, therefore, New Labour both turned its back on electoral reform for Westminster, but also set in place a wide range of other electoral systems for other elected bodies – an odd mix of electoral conservatism and radicalism.

Electoral reform for Westminster elections returned to the politi-cal mainstream in 2010 when that year's general election produced a hung parliament. Both Labour and the Conservatives proposed referendums on changing to AV in an effort to woo the Liberal Democrats. When the Liberal Democrats agreed to form a coalition with the Conservatives, the AV referendum was written into their agreement.

The potential attractions of AV for both the Conservatives and Labour were clear. Both needed Liberal Democrat support, making some sort of deal on electoral reform a likely price. And, if reform had to be considered, AV was the 'least worst' option for the two largest parties, as it involved least disruption to the FPTP system from which both benefited. For the Liberal Democrats, the benefits were less clear (and Liberal Democrat leader Nick Clegg had previously described AV as 'a miserable little compromise' – albeit also 'a baby step in the right direction').[18] They stood to gain some extra seats as they were often the 'second choice' of a significant number of Conservative and Labour voters.[19] However, they would still have almost certainly done considerably worse under AV than under most forms of PR. But by putting reform back on the agenda, the AV referendum did raise the prospect of further reforms which might prove more advantageous.

Arrangements for the AV Referendum were included in the 2011 Parliamentary Voting System and Constituencies Act, which also changed the rules for redrawing parliamentary constituencies (see Chapter 5). The referendum was held on 5 May 2011. With 68 per cent of voters opposing AV, electoral reform for Westminster was once again off the mainstream agenda. When the Conservatives achieved an overall parliamentary majority at the 2015 general election, it seemed likely that it would remain so.

But was the 2011 Referendum quite the death knell for reform efforts that it seemed? Perhaps not. As political conditions change, pressure for reform could rise.

One mechanism might be if conventional FPTP elections are perceived as producing anomalous and unfair results. This is what happened in New Zealand where in 1978 the New Zealand Labour party won (narrowly) more votes that the National Party, but under the country's FPTP election rules the latter gained more MPs and remained in government (having used its FPTP-induced majority to push through controversial legislation in the preceding Parliament). Labour initiated a national conversation on reform in 1979, which continued through the 1980s, eventually resulting in referendum votes in 1992 and 1993 endorsing the adoption of an AMS system for national elections.[20]

Does it have to be this way?

An alternative mechanism might be produced by a sustained period of minority government. Two of the three UK general elections between 2010 and 2017 failed to produce a one-party majority government (and in 2017 this was despite Labour and Conservatives both increasing their vote shares substantially to gain the largest joint share of the vote in almost 50 years). Analysis of the results led some commentators to suspect that FPTP in the UK may have lost its tendency to produce majority governments, making minority governments the 'new normal'.[21] If they are right, there is scope for a smaller party advocating a more proportional system once again to make that the price of its participation in a coalition – but the 2019 result, which delivered a 'stonking majority' to the Conservatives with 43.6 per cent of the vote, suggested that 'normal service had been resumed'.

Comparing electoral systems

As discussed above, only a few of the myriad possible electoral systems have been seriously considered in the UK. In addition to FPTP (a plurality system), they are: the Alternative Vote; the Single Transferable Vote; the Additional Member System; and List PR. In this section, we look in more detail at how these different electoral systems actually work, and compare their performance to FPTP.[22]

The Alternative Vote

We begin with the Alternative Vote, a system which requires the smallest change from FPTP. Like FPTP, AV takes place in single-member constituencies. It not only maintains the link between MPs and territorial communities which many British voters say they value, therefore, but could also be implemented quickly, with no need to change the constituency map from that employed in FPTP contests. The extent of disruption experienced by voters and parties would therefore be minimal (though, as with FPTP, AV constituencies would need to be reviewed periodically to take account of changing electorates).

Like FPTP, AV is a 'winner takes all' system: the most popular candidate in the constituency wins. They differ, however, in how each identifies the most popular candidate. In FPTP, voters only indicate which one of the candidates standing in their seat they support. The votes for all candidates are then tallied, and the candidate with the largest number of votes is elected as MP for the constituency. So far, so familiar – and so easy.

However, in a multi-party contest, this almost inevitably means that some MPs are elected with less than a clear majority (i.e. 50 per cent + 1 vote) of the votes cast in their constituency. If three parties stand in a constituency, for instance, it would be possible (if all three were just about equally popular in the seat) for the winning candidate to be elected on only a little more than 33.3 per cent of the vote. Almost two-thirds of the new MP's constituents would have voted for someone else – hardly a ringing endorsement. The winner would have a plurality of the vote (i.e. more votes than rival candidates), but not a majority (i.e. over half) – hence FPTP is often described as a plurality rather than a majoritarian system.

Nor is this a purely hypothetical problem. For much of the last 50 years, British elections have been multi-party affairs. True, elections in most constituencies are dominated by just two parties, with the others in a distant third place or worse.[23] At the 2019 general election, 34 per cent of MPs were elected with less than half of the votes in their constituency (Figure 7.1: the vertical line indicates the 50 per cent point). And in some constituencies, the winner's vote was very substantially below 50 per cent. The MP with the lowest winning vote share in Great Britain in 2019 was Labour's Olivia Blake, elected to represent Sheffield Hallam with just 34.6 per cent of the local vote. Although the point is seldom made too loudly, all MPs in this posi-

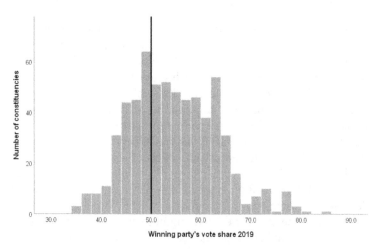

Figure 7.1 Winning party's per cent vote share, 2019 general election, Great Britain

tion face a slight legitimacy problem, as it is possible for opponents to argue that a majority of voters in their constituency voted against them.

AV is intended to deal with this problem by ensuring every MP is endorsed by a majority of voters in their area. To achieve this, voters in AV elections place as many of the candidates in their constituency as they want in rank order, from their first preference to their last. At the count, the first preference votes for each candidate are tallied. If a candidate gains over 50 per cent of first preference votes, that person is automatically elected as MP for the constituency. As Figure 7.1 suggests, it is therefore likely that in many constituencies, the outcome of an AV election would be the same as under FPTP rules. Where no candidate gets over the 50 per cent threshold, the candidate with fewest first preference votes is eliminated[24] and the second preferences of his or her voters are redistributed to the other candidates. This continues until one candidate gets over 50 per cent – and is duly elected.

Advocates of AV argue that this has a number of desirable outcomes, over and above maintaining the clear link between MPs and geographical constituencies. Because of the way votes are counted, they argue, almost all MPs will be able to say that they have at least the broad support of over half of their voters. (Occasionally, a stronger claim is made, that all MPs will have 50 per cent+ support. This, however, is not true. Because voters do not have to rank all candidates in an AV election, it is possible that the eventual winner's vote will fall short of the 50 per cent mark, even when all but the two most popular candidates have been eliminated.) What is more, they argue, AV removes pressure for tactical voting, as voters supporting less popular candidates or parties locally can still give them a first preference vote, knowing that their second (and possibly lower) preferences can still have an influence on the outcome of the election.

AV involves relatively minor shifts from FPTP, therefore. But how would it affect real elections? Luckily, researchers have used survey data on voters' relative rankings of the major parties to simulate how the 1992, 1997, 2010 and 2017 general elections in Great Britain might have turned out under AV rules.[25] Table 7.1 shows their estimates of the numbers of seats the parties would win under AV at each election, alongside the actual number of seats won, and the number each party would win on a strict proportional basis. In all four elections, the Conservatives stood to lose seats (from 11 seats in 1992

Table 7.1 Estimating the results of the 1992, 1997, 2010 and 2017 general elections in Great Britain under the Alternative Vote

	Per cent vote share (FPTP)	Seats (pure PR)	Actual seats (FPTP)	Estimated seats (AV)	Seat difference (AV – FPTP)
1992:					
Conservative	42.8	271	336	325	–11
Labour	35.2	223	271	270	–1
Liberal Democrat	18.3	116	20	30	10
Other	3.7	23	7	9	2
1997:					
Conservative	31.5	202	165	110	–55
Labour	44.3	284	418	435	17
Liberal Democrat	17.2	110	46	84	38
Other	7.0	45	12	12	0
2010:					
Conservative	36.9	233	306	283	–23
Labour	29.7	187	258	248	–10
Liberal Democrat	23.6	149	57	89	32
Other	9.8	62	10	10	0
2017:					
Conservative	43.5	274	317	304	–13
Labour	41.0	259	262	286	24
Liberal Democrat	7.6	48	12	11	–1
Other	7.9	50	40	30	–10

Sources: The estimates are taken from P. Dunleavy, H. Margetts and S. Weir, 'How Britain would have voted under alternative electoral systems in 1992', *Parliamentary Affairs*, 45 (1992), 640–655; P. Dunleavy, H. Margetts, B. O'Duffy and S. Weir, 'Remodelling the 1997 general election: how Britain would have voted under alternative electoral systems', *British Elections and Parties Review*, 8 (1998), 208–231; J. Garland and C. Terry, *The 2017 General Election: Volatile Voting, Random Results*, London, Electoral Reform Society, 2017 (https://www.electoral-reform.org.uk/latest-news-and-research/publications/the-2017-general-election-report/).

to 55 in 1997), as the balance of second preferences tended to work against them. The Liberal Democrats, meanwhile, have often been a favoured second preference choice, and so generally stood to gain from AV – but not dramatically so. One estimate suggests that, had the UK's general elections between 1983 and 2005 been re-run under AV rules, the Liberal Democrats would have gained in the order of

25 extra seats.[26] In the four elections reported in Table 7.1, estimates suggest the party would have gained on average just under 20 seats – though in 2017, they might have lost one. Labour, meanwhile, could have gained from AV in both 1997 and in 2017 (by around 20 seats), but might have had slightly fewer MPs in 1992.

In close elections, the overall outcome of the election might have been different had AV been in place. On these estimates, for instance, John Major's slender 1992 majority would have been wiped out, and he would have been one seat short of a Commons majority. In 2010, the dynamics of the coalition discussions which followed the election might have been different. In the actual event, even had the Liberal Democrats been willing to enter a coalition with Labour, the two parties would still have been short of an overall majority and would have needed a third partner, complicating the discussions. Under AV, they could have formed a viable two-party majority coalition – and with an enhanced parliamentary group, the Liberal Democrats would have been in a stronger position to wrest concessions from either of the two largest parties as a condition of joining a coalition.

However, compared to the numbers of seats the parties might have expected to get had a very pure form of proportional representation been in place (and assuming that the vote shares obtained by the parties under FPTP would have been much the same in that PR contest), the estimated AV results still fall well short of proportionality. To see just how far short, we re-use the disproportionality index employed

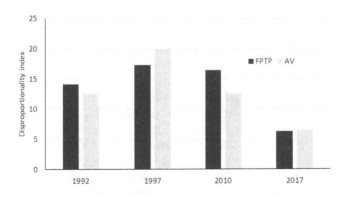

Figure 7.2 Disproportionality in British general elections under FPTP and AV

in Chapter 6 (Figure 7.2). At the 1992 and 2010 elections, AV would probably have produced a somewhat less disproportional result than FPTP. But in general, the difference between the two systems is small – and in 1997 AV could have been even more disproportional than FPTP, as Labour stood to gain more MPs in what was already a landslide year for the party. And, as shown by analyses of voting in AV elections to the Australian House of Representatives, electoral bias (described in Chapter 6) can be about as severe under AV as under FPTP.[27]

If disproportionality, the under-representation of smaller parties, and bias are seen as a failing of FPTP, therefore, AV is hardly the solution. It involves minimal changes to existing systems. But that comes at the cost of minimal improvements in (and even, in some cases worsening) proportionality.

Single Transferable Vote

The other system frequently canvassed as an alternative to FPTP for Westminster elections is the Single Transferable Vote (STV). Like FPTP and AV contests, STV elections take place in geographical constituencies, maintaining the link between MPs and communities. And, like AV, STV requires voters to rank the candidates standing in their seat. However, in other respects, STV is rather different.

An immediate difference is that, unlike FPTP and AV, STV elections use multi-member and not single-member constituencies. For instance, in the Republic of Ireland (where STV is used), each constituency returns between three and five TDs (members of the Dáil, the Irish Parliament). Within the UK, STV is used in Scotland for local government elections with wards returning either three or four councillors. It is also used for all non-Westminster elections in Northern Ireland: for the Northern Ireland Assembly, each constituency (the same constituencies are used for Assembly and Westminster elections) returns five (originally six) AMs; for local government district electoral areas return between five and seven councillors each; and for European Parliament elections (the entire province is one constituency for this purpose), there are three MEPs. The size of the multi-member constituencies (the district magnitude, or number of candidates elected) is important to the proportionality of an election result: the larger the number of MPs elected from a district, the more proportional the election result, and the more likely independent and very minor party candidates are to be elected.

Does it have to be this way?

Because each STV constituency is multi-member, parties usually field several candidates in those where they stand: they do not have to put up as many candidates as there are MPs to be elected there – though they often do. As a result, voters are faced with a ballot paper containing rather more candidate names than in an FPTP or AV contest. If four parties stand in an FPTP/AV single-member constituency, voters will see four names (one for each party's candidate) on the ballot paper. But their counterparts in an STV election will see up to twelve names on the ballot paper if they live in a constituency electing three MPs (three places times four parties), and up to 28 names if they live in a district electing seven MPs.

As in AV, STV voters rank the candidates on the ballot paper from their first to their last preference (usually, they do not have to rank all candidates). But, because each seat is multi-member, the voter is able to make use of more information. Under FPTP and AV, as each party fields just one candidate in a constituency there is no way to clearly differentiate between support for the party and support for the individual. In STV, however, voters can disentangle the two, can split their support across parties, and can express opinions on each candidate standing for a particular party. One might give first preference to the second candidate standing for Party A, second preference for the third candidate standing for Party C, and so on. As a result, in STV elections candidates are in competition not only with candidates from other parties, but also with their own party's other candidates there.

Before the votes for each candidate can be counted in an STV contest, the minimum number of votes needed to elect a candidate in the constituency is worked out. This is a function of the total number of votes cast and the number of MPs to be elected there, and is most commonly calculated using the Droop quota:

$$\left(\frac{total\ number\ of\ valid\ votes}{MPs + 1} \right) + 1$$

A valid vote is a single correctly completed ballot paper. If there is just one MP to be elected in a constituency where 40,000 votes were cast, the Droop quota would be:

$$\left(\frac{40,000}{1 + 1} \right) + 1 = \left(\frac{40,000}{2} \right) + 1 = 20,001$$

In other words, a candidate in a one-seat constituency would need at least 50 per cent of the vote plus one vote to win: in effect, an AV election. If our constituency was electing three MPs, however, the Droop quota (assuming there are still 40,000 votes cast in total) would be:

$$\left(\frac{40,000}{3+1}\right) + 1 = \left(\frac{40,000}{4}\right) + 1 = 10,001$$

A candidate here would have to be supported by at least a quarter (plus one) of all voters to be elected.

Once the Droop quota is calculated, the next task (as in AV) is to count the first preference votes going to each candidate. Any candidate whose first preference votes exceed the Droop quota is automatically elected. If a candidate gets more votes than the quota, their 'surplus votes' (i.e. their excess votes over the quota) will be redistributed to other candidates, based on the voters' preference rankings of those other candidates.

An example might make this more straightforward. In our hypothetical constituency electing three MPs and with a Droop quota of 10,001, let's say Candidate A gets 14,259 first preference votes. That clearly exceeds the quota, and Candidate A is duly elected. But Candidate A has 14,251–10,001 = 4,250 votes which are surplus to requirement. Now let's say 40 per cent of those who gave their first preference vote to Candidate A gave their second preference to Candidate B, while 30 per cent gave it to Candidate C, 20 per cent to Candidate D and 10 per cent to Candidate E. The surplus votes are then redistributed to the remaining candidates in those proportions. So 0.4*4250 = 1700 votes will be added to Candidate B's tally, 0.3*4,250 = 1275 will be added to Candidate C, 0.2*4,250 = 850 will go to Candidate D, and Candidate E will get 0.1*4,250 = 425 extra votes.

If any of the remaining candidates' votes now exceed the quota, they too are elected, and their surplus votes are redistributed among the remaining candidates in the same way. If at any stage there are no candidates whose vote exceeds the quota, the candidate with fewest votes is eliminated, and their votes are redistributed among the remaining candidates using their voters' preference ordering. The process continues until all MPs for the constituency have been elected.

This is clearly a more convoluted process than either FPTP or AV.

And there are some further complications. For instance, once the first MP has been identified it is almost inevitable that some of those who support candidates elected later in the process will have put the first winning candidate as their second preference. But there is no point in redistributing further surplus votes to candidates who have already been elected. In those cases, the third, and potentially lower, preferences of those voters come into play. What is more, small variations in the order in which candidates are either elected or eliminated can make a difference to the outcome of the contest in a constituency, as this can affect the numbers of votes to be redistributed to the remaining candidates (and hence who is elected next).

STV affects how parties campaign in elections, as the candidates standing for each party in a constituency are in competition with candidates standing not only for rival parties but also for their own party. Parties try to turn this to their advantage. For instance, parties may issue 'how to vote' leaflets in a constituency, showing their preferred candidate rank order and encouraging supporters to vote accordingly. Where voters have a strong preference for local candidates, parties can field candidate lists to appeal to different parts of the constituency. The hope, for the party, is that in each part of the constituency the more 'local' candidate will tend to get the higher preference rankings, and the party will increase its chances of electing both. There is evidence from Irish elections that such strategies can pay off.[28]

How does STV compare to FPTP? Scottish local government elections changed in 2007 from FPTP to STV. Comparing the outcomes of the last three rounds of local elections under FPTP (in 1995, 1999 and 2003) with the first three rounds under STV (in 2007, 2012 and 2017) gives an idea of the effects of moving from one to the other (Table 7.2). For the STV contests, the vote shares are the percentage of first preference votes for each party. The actual number of councillors elected for each party at each election is compared to the number we would expect under a very pure form of PR.

Two things are immediately clear. First, Labour was the major beneficiary from FPTP in Scottish local government elections, while the SNP was the largest loser. While the former won on average 108 more councillors under FPTP than it might have expected under pure PR, the SNP fell on average 126 councillors short. Under STV rules from 2007 onwards, Labour's advantage fell to just 10 more councillors than a pure PR system might give them (a negligible difference), while the SNP's FPTP disadvantage evaporated, to be

Table 7.2 Switching to STV: Scottish local government elections, 1995–2017

	Per cent vote share[A]	Councillors (Pure PR)	Elected councillors	Elected councillors – Pure PR councillors
FPTP elections				
1995				
Conservative	11.5	133	82	–51
Labour	43.6	503	613	110
Liberal Democrat	9.8	113	121	8
SNP	26.1	302	181	–121
Other	9.0	104	158	54
1999				
Conservative	13.5	164	156	–8
Labour	36.6	446	550	104
Liberal Democrat	12.7	155	108	–47
SNP	28.7	350	204	–146
Other	8.5	104	200	96
2003				
Conservative	15.1	184	122	–62
Labour	32.6	398	509	111
Liberal Democrat	14.5	177	175	–2
SNP	24.1	294	181	–113
Other	13.7	167	234	67
STV elections				
2007				
Conservative	15.6	191	143	–48
Labour	28.1	343	348	5
Liberal Democrat	12.7	155	166	11
SNP	27.9	341	363	22
Other	15.8	193	202	9
2012				
Conservative	13.3	162	115	–47
Labour	31.4	384	394	10
Liberal Democrat	6.6	81	71	–10
SNP	32.3	395	425	30
Other	16.4	200	218	18
2017				
Conservative	25.3	310	276	–34
Labour	20.2	248	262	14
Liberal Democrat	6.9	85	67	–18
SNP	32.3	396	431	35
Other	15.2	187	191	4

[A] From 2007 to 2017, vote shares are the percentage of first preference votes for each party.

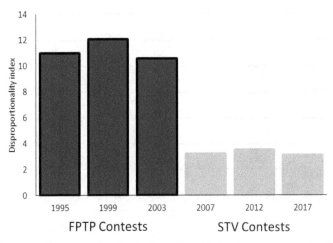

Does it have to be this way?

Figure 7.3 Disproportionality indices, Scottish local government elections
1995–2017

replaced by a 29-councillor advantage. The Conservatives and Liberal
Democrats, meanwhile, lost out by roughly the same amounts under
both systems – around 40 and 10 councillors down, on average, from
their PR 'entitlement' under both systems.

Comparing the disproportionality indices for both sets of local elections confirms the impression (Figure 7.3). In the last three FPTP
elections, the disproportionality index was around 11. In the first
three under STV, it dropped by almost three-quarters, to just over
3. Adopting STV for elections to Scotland's local authorities led to
a much more proportional outcome than had been the case under
FPTP.

One complication with this comparison, however, is that the two
sets of elections took place at different times. There were major
changes in Scottish politics over the period covered, not least the
strong growth of SNP support and Labour's decline (and after 2014,
a Scottish Conservative recovery). That makes a simple comparison
tricky, as the disproportionality index will vary somewhat from election to election even under the same election rules, just because of
how party support changes over time. Although it is likely that the
shift in disproportionality reflects a change in electoral system, therefore, we cannot be absolutely sure.

To get around this problem, we need to know how the same

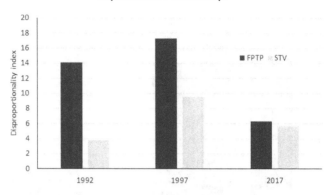

Figure 7.4 Disproportionality in British general elections under FPTP and STV

election might have turned out had it been fought under different rules. While we cannot re-run an actual election, we can (as we did with AV) look at estimates of the effects of STV on the 1992 and 1997 elections provided by Patrick Dunleavy and his co-workers, and at similar estimates for the 2017 election, calculated by Jess Garland and Chris Terry.[29] Their estimates are shown in Table 7.3 (again with the actual number of MPs and the 'pure PR' allocations for comparison), and the disproportionality indices are shown in Figure 7.4.

One caveat is that the estimates depend on assumptions about voters' preference rankings of parties, and about how many MPs are elected from each constituency under STV. In the examples looked at here, survey data provided voters' reference rankings. Dunleavy et al. assumed five-member STV constituencies, built from then-existing Westminster seats. Garland and Terry, meanwhile, combined existing constituencies into STV seats which varied in size from three to six MPs. That, plus the exact configuration of the seats, will have some effect on how the simulated election results will turn out. Hence the three sets of estimates are not precisely comparable with each other. However, they do give some indication of the likely effects of moving to STV for Westminster elections.

At all three elections STV would have benefited the Liberal Democrats very substantially. Their parliamentary representation would have increased by between 17 and 85 seats – in all cases giving them more than double their actual haul of MPs (and in 1992, almost five times more). The Conservatives, meanwhile, would have been

Table 7.3 Estimating the results of the 1992, 1997 and 2017 general elections in Great Britain under the Single Transferable Vote

	Per cent vote share (FPTP)	Seats (pure PR)	Actual seats (FPTP)	Estimated seats (STV)	Seat difference (STV – FPTP)
1992					
Conservative	42.8	271	336	256	−80
Labour	35.2	223	271	250	−21
Liberal Democrat	18.3	116	20	102	82
Other	3.7	23	7	26	19
1997					
Conservative	31.5	202	165	144	−21
Labour	44.3	284	418	342	−76
Liberal Democrat	17.2	110	46	131	85
Other	7.0	45	12	24	12
2017					
Conservative	43.5	274	317	282	−35
Labour	41.0	259	262	297	35
Liberal Democrat	7.6	48	12	29	17
Other	7.9	50	40	23	−17

Sources: The estimates are taken from P. Dunleavy, H. Margetts and S. Weir, 'How Britain would have voted under alternative electoral systems in 1992', *Parliamentary Affairs*, 45 (1992), 640–655; P. Dunleavy, H. Margetts, B. O'Duffy and S. Weir, 'Remodelling the 1997 general election: how Britain would have voted under alternative electoral systems', *British Elections and Parties Review*, 8 (1998), 208–231; J. Garland and C. Terry, *The 2017 General Election: Volatile Voting, Random Results*, London, Electoral Reform Society, 2017 (www.electoral-reform.org.uk/latest-news-and-research/publications/the-2017-general-election-report/).

losers under STV, as would Labour in 1992 and 1997 (though not, on Garland and Terry's estimate, in 2017). And other parties would have gained in 1992 and 1997 – but would have lost out in 2017 (largely, in the latter case, because the huge boost the SNP gained from FPTP in Scotland would have been reduced substantially under STV rules). And, whatever the precise details of the estimation process, the overall disproportionality of British general elections would have fallen substantially in STV contests.

The Additional Member System

Another contender which maintains a constituency link but which promises greater proportionality than FPTP is the Additional Member System. AMS is not only used in many countries worldwide (including Germany and New Zealand), but was also the basis of the system proposed for Westminster elections by the Jenkins Commission in 1998 and is used for elections to the Scottish Parliament and the Welsh Assembly.

In an AMS election, there are two ways to elect an MP. Some MPs are elected (usually using FPTP) in single-member constituencies, while others are elected via a closed party list PR system in larger regions covering a number of constituencies (in New Zealand, the entire country is treated as a single region). Voters have two votes: one for a candidate in the constituency contest, and one for a party list in the regional PR contest.

The constituency counts are straightforward: the plurality winner is elected as MP for the seat. Things get more involved in the regional count, however. Each party's regional vote share gives an indication of how many MPs in total (both constituency and regional list) it is entitled to in that region. In principle, therefore, this second vote is the most important for the composition of the Parliament, as it determines the overall party make-up of the elected chamber.

How many MPs a party elects from its regional list will depend on both its vote in the regional list ballot and on the number of constituency MPs elected for the party in the region. In elections to the Scottish Parliament, for instance, this is determined by the d'Hondt system. Each party's regional vote is divided by the number of constituency MPs it has won in the region plus one. The party with the largest total based on this calculation will be allocated the first regional MP, who is taken from that party's candidate list (in closed-list systems, the most common for AMS, candidates are elected in the order a party presents them on the regional list). The divisor for the party just allocated a regional MP is increased by one (to reflect that extra MP), and then the calculation is repeated – and the party with the largest total at the next stage gets the next regional MP. This process continues until all the regional list MPs for the region have been allocated. At each round, the system in effect allocates the next regional seat to the party with the highest average vote per candidate already elected.

Some parties may gain so many constituency MPs in a region that they will win no further MPs there through the regional list (in effect, their constituency haul has already reached – or exceeded – their proportional allocation). Other parties may win no constituency MPs but still pick up regional list MPs. And, of course, some parties will win MPs through both the constituency and regional list ballots.

It is sometimes claimed that the second, regional, vote in AMS elections is 'sincere', in the sense that voters will always vote for their most preferred party. As it is the regional vote which controls how many MPs are elected for a party, goes the argument, voters will want to make sure their party's support is properly reflected at that stage. However, this is not strictly the case. Voters can opt to vote tactically in AMS elections in both the constituency and the regional ballots. Supporters of parties which are unlikely to win the constituency contest in their seat might reasonably vote for their preferred party in the regional ballot (to maximise the chances of the party picking up some MPs through that route), while opting to cast their constituency vote for another party with a better chance of winning in the constituency if that seems to offer a better chance of defeating a party they dislike. But a similar calculation also applies to voters whose party is likely to elect its entire quota of MPs for the region from the constituency contests. For them, it makes sense to vote for their preferred party in the constituency vote but to vote tactically for another party in the regional ballot (knowing their preferred party is unlikely to win any regional MPs). That helps maximise the representation of parties they see as congenial.

Parties, too, have incentives to make tactical choices in AMS elections. For instance, if a party has little chance of winning any constituency votes, but thinks it might pick up some MPs via the regional list, it is rational for the party to field candidates only in the regional ballot.

An example illustrates the point. In the 1999 Scottish Parliament election, the city of Glasgow was one of the second vote regions. It elected 17 MSPs, ten through the constituency ballot, and a further seven through the regional vote (Table 7.4). Labour took 49.3 per cent of the vote in the constituency contest and won all ten constituency seats. Its chances of winning any further seats through the regional vote were minimal, therefore. Not surprisingly, the party's vote share in the regional contest was noticeably lower, at 43.9 per cent. Support for minor parties jumped, however, from 7 per cent in the constituency vote to 15 per cent in the regional vote. Most of that increase

Table 7.4 The 1999 Scottish Parliament election in Glasgow region

	Constituency vote per cent	Constituency MSPs	Regional vote per cent	Regional MSPs
Conservatives	7.7	0	7.9	1
Labour	49.3	10	43.9	0
Liberal Democrats	8.1	0	7.2	1
SNP	27.9	0	25.5	4
Other	7.0	0	15.5	1

came from two parties. The Scottish Socialist party did field candidates in some Glasgow constituencies and took 6.3 per cent of the constituency vote (nowhere near enough to win via that route). But its vote share in the regional ballot went up to 7.2 per cent, enough to give the party one regional MSP. The Scottish Greens, meanwhile, did not field any constituency candidates in Glasgow, but did stand in the regional ballot, gaining 4 per cent of the vote. Other minor parties also followed the Greens' example, standing only in the regional ballot and picking up a further 4 per cent in the process.

AMS is broadly proportional in its operation, as can be demonstrated by exploiting its two-ballot design. In an AMS election, the constituency vote gives us an indication of just how proportional the election would be if fought solely on FPTP rules, while the overall result reveals its true proportionality. For all Scottish Parliament and Welsh Assembly elections between 1999 and 2016, we have calculated the disproportionality index for the constituency context alone, and for the overall election result (Figure 7.5).[30] As we are looking at real behaviour in the same election, this is a particularly telling comparison.

While the constituency votes clearly would have produced substantially disproportional outcomes, the addition of the MSPs/AMs elected through the regional list makes for a more proportional overall result.[31] This is particularly clear in elections to the Scottish Parliament where in 2016, for instance, the disproportionality measure for the constituency contest is almost six times larger than that for the overall result. However, AMS tended to produce more proportional results in Scotland than in Wales, where the relative difference in disproportionality between the constituency and overall results declined over time.

Does it have to be this way?

a) Elections to the Scottish Parliament

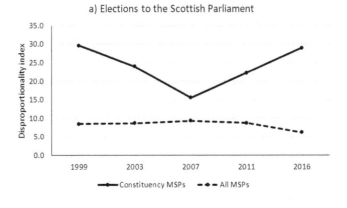

b) Elections to the Welsh Assembly

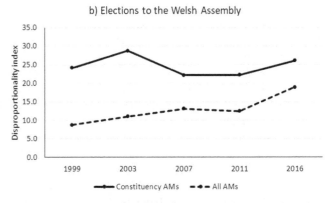

Figure 7.5 Disproportionality in AMS elections to the Scottish Parliament and the Welsh Assembly

In large measure, this is because a higher proportion of all Welsh AMs than of Scottish MSPs are constituency representatives. While 66.6 per cent (40 out of 60) of the former are elected from the constituency contest, only 56.6 per cent (73 out of 129) of the latter are. This matters, as the lower the proportion of members elected through the regional list competition, the less efficient that part of the AMS process is at compensating for disproportionalities in the constituency element.

One further aspect of AMS is worth considering. What sort of mandate MPs can claim, and what they see as their main parliamentary responsibilities, can depend on whether they are elected through the constituency or the regional PR route. MPs elected through the regional list owe their election to their party's popularity and to their place on the party list for their region. To that extent they have a party, but not a personal, mandate. MPs elected via the constituency contest, however, can claim more of a personal vote, as some voters may have opted to support them based not on their party label but on their record (actual or potential) as a constituency representative. This affects how MPs elected under AMS approach their jobs. Constituency MPs have to pay attention to constituency work. List MPs need to burnish their party credentials.[32] In order to find time to meet their constituency responsibilities (which they both feel are important and know may help them win re-election) members of the Scottish Parliament and the Welsh Assembly elected via the constituency system spend less time on parliamentary work (like committee membership), and more on constituency work, than do those who are elected via the regional list (though this is not a complete division of labour: both constituency and regional list representatives attend to the concerns of voters in their areas, and both are involved in all aspects of their party's parliamentary work).[33] And those who stand both as constituency candidates and as candidates on the regional list seem to form a 'half-way house' between 'pure' constituency and 'pure' list MSPs in terms of the balance they strike between constituency and Parliament. This can create tensions between representatives depending on which route they were elected through. Constituency representatives, for instance, can feel that their regional list colleagues have less of a personal mandate, or (where the latter do take up local issues) are encroaching on their constituency role.

Regional Closed List PR

A more radical approach to reforming Westminster elections would be to break the constituency link and to move to a system in which all MPs were elected in large multi-member regions, using some form of proportional representation. This would clearly push against the widely expressed public preference for 'local' MPs, as expressed in the recent rapid growth in MPs' constituency caseloads (see Chapter 2) – which could be countered by the elected candidates dividing the region among themselves. But such a change is not entirely inconceivable – particularly if devolution is extended beyond Scotland, Wales and Northern Ireland to the English regions. A more comprehensive devolution settlement across all parts of the UK would create a substantial layer of government at sub-national level which could deal with many of the welfare state issues currently filling MPs' post-bags. As a result, the need for local communities to have their own Westminster representative might be diminished – opening the door to a more root-and-branch approach to Westminster elections.

One vision of how this might work in practice is provided by the Regional Closed List form of PR used in European Parliament elections in Great Britain (but not Northern Ireland) from 1999. This system divided Britain into eleven regions: Scotland, Wales, and the nine English government regions. Each region was a large multi-member constituency. The European Parliamentary Elections Act 2002 stipulated that the number of MEPs elected from each region should be a function of the total number of MEPs allocated to Great Britain (in 2019, there were 70, plus three more in Northern Ireland), and the electorate in each region. No region was to elect fewer than three MEPs and (with that proviso), the same (more or less) ratio of electors to MEPs was to be used in each region. On that basis, the allocation of MEPs to regions for the 2019 elections ranged from just three in the North East of England, to ten in the South East of England (Table 7.5).

In closed list PR elections, each party fields a list of candidates in each region, with the candidates listed in the order the party wishes them to be elected (the party's top candidate appearing at the top of the list). Voters have just one vote, which they cast for one of the

Table 7.5 Allocation of MEPs to regions, 2019 European Parliament election in Great Britain

Region	MEPs	Lijphart Effective Threshold
Scotland	6	10.7
Wales	4	9.4
East Midlands	5	12.5
East of England	7	9.4
London	8	8.3
North East England	3	18.8
North West England	8	8.3
South East England	10	6.8
South West England	6	10.7
West Midlands	7	9.4
Yorkshire & the Humber	6	10.7

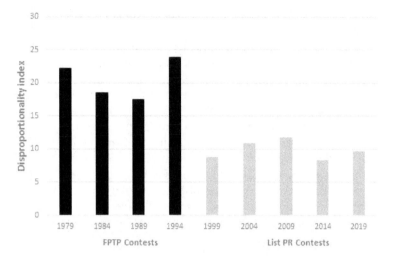

Figure 7.6 Disproportionality indices, European Parliament elections in Great Britain 1979–2019

parties (or for an independent candidate, should any stand). There is no need to worry about relative preference ordering of candidates or parties. And as the system is proportional, the pressure to consider tactical voting is reduced (though not entirely removed). The votes are then counted for each party in each region. The allocation of seats takes place in a series of rounds, using the d'Hondt system for the regional vote under AMS.

Just how much more proportional EU elections in Britain became as a result of the adoption of list PR is clear from a comparison of the disproportionality indices for contests from 1999 (when the system changed) with those for elections before then which were fought using FPTP in single-member constituencies (Figure 7.6). The change is very noticeable indeed. Prior to 1999, almost all British MEPs came from just a handful of parties. From 1979 until 1989, all bar one (an SNP MEP) were either Conservative or Labour. No other party sent a representative to Brussels, even though they won on average 21 per cent of the vote. In 1994, the Liberal Democrats managed to win two seats (as did the SNP). But they were still heavily under-represented: despite gaining almost 17 per cent of the national vote that year, they provided just over 2 per cent of the MEPs.

Does it have to be this way?

The adoption of regional list PR in 1999 broke the two-party duopoly over British MEPs. Fewer Labour and Conservative candidates were elected, and more came from other parties. Between 1999 and 2014, the two parties' average share of Britain's MEPs dropped to 65 per cent (and by 2014, only 55 per cent). And in 2019, their combined share of both votes and seats fell even further (to 23 per cent and 20 per cent), as they were pushed into third and fifth place respectively by the Brexit Party (which gained 32 per cent of the vote and 40 per cent of the MEPs), the Liberal Democrats (20 per cent of the vote and 23 per cent of MEPs) and the Greens (12 per cent of the vote netting 10 per cent of MEPs).

The degree of proportionality in a system of regional list PR will vary from region to region, depending on the number of individuals to be elected in each region. Although there is no precise linear relationship between the two, the larger the number of individuals to be elected, the more proportional the system will be between parties (and hence the easier it will be for smaller parties to gain some representation). This is because, even in the most proportional of systems (and even where there is no legal threshold for representation), there is a minimum effective threshold of support a party must reach in order to elect at least one of its candidates, which is a function of the number of votes cast and the number of seats to be filled. The political scientist Arendt Lijphart estimates this as:[34]

$$Threshold\ vote = \left(\frac{75\ per\ cent\ of\ the\ total\ votes\ cast}{number\ of\ seats + 1} \right)$$

That has had consequences in Britain's Euro-elections, especially for smaller parties. In the 2019 Euro-election, the South East region elected ten MEPs. The effective threshold there was 6.8 per cent of the vote (Table 7.5), and every party with a vote share higher than that got at least one MEP. The Brexit Party took 36 per cent of the vote in the region and gained four MEPs; the Liberal Democrats' 26 per cent of the vote netted three MEPs; and the Greens, the Conservatives and Labour got one MEP each, on 14 per cent, 10 per cent and 7 per cent of the vote respectively. But at the same election, the North East region elected only three MEPs, and the effective threshold was therefore 18.8 per cent. Only two parties (the Brexit Party and Labour) exceeded this vote share. The Brexit Party, with 39 per cent of the vote, won two MEPs, while Labour got one MEP with 19 per cent of the vote. The

Table 7.6 Effective regional vote thresholds for Regional Closed List PR at general elections, 2010–19

Region	MPs	Lijphart Effective Threshold
Scotland	59	1.3
Wales	40	1.8
East Midlands	46	1.6
East of England	58	1.3
London	73	1.0
North East England	29	2.5
North West England	75	1.0
South East England	84	0.9
South West England	55	1.3
West Midlands	59	1.3
Yorkshire & the Humber	54	1.4

next most popular party in the region, the Liberal Democrats, won 17 per cent of the vote, but received no MEPs – despite gaining a larger vote share in the region than the Greens, Labour or the Conservatives had in the South East.

That said, the number of MEPs returned per region in a Euro-election is considerably smaller than the number of Westminster MPs elected for the same region. If Regional Closed List PR was introduced for Westminster elections, therefore, the effective vote threshold would be much lower in any given region than it was in the 2019 EU elections. Had the general elections between 2010 and 2019 been fought using regional list PR an in the regions used for Euro-elections, for instance, the effective threshold would have ranged from 0.9 per cent of the vote in the South East of England to 2.5 per cent in the North East (Table 7.6). As a consequence, the election result would have been highly proportional, even in regions with relatively few MPs; it could have encouraged many small parties to nominate candidates with a good chance of achieving election.

To illustrate this, we estimate the outcomes of the 2015, 2017 and 2019 UK general elections in the North East region of England, had those elections been fought using the regional list PR system employed in Britain's EU elections, assuming the parties obtained the same overall vote shares there as they did in the actual election (Table 7.7). The results are striking. Labour won 47 per cent of the regional vote in 2015 and 55 per cent in 2017. Under FPTP, that gave

Table 7.7 The 2015, 2017 and 2019 UK general elections in the North East of England: FPTP and Regional Closed List PR compared

	2015			2017			2019		
	Vote per cent	MPs (FPTP)	MPs (list PR)	Vote per cent	MPs (FPTP)	MPs (list PR)	Vote per cent	MPs (FPTP)	MPs (list PR)
Conservative	25.3	3	7	34.4	3	10	38.3	10	12
Labour	46.9	26	14	55.4	26	17	42.6	19	13
Liberal Democrats	6.5	0	2	4.6	0	1	6.8	0	2
UKIP/Brexit	16.7	0	5	3.9	0	1	8.1	0	2
Greens	3.6	0	1	1.3	0	0	2.4	0	0
Others	0.9	0	0	0.5	0	0	1.9	0	0
Disproportionality		34.5	1.5		29.9	2.6		18.2	3.6

the party all bar three of the region's 29 seats at both elections – just under 90 per cent. The only other party to gain representation was the Conservative, netting just under 10 per cent of the seats (three MPs!) in both election years, with 25 per cent and 34 per cent of the vote respectively. Perhaps the most dramatic loser in the region was UKIP in 2015: despite gaining 17 per cent of the vote, they won no seats. Not surprisingly, the disproportionality scores for both FPTP contests are poor: 34.5 in 2015 and 29.9 in 2017. Things weren't quite so disproportional in 2019, thanks entirely to the dramatic change in the relative fortunes of Labour and the Conservatives: the former's vote share in the region dropped by almost 13 percentage points to just 42.6 per cent while the latter's share rose by a more modest 3.9 percentage points to 38.3 per cent. But that was enough to shift seven seats from Labour to Conservative, reducing the disproportionality index to 18.2.

Under regional list PR, however, the result would have been very different. Labour (as the most popular party in the region) would still have had most seats at these elections. But with just 14 (48 per cent) in 2015, 17 (59 per cent) in 2017 and 12 (45 per cent) in 2019, it would not have been so dominant. Conservative representation would have increased from three seats to seven in 2015 and ten in 2017, and from ten to twelve in 2019. And both UKIP (or the Brexit Party in 2019) and Liberal Democrat voters (and Greens in 2015) in the region would have had some parliamentary representation. In 2015, for instance, UKIP would have returned five MPs from the North East. Not surprising, disproportionality would have been considerably reduced – with indices of 1.5 in 2015, 2.6 in 2017 and 3.6 in 2019 (the slightly higher figures in the later years reflecting the fact that fewer parties got over the effective threshold in those contests – largely because of the increase in Labour and Conservative voting, and the drop in support for UKIP/the Brexit Party).

One large obstacle to the adoption of regional list PR for Westminster elections, however, is that it represents the largest move away from the constituency system of any of the electoral systems reviewed here. If voters' attachment to the idea of constituency representation really is strong, moving to a system where MPs represent an entire region is a very large step. The North East region, for instance, covers a very wide array of different communities, including remote rural areas, affluent towns and suburbs, deprived inner cities, and former mining communities. Voters might feel

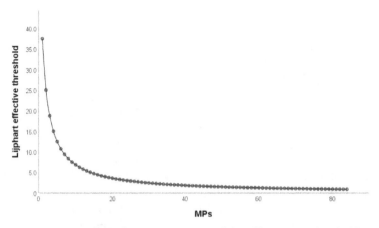

Figure 7.7 Number of MPs in a region and the effective vote threshold

that MPs elected from such a large region are too remote from their particular local interests. One option, therefore, might be to base the system around more, but smaller, regions. Inevitably, this would come at some cost to proportionality. But Lijphart's formula for the effective minimum vote threshold needed to return an MP is not linear (Figure 7.7). As the number of MPs in a region increases, the effective threshold needed to win at least one MP declines – but at a decreasing rate. The marginal benefits of increasing the number of MPs diminish rapidly once a region returns around 10–12 MPs. The smallest parties would lose out from smaller rather than larger regions, but MPs for moderately popular parties would still be returned to Westminster in larger numbers than at present. Regions would not have to be very large to produce 'acceptably' proportional results. To put this into context, in 2017 the city of Sheffield returned six MPs (one of whom represented a seat which straddled the Sheffield-Barnsley border). If Sheffield was a list PR region, a party gaining just over 10 per cent of the vote there would have a good chance of electing one of the local MPs. It is possible, therefore, to think of list PR operating reasonably in regions with electorates similar to a large city – still quite large, but not, perhaps, insuperably so for those attached to the ideal of MPs representing defined geographical communities.

Conclusions

Throughout most of this book, we have traced the development and operation of the FPTP single-member constituency system used for many years to elect the UK's MPs. But, as we outline in this chapter, FPTP has not been the only electoral system to be considered for Westminster (and other) elections in the UK. We have looked in more detail at the four alternative systems which have dominated debate here: the Alternative Vote; the Single Transferable Vote; the Additional Member System; and Regional Closed List PR. But there are many (very many)[35] others too – both variants on the systems we have discussed, and systems which operate in rather different ways.

No electoral system is perfect, however. All have pros and cons. FPTP is simple, quick, and easily understood. Voters may not always be happy with the politicians and the governments elected via FPTP. But survey after survey suggests that (in so far as they do think about it) most British voters value key aspects of FPTP – not least the close relationship between MPs and their constituents, and FPTP's tendency to produce single party governments with clear parliamentary majorities (though the latter looks somewhat hollow in the light of general election results since 2010). Even so, it produces not only highly disproportional results (a feature which horrifies its opponents and delights its supporters) but also (and potentially more seriously) biased outcomes which, as shown in the previous chapters, can benefit one party greatly over another, even when they obtain the same shares of the vote. Supporters of smaller parties can feel semi-permanently excluded from the front pages of politics. And the link between votes and seats is neither consistent nor transparent. Under FPTP, a party can increase its vote share substantially, and yet see the number of MPs representing it decline (as happened to the Conservative Party between the 2015 and 2017 general elections), especially in areas where it is not the largest party. AV, as we have indicated, largely mirrors the pros and cons of FPTP.

STV, AMS and List PR are all much more proportional in their operation than are either FPTP or AV (a tick in their favour for those who prefer proportionality in election results). But, partly as a consequence, they are less likely to produce strong one-party majority governments and more likely to result in coalitions (again something that some will see as desirable and others as dreadful). And all three would change the nature of the constituency system to some degree.

Constituencies would be larger than at present (and under regional list PR substantially so). And both STV and List PR would require multi-member constituencies, while AMS would create two different 'classes' of MPs. None of these problems is insuperable or a deal-breaker. After all, each of these systems is used elsewhere – and many of the countries which use them are well-governed and successful (though whether that is a result of the election systems they use is an open question).[36]

But reforming Westminster elections is liable to be an uphill struggle. One obstacle is that electoral reform is hardly a major priority for most members of the British public. The only time electoral reform has been put to the British public (in the 2011 referendum on AV), it was rejected (even though – as we have seen – AV is only marginally different from FPTP) – and on a relatively low turnout (42 per cent). Government time and energy is limited, and in the absence of a loud and persistent public clamour for change, other more pressing issues are likely to take precedence.

What is more, perhaps the largest obstacle against electoral reform for Westminster is the reluctance of the largest parties to sponsor it – for very clear reasons of practical politics. Labour and the Conservatives have benefited substantially from FPTP, and one or other has been in government (usually alone, very occasionally with the support of other parties) continuously for most of the period since the introduction of the universal franchise in the UK early in the twentieth century. As things stand, their agreement is essential if electoral reform for Westminster is to move beyond tinkering with details of FPTP – and it is hard to see why they should agree to the adoption of systems which would substantially reduce their power and advantage. It isn't hard to see, therefore, why AV is the only system that either party has come close to offering as a serious alternative to FPTP (as both did in 2010, under the pressure of neither gaining a majority in that year's election). AV, as we have seen, can be even less proportional – and even more advantageous for the 'big two' parties – than FPTP.

Where UK governments have introduced more proportional electoral systems, it has been for elected bodies away from Westminster, and for distinctly political ends. For instance, STV was used for the Northern Ireland Assembly to minimise the risk of one community establishing majority control over the body to the detriment of other communities – and hence to encourage power-sharing.[37]

Northern Ireland, of course is a region where neither Labour nor the Conservatives have any real electoral interests. In Scotland and Wales, meanwhile, an important incentive behind the introduction of AMS for the newly devolved governments was to limit the risk of nationalist majorities in the new devolved Scottish and Welsh governments (though the 2011 Scottish election, when the SNP won 44 per cent of the regional vote and a slim majority in Holyrood, shows the limits of that strategy).

It would be premature, however, to conclude that electoral reform for Westminster is a dead duck. While voters' preferences for the main features of FPTP elections (the constituency MP, strong government, etc.) may be relatively wide, they may also be quite shallow. Many voters' real understanding of how different electoral systems work – and of their pros and cons – is rather limited.[38] And when actually faced with new electoral systems, voters and parties easily adapt. Prior to the adoption of AMS there in 1996, New Zealand was often discussed as one of the strongest examples of an FPTP-based plurality electoral system outside the UK. Yet the change to AMS proved broadly popular (in a 2011 referendum, a clear majority – 58 per cent – voted to retain it) and seems to have bedded in successfully. In Scotland, voters have used four very different electoral systems: STV for local government, AMS for the Scottish Parliament, regional list PR for the European Parliament, and FPTP for Westminster. There is little sign that they are confused as a result – or that they have a strong preference for one system over the others.

What is more, the political environment is currently very fluid, and may in future provide more conducive conditions for reform. Two of the last four British general elections have resulted in hung parliaments and major party governments dependent on the support of smaller parties (in either formal coalition or informal agreements). And the fall-out from the 2016 Brexit referendum shows the difficulties major parties can face in adapting to shifting voter preferences. FPTP does give large parties major advantages and makes it very hard for new challengers to break through. But that only holds while the largest parties stay relatively large. If their support fragments, the benefits they receive from FPTP can diminish rapidly, as Scottish Labour has found to its cost. Previously dominant in Scottish politics – in the 2010 general election, it secured 42 per cent of the votes and 41 out of 59 MPs – its vote collapsed to just 24 per cent in 2015 in the face of an SNP surge, and it elected just one MP. Similar threats could face both

Labour and Conservatives in the rest of Britain too – not least if they lose support in their traditional heartlands. (Labour lost a number of seats in 2019 that it had won at previous elections in the Midlands and North of England, but it gained only one from the Conservatives – in London.) Pressure to reform the electoral system could come either from renewed demands from potential coalition partners after future elections, or from public disquiet if a large body of voters are consistently grossly under-represented as a result of FPTP. UKIP's 2015 experience could be a harbinger. At that election, the party was the third most popular in Britain, securing just under 13 per cent of all votes cast. But although almost 4 million people supported them, they gained just one MP. In the event, UKIP's 2015 success proved ephemeral, and just two years later the party slumped to fifth place, with around 600,000 votes (1.8 per cent). But had UKIP's support proved more durable, and had FPTP continued to so substantially under-reward it, it is possible that public discontent with FPTP might have grown. Given the UK party system's current volatility, similar situations in future cannot be ruled out – and that may begin to erode public support for 'business as usual' for the electoral system.

Given these upheavals, it would be a brave person who would predict either that British parliamentary elections will return any time soon to consistently producing strong one-party majority governments, or that the party system itself will revert to the two-party dominance of the past. The 2019 European Parliament election result showed that, outside Scotland, the 2017 return to two-party predominance had rather flimsy foundations. And – given growing discontent with the 'business as usual' of Westminster politics – it would also be a bold prediction to say that questions of political reform in general – and of electoral reform in particular – will remain the preserve of a few keen enthusiasts, and marginal to the interests and concerns of most voters. These are turbulent times – and Westminster's FPTP system could yet be a casualty.

8

Conclusion

Throughout its history, the UK's House of Commons has comprised MPs elected to represent places. Furthermore, from 1885 on, accepted practice has been that each MP should be her or his place's sole representative; single-member constituencies have predominated since then and have been the only type since 1950 when university representation was abolished. The UK's representative democracy has been territorially grounded.

Places differ in their population size, however, and increasingly over the last two centuries it has been realised that allowing those differences to be reflected in the composition of the House of Commons means that some places have greater weight and influence than others in its debates and decision-making. As a consequence, steps were increasingly taken to ensure that, as far as possible, constituencies have the same number of electors. This created challenges for those determining the boundaries of new constituencies at redistributions – from 1944 non-partisan Boundary Commissions operating in ignorance of their decisions' likely political consequences. Drawing a new constituency map thus involved addressing a tension between the particularities of places and the mathematics of equality – between an organic criterion of defining constituencies that encompassed populations with communities of interest and an arithmetic criterion linked to the maxim of 'one person, one vote, one vote, one value'. Changes to the Commissions' guidelines and rules reflected the relative importance those in power at the time gave to the two criteria; the most recent changes made the arithmetic criterion predominant, though in its application the Commissions – and the politicians and others seeking to influence their decisions – strove to give as much recognition as possible to the organic criterion within the strict arithmetic rules they are bound to apply. Whether this has any clear impact on political practice remains to be seen.

The organic versus arithmetic tension operates within a geographic matrix created by the degree of spatial clustering of each party's supporters into particular areas and the degree to which those clusters are concentrated together. The boundary drawers have to superimpose a map of constituencies onto those geographies and – even using the building blocks they largely rely on (local authority wards) – a large number of different maps can be created within the rules, with different configurations perhaps having different electoral consequences – not least in the degree to which parties are significantly under-represented in some parts of the country and over-represented in others. The Boundary Commissioners operate in ignorance of those possible consequences, but political parties and others who seek to influence their decisions do not; they promote alternative boundaries which might enhance their prospects of electing MPs from the affected areas. The tension is played out geographically, therefore; the Commissions and those who seek to influence them are geographical actors.

Operation of this system has favoured some political actors much more than others. It is typical of single-member constituency systems using plurality voting that small parties – especially those whose voters are neither spatially clustered nor spatially concentrated enough – rarely get a proportion of the seats commensurate with their share of the votes. But larger parties are unequally treated as well. Throughout the long nineteenth century the Tories gained larger shares of the seats than votes at nearly every election because their voters were clustered and concentrated in the countryside and small towns, where constituencies were much smaller than those in the big cities – something that Lord Salisbury was careful to maintain when negotiating with Charles Dilke over the details of the 1885 redistribution. In the twentieth century, Labour built its strength in the large cities: the depopulation of their inner regions during the first decades following the Second World War II meant that constituencies there tended to have fewer voters than in the suburbs and shires, increasingly so over time, which operated to the Conservatives' disadvantage. The Conservatives sought to rectify that in 2011, probably successfully, but no new sets of constituencies have yet been put into place implementing their strict arithmetic criterion.

Disproportionality of this type is common in such electoral systems.

Less noted, but just as pervasive, is bias whereby – again for the same geographic reasons – one party may have a considerable advantage over another, even if they achieve the same vote totals. That bias can be extensive, sometimes worth more than 50 seats to the advantaged party even when the two largest are very close in their vote shares. The potential for such unequal treatment casts considerable doubt on the fairness of such a system and its implications for representative democratic practice.

Can that unfairness be removed? Part of it, as the decomposition of the bias measure has shown, results from variations in turnout that could be removed with compulsory voting. But, as stressed throughout this book, most of it is a function of the geographies of support for each party over which a matrix of constituency boundaries is superimposed. Those geographies will almost always create disproportional and biased election results, some more than others. Many Americans are concerned with the growing extent of gerrymandering district boundaries there, for example,[1] but research has clearly shown that because support for the Democrats is spatially more clustered and concentrated than that for the Republicans the latter is almost certain to benefit, even without gerrymandering of boundaries.[2]

Any electoral map produced by independent cartographers is very likely to be, in effect, an unintentional gerrymander. That is the situation in the UK; a set of geographies that significantly, often substantially, exaggerates the electoral prospects of one of the two largest parties and leads to the under-representation of others, unless – like the SNP in Scotland at the 2015 general election – they win a near-majority of the votes nearly everywhere. Those geographies can be challenged by campaigning strategies. For most of the post-1945 period the Conservatives have benefited from the distributional component of the bias measure because Labour's votes have been spatially more clustered and concentrated. But when Labour won substantial support outside its traditional working-class heartlands, in 1966 and again in 1997–2005, it overcame the apparently in-built gerrymander; assisted in 1997 and 2001 by tactical anti-Conservative voting it changed its geography of support and the direction of the unintentional gerrymander. From 2010 the pro-Conservative status quo was reinstated.

While the UK retains the current electoral system, therefore, disproportional and biased election results will continue to be the norm, whatever tweaks to the system – tackling the organic versus arithmetic tension – are introduced by an injured party with the power to do so. Only extensive electoral reform, to a system that delivers proportional representation, will remove the disproportionality and bias, and such systems very substantially downplay the organic criterion. Electoral reform has never attracted substantial support in the UK, among the political parties let alone the general population; there are protagonists within both the Labour and Conservative parties but they are few and when it has seemed that they might gain some influence – as before and just after the election of New Labour in 1997 – that has soon been dissipated. The Conservatives and their Tory predecessors have never embraced PR; they have been the main beneficiaries of the disproportionality and bias for two centuries, occasionally losing elections but being in power for much longer during that time than their voting support might justify on other grounds. Geography has largely worked for them and they have no desire to change it, save at the margins. As a small party until the 1920s Labour generally favoured reform but as they replaced the Liberals as the second party and realised they could gain power through the existing system reform's popularity waned and Labour now sustains the current system. And the Liberals were content with that system until too late: they only embraced reform and PR after they became the third party and despite their arguments have since lacked the power to achieve change.

The UK's political parties are not totally averse to other electoral systems, however – only where it affects their prospects at general elections. A quasi-proportional system was introduced as part of Irish Home Rule in 1922 to protect the Protestant minority and has since been deployed in Northern Ireland to protect the nationalist minority. And a proportional system was deployed for the new Scottish Parliament and Welsh Assembly in 1999 to try and ensure that nationalists never won power – a stratagem that failed in Scotland in 2011 given the SNP's popularity then. But for general elections neither Labour nor the Conservatives is prepared to consider seriously any alternative to first-past-the-post: they are content to allow the geographies that underpin the translation of votes into seats to influence election outcomes – until it becomes clear to at least one of them that the likelihood of them forming a majority government again is remote.

And what of the citizen? Whether we subscribe to a Burkean viewpoint or not, it is clear that the political establishment has achieved effective control of the country's electoral system. The UK is spared the messiness of coalitions, by and large, but that comes at a price in terms of both proportionality and, occasionally, bias. The current major beneficiary of that system, the Conservative Party, is set to gain further advantage as a result of the reforms legislated for in 2011 but still to be implemented. It is not necessary to be a cynic to note the irony in the manifesto pledge that 'a Conservative government will ensure every vote will have equal value'. As the country with the largest mismatch between the preferences of the people as expressed through an election and the reflection of that in its legislature, the UK falls a long way short of that Chartist ideal. There are alternatives available, many of which have a proven track record in various parts of the country. There are valid debates to be had as to the degree of proportionality which might be desirable, and we do not see it as our role to point in any one direction. It is our hope, however, that by documenting the evolution of our electoral system and explaining how it translates votes to seats, the reader will be better placed to judge exactly where that balance should lie.

Notes

Preface

1   The first of those monographs was D. J. Rossiter, R. J. Johnston and C. J. Pattie, *The Boundary Commissions: Redrawing the UK's Map of Parliamentary Constituencies*, Manchester: Manchester University Press, 1999; followed by R. J. Johnston, C. J. Pattie, D. Dorling and D. J. Rossiter, *From Votes to Seats: the Operation of the UK's Electoral System since 1945*, Manchester: Manchester University Press, 2001. The overview volume was R. J. Johnston and C. J. Pattie, *Putting Voters in Their Place: Geography and Elections in Great Britain*, Oxford: Oxford University Press, 2006.

Chapter 1

1   To Patrick Dunleavy this reflects the British electoral system's favouring of parties with particular features to the geography of their support, producing the disproportionality and biases described later in this book. P. Dunleavy, 'First-past-the-post – normal (disproportionate) service has resumed', *Democratic Audit* (16 December 2019), www.democraticaudit. com/2019/12/16/first-past-the-post-normal-disproportionate-service-has -resumed/#more-29202.

2   Though ten MPs have been returned with less than that share, most notably the Member for Belfast South who was returned on a share of 25.5 per cent of the votes cast at the 2015 general election.

3   See R. Johnston, G. Borisyuk, M. Thrasher and C. Rallings, 'Unequal and unequally distributed votes: the sources of electoral bias at recent British general elections', *Political Studies*, 60 (2012), 877–898.

4   Full details are given in R. McInnes, *General Election 2019: Marginality*. House of Commons Library, *Insight*, 7 January 2020. This continues a long-term trend in the decline of marginal seats: J. Curtice, 'How the electoral system failed to deliver – again', in J. Tonge, C. Leeston-Bandeira and S. Wilks-Heeg (eds), *Britain Votes 2017*, Oxford: Oxford University Press, 2018, p. 32.

Notes

5   R. J. Johnston and C. J. Pattie, *Money and Electoral Politics: Local Parties and Funding in General Elections*, Bristol: The Policy Press, 2014; Johnston and Pattie, *Putting Voters in Their Place: Geography and Elections in Great Britain*.

6   Until 1832 many constituencies lacked boundaries with legal definitions.

7   G. Gudgin and P. J. Taylor, *Seats, Votes and the Spatial Organisation of Elections*, London: Pion, 1979 (reprinted Colchester: ECPR Press, 2012).

8   These two chapters draw considerably on, in a condensed form, our detailed study of the period in Rossiter, Johnston and Pattie, *The Boundary Commissions: Redrawing the UK's Map of Parliamentary Constituencies*.

9   Whereas the previous two chapters draw extensively on our 1999 book, the material in Chapter 5 is entirely new, recording changes since that book was written.

10 A. M. Carstairs, *A Short History of Electoral Systems in Western Europe*, London: Routledge, 2009.

11 J. Hart, *Proportional Representation: Critics of the British Electoral System, 1820–1945*, Oxford: The Clarendon Press, 1992.

12 See D. M. Farrell, *Electoral Systems: a Comparative Introduction* (2nd edn), Basingstoke: Palgrave-Macmillan, 2011. S. Hix, R. J. Johnston and I. McLean, *Choosing an Electoral System*, London: The British Academy, 2010.

13 See www.telegraph.co.uk/news/politics/av-referendum/8332801/AV-referendum-its-a-once-in-a-generation-opportunity-says-Nick-Clegg.html (accessed 29 October 2019).

14 A. Renwick, *Politics of Electoral Reform: Changing the Rules of Democracy*, Cambridge: Cambridge University Press, 2011.

Chapter 2

1   E. Burke, 'Speech at Mr Burke's arrival in Bristol', in I. Kramnick (ed.), *The Portable Edmund Burke*. Harmondsworth: Penguin, 1999, p. 156.

2   Rotten and pocket boroughs are discussed in greater detail in Chapter 3 (see p. 37).

3   J. A. Schumpeter, *Capitalism, Socialism and Democracy*, New York: Harper and Brothers Publishers, 1942.

4   A. Haugsgjerd, 'Political distrust amidst the Great Recession: the mitigating effect of welfare state effort', *Comparative European Politics*, 16 (2018), 620–648; C. Hay, *Why We Hate Politics*, Cambridge: Polity Press, 2007; B. Seyd, J. Curtice and J. Rose, 'How might reform of the political system appeal to discontented citizens?', *British Journal of Politics and International Relations*, 20 (2018), 263–284; G. Stoker, *Why Politics Matters: Making Democracy Work*, Basingstoke: Macmillan, 2006.

5   Data are from the 2019 British Election Study face-to-face survey.

Notes

6 J. R. Hibbing and E. Thiess-Morse, *Stealth Democracy: Americans' Beliefs about how Government Should Work*, Cambridge: Cambridge University Press, 2002.

7 P. Webb, 'Who is willing to participate? Dissatisfied democrats, stealth democrats and populists in the United Kingdom', *European Journal of Political Research*, 52 (2013), 747–772.

8 R. Campbell and J. Lovenduski, 'What should MPs do? Public and parliamentarians' views compared', *Parliamentary Affairs*, 68 (2015), 690–708.

9 N. Vivyan and M. Wagner, 'What do voters want from their local MP?', *The Political Quarterly*, 86 (2013), 33–40.

10 www.stokesentinel.co.uk/news/stoke-on-trent-news/jumping-before-hes-pushed-3294525

11 www.theguardian.com/commentisfree/2019/feb/05/parliament-vote-brexit-deal-now

12 www.theguardian.com/politics/2019/feb/14/backing-tory-brexit-could-wipe-out-labour-warns-clive-lewis

13 D. Cannadine, *Victorious Century: the United Kingdom 1800–1906*, Harmondsworth: Penguin, 2017.

14 R. S. Katz and P. Mair, 'Changing models of party organization and party democracy: the emergence of the cartel party', *Party Politics*, 1 (1995), 5–28.

15 P. Cowley, *Revolts and Rebellions: Parliamentary Voting Under Blair*, London: Politico's Publishing, 2002.

16 R. Ford, 'Of mousers and men: how politics colours everything we see', in P. Cowley and R. Ford, *Sex, Lies and the Ballot Box: 50 Things You Need to Know About British Elections*. London: Biteback Publishing, 2014.

17 D. Searing, *Westminster's World*, Cambridge MA: Harvard University Press, 1994; P. Norton, 'Roles and behaviour of British MPs', *Journal of Legislative Studies*, 3 (1997), 17–31.

18 P. Seyd, 'In praise of party', *Parliamentary Affairs*, 51 (1998), 198–206.

19 Data from the British Election Study 2017 post-election face-to-face survey (www.britishelectionstudy.com/).

20 R. Plant, 'Criteria for electoral systems: the Labour party and electoral reform', *Parliamentary Affairs*, 44 (1991), 549–557.

21 For a detailed discussion of arguments regarding the nature of representation in nineteenth-century debates on electoral reform see G. Conti, *Parliament the Mirror of the Nation. Representation, Deliberation and Democracy in Victorian Britain*, Cambridge: Cambridge University Press, 2019.

22 Data from the British Election Study 2017 post-election face-to-face survey. The question, it must be said, is rather leading: who would want ineffective government?

23 S. Childs and P. Cowley, 'The politics of local presence: is there a case for descriptive representation?', *Political Studies*, 59 (2011), 1–19.

24 P. Allen, *The Political Class: Why it Matters Who Our Politicians Are*, Oxford: Oxford University Press, 2018.

25 G. Allen, *General Election 2019: How Many Women Were Elected?* House of Commons Library, *Insight*, 15 January 2020.

26 D. Butler and D. Kavanagh, *The British General Election of 1979*, Basingstoke: Macmillan, 1980, p. 287: R. Campbell and J. Hudson, 'Political recruitment under pressure: MPs and candidates', in P. Cowley and D. Kavanagh, *The British General Election of 2017*, Basingstoke: Macmillan, 2018, p. 401.

27 R. Campbell and P. Cowley, 'What voters want: reactions to candidate characteristics in a survey experiment', *Political Studies*, 62 (2014), 745–765.

28 Childs and Cowley, 'The politics of local presence: is there a case for descriptive representation?', 1–19.

29 Campbell and Cowley, 'What voters want: reactions to candidate characteristics in a survey experiment', 756.

30 The findings in this paragraph are from S. Collignon and J. Sajuria, 'Local means local, does it? Regional identification and preferences for local candidates', *Electoral Studies*, 56 (2018), 170–178.

31 K. Arzheimer and J. Evans, 'Geolocation and voting: candidate-voter distance effects on party choice in the 2010 general election in England', *Political Geography*, 31 (2012), 301–310; J. Evans, K. Arzheimer, R. Campbell and P. Cowley, 'Candidate localness and voter choice in the 2015 general election in England', *Political Geography*, 59 (2017), 61–71.

32 R. Campbell, P. Cowley, N. Vivyan and M. Wagner, 'Why friends and neighbors? Explaining the electoral appeal of local roots', *The Journal of Politics*, 81(3); published online, 6 May 2019, doi: 10.1086/703131.

33 M. Rush and P. Giddings, *Parliamentary Socialisation: Learning the Ropes or Determining Behaviour?* Basingstoke: Palgrave Macmillan, 2011, pp. 108–9.

34 R. Gandy, *Are UK Politicians 'local'? General elections and the trend towards greater English regionalism.* LSE Politics and Policy blog, 19 March 2019, http://blogs.lse.ac.uk/politicsandpolicy/increasingly-local-parliament.

35 P. Norton, 'The growth of the constituency role of the MP', *Parliamentary Affairs*, 47 (1994), 705–720.

36 C. J. Pattie and R. J. Johnston, 'The electoral impact of the UK 2009 MPs' expenses scandal', *Political Studies*, 60 (2012), 730–750.

37 Rush and Giddings, *Parliamentary Socialisation: Learning the Ropes or Determining Behaviour?*, p. 109ff.

38 C. Mullin, 'Short cuts', *London Review of Books*. 40(10), 24 May 2018, 20.

39 D. M. Willumsen, 'So far away from me? The effect of geographi-

cal distance on representation', *West European Politics*, 42 (2019), 645–669.

40 R. J. Johnston, P. Cowley, C. J. Pattie and M. Stuart, 'Voting in the House or wooing the voters at home: Labour MPs and the 2001 General Election campaign', *Journal of Legislative Studies*, 8 (2002), 9–22.

41 P. Norton and D. Wood, 'Constituency service by Members of Parliament: does it contribute to a personal vote?', *Parliamentary Affairs*, 43 (1990), 196–208; D. Wood and P. Norton, 'Do candidates matter? Constituency-specific vote changes for incumbent MPs, 1983–1987', *Political Studies*, 40 (1992), 227–238.

42 A. Middleton, 'The personal vote, electoral experience and local connections: explaining retirement underperformance at UK elections 1987–2010', *Politics*, 39 (2019), 137–153.

43 Pattie and Johnston, 'The electoral impact of the UK 2009 MPs' expenses scandal', 730–750.

44 M. Kellerman, 'Electoral vulnerability, constituency focus and parliamentary questions in the House of Commons', *British Journal of Politics and International Relations*, 18 (2016), 90–106; Willumsen, 'So far away from me? The effect of geographical distance on representation', 645–669.

45 On which see the examples quoted in Rossiter, Johnston and Pattie, *The Boundary Commissions: Redrawing the UK's Map of Parliamentary Constituencies*, pp. 308–316.

Chapter 3

1 J. Riding, *Peterloo: the Story of the Manchester Massacre*, London: Head of Zeus, 2018.

2 On Chartism see M. Chase, *Chartism: A New History*, Manchester: Manchester University Press, 2007.

3 Much of the material in this and the next chapter is based on the more detailed coverage in Rossiter, Johnston and Pattie, *The Boundary Commissions: Redrawing the UK's Map of Parliamentary Constituencies*.

4 Cannadine, *Victorious Century: the United Kingdom, 1800–1906*, p. 156.

5 C. Seymour, *Electoral Reform in England and Wales: the Development and Operation of the Parliamentary Franchise 1832–1855*, New Haven, CT: Yale University Press, 1915, p. 533 (reprinted Newton Abbott: David & Charles, 1970).

6 Cannadine, *Victorious Century: the United Kingdom, 1800–1906*, p. 163.

7 For detailed discussions see E. Pearce, *Reform! The Fight for the 1832 Reform Act*, London: Pimlico, 2004; and A. Fraser, *Perilous Question: the Drama of the Great Reform Bill 1832*, London: Weidenfeld & Nicolson, 2014.

8 The quote is taken from J. Cannon, *Parliamentary Reform, 1640–1832*, Cambridge: Cambridge University Press, 1973, p. 208.

Notes

9   B. T. Robson, 'Maps and mathematics: ranking the English boroughs for the 1832 Reform Act', *Journal of Historical Geography*, 46 (2014), 66–79.

10 Cannadine, *Victorious Century: the United Kingdom, 1800–1906*, p. 265.

11 S. Bradford, *Disraeli*, London: Phoenix, 1983.

12 F. B. Smith, *The Making of the Second Reform Bill*, Cambridge: Cambridge University Press, 1966.

13 C. Seymour, *Electoral Reform in England and Wales: the Development and Operation of the Parliamentary Franchise, 1832–1885*, Newton Abbott: David & Charles, 1970, pp. 349–350.

14 Lord Salisbury, 'The value of redistribution: a note on electoral statistics', *The National Review*, 4 (20), 1884, 145–162. Salisbury's biographer quotes him as saying that 'enfranchisement without redistribution would lead to "the absolute effacement of the Conservative Party. It would not have reappeared as a political force for thirty years"': A. Roberts, *Salisbury. Victorian Titan*, London: Weidenfeld & Nicolson, 1999, p. 297. Chapter 18 of that book discusses the debates in detail.

15 R. Jenkins, *Dilke: a Victorian Tragedy*, London: Collins, 1965.

16 A. Jones, *The Politics of Reform 1884*, Cambridge: Cambridge University Press, 1972.

17 Salisbury had consulted Charles Dodgson (Lewis Carroll) – a mathematician who wrote widely on electoral issues: I. McLean, 'Voting', in A. Moktefi and R. Wilson (eds), *The Mathematical World of Charles L. Dodgson (Lewis Carroll)*, Oxford: Oxford University Press, 2019, pp. 123–141.

18 Evidence from poll books suggests that there was a strong class alignment to voting patterns by the 1880s: T. Dewan, J. Meriläinen and J. Tukiainen, 'Victorian voting: the origins of party orientation and class alignment', *American Journal of Political Science*, 2019, doi: 10.7910/DVN/AH2PEI.

19 Rodden shows, for example, that the countries that adopted PR devote much larger proportions of their national incomes on social expenditures than those, like the UK, with single-member district systems because the major parties collaborate and governments implement policies serving a majority of the population rather than the minority which voted for the party currently in power. J. Rodden, *Why Cities Lose. The Deep Roots of the Urban-Rural Political Divide*, New York: Basic Books, 2019.

20 Conti, *Parliament the Mirror of the Nation. Representation, Deliberation and Democracy in Victorian Britain*, p. 194.

21 T. R. Bromund, 'Uniting the whole people: proportional representation in Great Britain 1884–5, reconsidered', *Historical Research*, 74 (2001), 90.

22 R. J. Johnston, 'Electoral reform or not – party interests defeated principled arguments in the late nineteenth century, and have characterised the UK's electoral system since', *Political Studies Review*, 18 (2020). For further discussion of the 1885 legislation see M. E. J. Chadwick, 'The role

of redistribution in the making of the Third Reform Act', *The Historical Journal*, 19 (1976), 665–683; and M. Roberts, 'Resisting "arithmocracy": parliament, community and the Third Reform Act', *Journal of British Studies*, 50 (2011), 381–409.

23 Until 2011 the use of wards as the building blocks for constituencies was only specified in legislation for Northern Ireland.

24 Ireland was allocated 103 seats under the 1800 Act of Union, which meant that it was under-represented, relative to population and compared with Great Britain, by about 50 per cent. Because of depopulation there, especially following the famines of the 1840s, and growth elsewhere, by 1910 with the same number of seats Ireland was over-represented by about 50 per cent. If each part of the British Isles was equally represented, in 1912 Ireland would have been entitled to just 64 MPs (see P. Clarke, *Hope and Glory. Britain 1900–2000*, London: Penguin Books, 2004, pp. 63–66).

25 On Morrison-Bell and his cartography see M. Heffernan and B. J. Thorpe, '"The map that would save Europe": Clive Morrison-Bell, the tariff walls map, and the politics of cartographic display', *Journal of Historical Geography*, 60 (2018), 24–40.

26 The Conference is covered in detail in M. Pugh, *Electoral Reform in War and Peace 1906–1918*, London: Routledge & Kegan Paul, 1978. See also D. E. Butler, *The Electoral System in Britain since 1918*, Oxford: The Clarendon Press, 1963.

27 Calculating the percentage of the votes won is difficult at all nineteenth-century elections because of the large number of uncontested seats, so Figure 3.3 is based on rough estimates only.

Chapter 4

1 Hart, *Proportional Representation: Critics of the British Electoral System, 1820–1945*, p. 261.

2 See I. McLean, 'Are Scotland and Wales over-represented in the House of Commons?', *The Political Quarterly*, 66 (1995), 250–268.

3 Table 4.2 excludes data on Northern Ireland since the number of constituencies there was fixed in the legislation.

4 H. F. Rawlings, *Law and the Electoral Process*, London: Sweet & Maxwell, 1988, p. 38.

5 A term coined in the *New Society* magazine based on the notorious Gerrymander in the United States (see Chapter 6).

6 Boundary Commission for England, *Second Periodical Report* (Cmnd, 4084), London: HMSO, 1969, p. 5.

7 There was just one order for each country not a large number for separate groups of counties and boroughs as in the 1940s and 1950s. This was not the result of a legislative decision but rather one made by those

responsible for managing the House's business, presumably after political consultations.

8   A lengthy footnote is in order here. In the late 1970s one of us (RJ, then working at the University of Sheffield) had undertaken a number of research projects with Peter Taylor, then of the University of Newcastle upon Tyne, who with Graham Gudgin had done pioneering work – discussed in Chapter 6 – on the issue of alternative constituency configurations in two boroughs (Newcastle upon Tyne and Sunderland). RJ suggested that this could be extended by developing a computer algorithm to identify all possible configurations in each area. Taylor and Gudgin had changed their research interests and encouraged RJ to pursue this. He obtained a grant from the Social Science Research Council for that, and DR, then completing his PhD on coalfield voting patterns, was employed to work on the project. When the Boundary Commission published its provisional proposals for six new constituencies in Sheffield in 1981 DR ran the computer algorithm and identified what we considered a better set of six constituencies than the Commission's proposal and it was submitted as a representation to the Commission. All representations were published prior to the Local Inquiry and we were approached by an official of Labour-controlled Sheffield City Council asking to join us in their representation but we decided to retain independence. At the week-long Inquiry we were asked how we had developed our alternative configuration, which had not been set out in our brief representation, and we indicated that it was the output of a computer simulation. When the Commission published its revised proposals it had accepted our configuration. After the Inquiry, Gerry Bermingham contacted us and we agreed to be expert witnesses in the case that he and Marshall were developing for Michael Foot – we provided written evidence that was submitted as part of the case.

9   1983 2 *WLR*, 484.

10 For a fuller discussion of the case see Rossiter, Johnston and Pattie, *The Boundary Commissions: Redrawing the UK's Map of Parliamentary Constituencies*, pp. 113–117.

11 Note the change from Periodical to Periodic.

12 A full discussion of these issues is in D. Butler and I. McLean, 'The redrawing of Parliamentary boundaries in Britain', in I. McLean and D. Butler (eds), *Fixing the Boundaries: Defining and Redefining Single-Member Electoral Districts*, Aldershot: Dartmouth, 1996, pp. 1–38.

13 A clause of the Act said that a Commission's failure 'to submit a report within the time limit which is appropriate shall not be regarded as invalidating the report for the purposes of any enactment'!

14 The conduct of that review is covered in detail in Rossiter, Johnston and Pattie, *The Boundary Commissions: Redrawing the UK's Map of Parliamentary Constituencies*.

15 Colin Rallings and Michael Thrasher, *Media Guide to the New Parliamentary Constituencies*, BBC/ITN/PANew/Sky, 1995; Colin Rallings and Michael Thrasher, *Media Guide to the New Parliamentary Constituencies*, BBC/ITN/PANew/Sky, 2007.

16 In Scotland the Commission also gained responsibility for reviewing local government ward boundaries and the boundaries for Scottish Parliament constituencies, requiring a larger permanent staff.

17 D. J. Rossiter, R. J. Johnston and C. J. Pattie, *The Boundary Commissions; Redrawing the UK's Map of Parliamentary Constituencies*, Manchester: Manchester University Press, 1999, pp. 237–245, discuss the ACs in detail.

Chapter 5

1 A. Tyrie, *Pruning the Politicians*, London: Conservative Mainstream, 2004.

2 For a critique of the bill, see R. J. Johnston, I. McLean, C. J. Pattie and D. J. Rossiter, 'Can the Boundary Commissions help the Conservative Party? Constituency size and electoral bias in the United Kingdom', *The Political Quarterly*, 80 (2009), 479–494.

3 Again, we should note that all three authors attended that meeting with (now Sir) Eric Pickles, then Chairman of the Conservative Party and (now Lord) Rob Hayward. We had previously published a draft set of rules, with a fixed number of MPs, a UK-wide quota, and a fixed percentage deviation around that quota: R. J. Johnston, C. J. Pattie, D. Dorling and D. J. Rossiter, *From Votes to Seats. The Operation of the UK Electoral System since 1945*, Manchester: Manchester University Press, 2001, pp. 213–214. These were adopted, slightly modified, in D. Butler and I. McLean, *Report to the Committee on Standards in Public Life: the Electoral Commission and the Redistribution of Seats*, Oxford: University of Oxford, Department of Politics and International Relations, 2006.

4 M. Balinski, R. J. Johnston, I. Mclean and H. P. Young, *Drawing a New Constituency Map for the United Kingdom. The Parliamentary Voting System and Constituencies Bill, 2010*, London: The British Academy, 2010.

5 The AV system is discussed in Chapter 7.

6 Note that the rule did not say that electorates should be as equal as possible only that they should fall within the tolerance: this was interpreted by the Boundary Commission for England which in its *Guide to the 2013 Review* stated that it was preferable to 'identify a constituency that had, say, a 4 per cent variance from the UK electoral quota, but which respected local ties ... to an alternative that produced a constituency with only a 1 per cent variance but which split communities'.

7   These two constituencies had electorates at the start of the first review using the new rules of 33,755 and 21,837 respectively.

8   This was the issue in the court case discussed later in this chapter (see p. 102).

9   A full discussion of the changes is in R. J. Johnston and C. J. Pattie, 'From the organic to the arithmetic: new redistricting/redistribution rules for the United Kingdom', *Election Law Journal*, 11 (2012), 70–89.

10 Few of the proposed amendments were adopted: see R. J. Johnston and C. J. Pattie, 'Parties and crossbenchers voting in the post-2010 House of Lords: the example of the Parliamentary Voting System and Constituencies Bill', *British Politics*, 6 (2011), 430–452.

11 As illustrated in Chapter 6, the impact of abstentions and third-party competition would not be affected.

12 On the extent of the disruption see D. J. Rossiter, R. J. Johnston and C. J. Pattie, 'Representing people and representing places: community, continuity and the current redistribution of Parliamentary constituencies in the UK', *Parliamentary Affairs*, 66 (2013), 856–886.

13 For more detail on the Hearings, see R. J. Johnston, C. J. Pattie and D. J. Rossiter, 'Local Inquiries or Public Hearings: changes in public consultation over the redistribution of UK Parliamentary constituency boundaries', *Public Administration*, 91 (2013), 663–679.

14 See R. J. Johnston, C., J. Pattie and D. J. Rossiter, 'MPs' responses to a proposed new constituency map: electoral prospects, community ties and party organisation', *Journal of Legislative Studies*, 20 (2014), 360–379.

15 These were done by Anthony Wells of the polling company YouGov – https://ukpollingreport.co.uk/: we are grateful to him for making all of his data available.

16 Further detail on the parties' counter-proposals is in R. J. Johnston, C. J. Pattie and D. J. Rossiter, 'Manipulating territories: British political parties and new Parliamentary constituencies', *Territory, Politics, Governance*, 1 (2013), 223–245.

17 Details of the English ACs for the review that reported in 2018 can be found at: https://boundarycommissionforengland.independent.gov.uk/about-us/assistant-commissioners/.

18 In its submission the Conservative Party noted that: 'If therefore the Commission were convinced of the advantages of keeping Beverley and Holderness CC and East Yorkshire CC unchanged, we believe that they should only do so if they are able also to keep Grimsby as they have proposed it, which can probably only be done by a reconfiguration of wards within Kingston upon Hull.' At the 2010 election two of Hull's seats were safe for Labour with the Conservatives in second place and the third was a marginal Labour victory over the Liberal Democrats. Grimsby was divided in the final proposals submitted after the next review in 2018.

19 Rossiter, Johnston and Pattie, 'Representing people and represent-ing places: community, continuity and the current redistribution of Parliamentary constituencies in the UK', 856–886.

20 R. J. Johnston, D. J. Rossiter and C. J. Pattie, *Equality, Community and Continuity: Reviewing the UK Rules for Constituency Redistributions*, London: The McDougall Trust, 2014.

21 House of Commons Political and Constitutional Reform Committee, *What Next on the Redrawing of Parliamentary Constituency Boundaries*. London: The Stationery Office, HC600, 2015.

22 *Government Response to the Political and Constitutional Reform Committee's Eighth Report of Session 2014–15. What Next on the Redrawing of Parliamentary Constituency Boundaries?* Cm 9203, 2016.

23 The DUP, which was sustaining the Conservative minority government, was thought to be opposed to the new constituencies in the belief that Sinn Féin might win more seats than them, and so the DUP might vote with the Opposition against the government when the Commissions' reports were laid before Parliament. Some Conservative MPs, who might lose their seats, were also believed to be opposed.

24 The legislation (the *Parliamentary Voting System and Constituencies Act 2011*, section 10) requires that on receipt of a Boundary Commission report the Secretary of State shall lay it before Parliament 'as soon as may be' after its submission and then that when reports have been submitted by all four Commissions 'as soon as may be' thereafter the Secretary of State shall 'lay before Parliament the draft of an Order in Council for giving effect to the recommendations contained in them' – but one year after the reports had been received and laid before Parliament no such Draft Order had been published.

25 Given that a general election was scheduled for 12 December 2019 the next, under the terms of the *Fixed-term Parliaments Act 2011*, is not due until December 2024 – although the 2019 election was called notwithstanding the 2011 Act following a simple-majority vote in the House of Commons and the viability of the fixed-term legislation is now in doubt.

26 House of Commons Public Administration and Constitutional Affairs Committee, *Parliamentary Boundary Reviews: What Next?* HC559, 6 February 2018.

27 Appendix to the Public Administration and Constitutional Affairs Committee Second Report: https://publications.parliament.uk/pa/cm201719/cmselect/cmpubadm/1072/107202.htm.

28 These words appeared in bold in the Boundary Commission for England, *Guide to the 2018 Review of Parliamentary Constituencies*, 2016, page 8.

29 Budding Boundary Commissioners can test this for themselves by refer-ence back to Figures 6.3 and 6.14 – if any of constituencies 1–6 in the

former is abolished, the level of disruption is far greater than if 7 is the victim.

30 Balinski, Johnston, McLean and Young, *Drawing a New Constituency Map for the United Kingdom. The Parliamentary Voting System and Constituencies Bill 2010*, p. 37.

31 For example, www.newsletter.co.uk/news/revamp-of-constituency-boun daries-may-put-unionist-seats-at-risk-1-7561703.

32 See www.northernslant.com/musical-chairs-latest-boundary-recommen dations-mean/.

33 One of its MPs was reported as claiming that the revised proposals were akin to a 'government gerrymander designed to placate the DUP': www.independent.ie/irish-news/politics/sinn-fein-mp-claims-proposed-new-electoral-map-for-northern-ireland-akin-to-unionist-gerrymander-36500073.html.

34 Northern Ireland Court of Appeal [2020] NICA 32 https://www.judici aryni.uk/judicial-decisions/2020-nica-32.

35 We are grateful to Professor Cowley for providing us with a copy of their unpublished paper on 'The length of Westminster constituency names – 1950–2020', which was later published as evidence to the Boundary Commissions – www.boundarycommission.org.uk/sites/bc/files/media-files/Cowley%2C%20Philip.pdf

36 The Conservatives' manifesto included a commitment to repeal the *Fixed-term Parliaments Act 2011* (as also did Labour's manifesto), which may be another reason why they might prefer to implement the 2018 proposals.

Chapter 6

1 Between 1950 and 2019 the Conservatives won 41 per cent of all votes cast at general elections but were in government (as a majority for all but five of the years) for 66 per cent of the time.

2 Gudgin and Taylor, *Seats, Votes and the Spatial Organisation of Elections*.

3 M. Gallagher, 'Proportionality, disproportionality and electoral systems', *Electoral Studies*, 10 (1991), 33–51.

4 According to Gallagher, the index 'penalizes a few large disproportionali-ties more than a host of small ones' (p. 41); in general, the percentage to be redistributed is slightly larger than the index.

5 www.tcd.ie/Political_Science/people/michael_gallagher/ElSystems/Docts/ElectionIndices.pdf.

6 A recent alternative definition is of 'excess' (i.e. surplus), 'redundant' (i.e. wasted) and 'decisive' (i.e. effective): see R. McInnes, *General Election 2019: Turning Votes into Seats.* House of Commons Library, Insight, 10 January 2020.

Notes

7   American analysts of electoral systems use a comparable measure, what they term the *efficiency gap*: see N. O. Stephanopoulos and E. M. McGee, 'Partisan gerrymandering and the efficiency gap', *University of Chicago Law Review*, 82 (2015), 831–848.

8   Irregular shapes have been the norm in American redistricting since Elbridge Gerry: for examples, see M. S. Monmonier, *Bushmanders and Bullwinkles: how Politicians Manipulate Electronic Maps and Census Data to Win Elections*, Chicago: University of Chicago Press, 2002.

9   The eight Welsh 'counties' shown here no longer exist; they were retained for use by the Boundary Commission after the local government reorganisation into 22 unitary authorities in 1996.

10 One seat was won by the Liberal Democrats.

11 From this we can infer that it is very unlikely that an index of disproportionality will reach 50, depending on what share of the votes cast is obtained by the party winning all seats. The largest percentages in 2010 were 55.1 per cent for the Conservatives in Surrey, which yielded all 11 seats, and 52.2 per cent in Merseyside for Labour, which yielded 86.7 per cent of the seats.

12 R. H. Brookes, 'Electoral distortion in New Zealand', *Australian Journal of Politics and History*, 5 (1959), 218–233; and R. H. Brookes, 'The analysis of distorted representation in two-party, single-member elections', *Political Science*, 12 (1960), 158–167.

13 R. J. Johnston, 'Manipulating maps and winning elections: measuring the impact of malapportionment and gerrymandering', *Political Geography*, 21 (2002), 1–32; R. J. Johnston, 'Which map? Which government? Malapportionment and gerrymandering UK-style', *Government and Opposition*, 50 (2015), 1–23; P. J. Taylor and G. Gudgin, 'The myth of non-partisan cartography: a study of electoral biases in the English Boundary Commission's redistribution for 1955–1970', *Urban Studies*, 13 (1976), 13–25.

14 At the first two post-1945 redistributions the Boundary Commission for England argued that rural constituencies should have fewer voters than urban because of MPs' problems serving a dispersed, lower-density population; it ended that practice in the 1960s. All three British Commissions used the rule that allowed them to create small constituencies – in electorate though not area – in areas with very low population densities, but this was discontinued by the English and Welsh Commissions from the 1970s on. (See Rossiter, Johnston and Pattie, *The Boundary Commissions: Redrawing the UK's Map of Parliamentary Constituencies*, pp. 164–166.)

15 R. J. Johnston, D. J. Rossiter and C. J. Pattie, 'Integrating and decomposing the sources of partisan bias: Brookes' method and the impact of redistricting in Great Britain', *Electoral Studies*, 18 (1999), 367–378, and *Electoral Studies*, 20 (2000), 649–650; Johnston, Pattie, Dorling and

Notes

Rossiter, *From Votes to Seats: the Operation of the UK Electoral System since 1945*. (For an updated presentation of the data see T. Smith, 'Why did the Conservatives' large lead in vote shares produced only an 80-seat majority?', *LSE British Politics and Policy Blog*, 15 January 2020, https://blogs.lse.ac.uk/politicsandpolicy/ge2019-bias/. For an animated description of the method, see M. Thrasher, *Ballots, Bias and Boundaries*, on YouTube (www.youtube.com/watch?v=cLLgLDkBDoo). An expansion of the method for three-party contests has been developed but is not deployed here which focuses on the two largest parties throughout the period studied: see G. Borisyuk, M. Thrasher, C. Rallings and R. J. Johnston, 'Measuring bias: from two-party to three-party elections', *Electoral Studies*, 27 (2008), 245–256.

16 According to Rodden, this is a characteristic affecting all left-leaning parties in first-past-the-post electoral systems – not least the Democrats in the United States and Labour in the UK. Their vote distributions tend to be more spatially clustered and concentrated than those of right-leaning parties (such as the Republicans and Conservatives). As a consequence, on average the former tend to win seats by larger majorities because their vote distributions contain a strong, if unintentional, 'packed gerrymander element', producing a bias against them. See Rodden, *Why Cities Lose: the Deep Roots of the Urban-Rural Political Divide*; and J. Chen and J. Rodden, 'Unintentional gerrymandering, political geography and electoral bias in legislatures', *Quarterly Journal of Political Science*, 8 (2013), 239–268.

17 G. Evans and J. Tilley, *The New Politics of Class: the Political Exclusion of the British Working Class*, Oxford: Oxford University Press, 2017.

18 See G. Evans, J. Curtice and P. Norris, 'New Labour, new tactical voting? The causes and consequences of tactical voting in the 1997 general election', *Journal of Elections, Public Opinion and Parties*, 8 (1998), 65–79.

19 Evans and Tilley, *The New Politics of Class; the Political Exclusion of the British Working Class*; C. J. Pattie, T. Hartmann and R. J. Johnston, 'A close-run thing? Accounting for changing overall turnout in UK general elections', *Representation*, 55 (2019), 101–116.

20 All calculations of the likely outcome in each constituency were undertaken by Anthony Wells of YouGov, using the method developed by Rallings and Thrasher, and reported on his website – http://ukpollingreport.co.uk/; we are grateful to him for allowing us to use those data.

21 Interactions between the various factors mean that the net total is not the arithmetic sum of the parts.

22 The estimates of the number of seats for each party if the 2019 election had been held in the 583 constituencies proposed by the Boundary Commissions come from Electoral Calculus: www.electoralcalculus.co.uk/homepage.html.

23 Once again, interactions mean the net total is less than the sum of the parts.

24 On Scotland in 2015 and 2017 see R. J. Johnston, C. J. Pattie, T. K. Hartman, D. Manley, D. J. Rossiter and K. Jones, 'Scotland's electoral geography differed from the rest of Britain's in 2017 (and 2015) – exploring its contours', *Scottish Geographical Journal*, 134 (2018), 24–38; R. J. Johnston, C. J. Pattie and T. K. Hartman, 'Local knowledge, local learning and predicting election outcomes: voter assessments of likely party success in Scotland's constituencies and the 2015 and 2017 general elections', *Scottish Affairs*, 28 (2019), 1–31.

Chapter 7

1 Plant, 'Criteria for electoral systems: the Labour party and electoral reform', 549–557.

2 V. Bogdanor, *The People and the Party System*, Cambridge: Cambridge University Press, 1981; Hart, *Proportional Representation: Critics of the British Electoral System 1820–1945*; P. Norris, 'The politics of electoral reform in Britain', *International Political Science Review*, 16 (1995), 65–78.

3 J. S. Mill, *Considerations on Representative Government*, Cambridge, Cambridge University Press, 2010.

4 House of Commons *Hansard*, 30 May 1867, Column 1357.

5 House of Commons *Hansard*, 30 May 1867, Column 1361.

6 G. Conti, *Parliament as the Mirror of the Nation. Representation, Deliberation and Democracy in Victorian Britain*, Cambridge: Cambridge University Press, 2019.

7 D. Butler, *The Electoral System in Britain 1918–1951*, Oxford: Oxford University Press, 1953, p. 7.

8 Norris, 'The politics of electoral reform in Britain', 65–78; A. M. Carstairs, *A Short History of Electoral Systems in Western Europe*, London: George Allen & Unwin, 1980.

9 Another Speaker's Conference in all but name: Butler, *The Electoral System in Britain 1918–1951*; D. Butler, 'Electoral reform', *Parliamentary Affairs*, 57 (2004), 734–743.

10 A. Heath, J. Curtice, R. Jowell, G. Evans, J. Field and S. Witherspoon, *Understanding Political Change: the British Voter 1964–1987*, Oxford: Pergamon Press, 1991; I. Crewe and A. King, *SDP: the Birth, Life and Death of the Social Democratic Party*, Oxford: Oxford University Press, 1995.

11 Plant, 'Criteria for electoral systems: the Labour party and electoral reform', 549–557.

12 A. Heath, R. Jowell, J. Curtice and B. Taylor (eds), *Labour's Last Chance? The 1992 Election and Beyond*, Aldershot: Dartmouth Publishing, 1994.

Notes

13 E. Shaw, *The Labour Party Since 1945*, Oxford: Blackwell, 1996; P. Gould, *The Unfinished Revolution: How the Modernisers Saved the Labour Party*, London: Abacus, 1998.

14 M. S. Shugart and M. P. Wattenberg (eds), *Mixed-Member Electoral Systems: the Best of Both Worlds?* Oxford: Oxford University Press, 2001.

15 To the disappointment of Paddy Ashdown, Liberal Democrat leader at the time: P. Ashdown, *Fortunate Life: the Autobiography of Paddy Ashdown*, London: Aurum Press, 2010, pp. 311–322.

16 See Farrell, *Electoral Systems: a Comparative Introduction (2nd edition)*, pp. 77–91.

17 C. Rallings, M. Thrasher and D. Cowling, 'Mayoral referendums and elections', *Local Government Studies*, 28 (4) (2002), 67–90.

18 P. Cowley and D. Kavanagh, *The British General Election of 2015*, Basingstoke: Palgrave Macmillan, 2016, pp. 20 and 39.

19 J. Curtice, 'Politicians, voters and democracy: the 2011 UK referendum on the alternative vote', *Electoral Studies*, 32 (2013), 215–223.

20 Although ironically both National and Labour opposed the change, and a referendum only happened because the Labour leader misread his briefing notes: K. Jackson and A. McRobie, *New Zealand Adopts Proportional Representation: Accident? Design? Evolution?* Aldershot: Ashgate, 1998.

21 Curtice, 'How the electoral system failed to deliver – again', 29–45; J. Curtice, 'So what went wrong with the electoral system? The 2010 election result and the debate about electoral reform', *Parliamentary Affairs*, 63 (2010), 622–638.

22 For a good overview, see A. Renwick, *A Citizen's Guide to Electoral Reform*, London: Biteback Publishing, 2011.

23 R. J. Johnston, D. Manley, D. J. Rossiter, C. J. Pattie, T. K. Hartman and K. Jones, 'Coming full circle: the 2017 UK general election and the changing electoral map', *The Geographical Journal*, 184 (2018), 100–108.

24 In one rarely used variant of AV, the first candidate to be eliminated is the one with most last preferences.

25 P. Dunleavy, H. Margetts and S. Weir, 'How Britain would have voted under alternative electoral systems in 1992', *Parliamentary Affairs*, 45 (1992), 640–655; P. Dunleavy, H. Margetts, B. O'Duffy and S. Weir, 'Remodelling the 1997 general election: how Britain would have voted under alternative electoral systems', *British Elections and Parties Review*, 8 (1998), 208–231; D. Sanders, H. D. Clarke, M. C. Stewart and P. Whiteley, 'Simulating the effects of the Alternative Vote in the 2010 UK General Election', *Parliamentary Affairs*, 64 (2010), 5–23; J. Garland and C. Terry, *The 2017 General Election: Volatile Voting, Random Results*, London: Electoral Reform Society, 2017 (www.electoral-reform.org. uk/latest-news-and-research/publications/the-2017-general-election-report/).

26 Curtice, 'Politicians, voters and democracy: the 2011 UK referendum on the alternative vote', 215–223.

27 R. J. Johnston. and J. Forrest, 'Electoral disproportionality and bias under the Alternative Vote: elections to Australia's House of Representatives', *Australian Journal of Political Science*, 44 (2009), 521–528.

28 A. J. Parker, 'Geography and the Irish electoral system', *Irish Geography*, 19 (1986), 1–14; M. A. Górecki and M. Marsh, 'A decline of "friends and neighbours voting" in Ireland? Local candidate effects in the 2011 Irish "earthquake election"', *Political Geography*, 41 (2014), 11–20.

29 The estimates are taken from Dunleavy, Margetts and Weir, 'How Britain would have voted under alternative electoral systems in 1992', 640–655; Dunleavy, Margetts, O'Duffy and Weir, 'Remodelling the 1997 general election: how Britain would have voted under alternative electoral systems', 208–231; Garland and Terry, *The 2017 General Election: Volatile Voting, Random Results*.

30 The disproportionality index for the constituency contests compares the share of constituency MPs won by each party with their shares of the constituency vote. For the overall disproportionality index, we compare the share of the regional list vote going to each party with that party's share of all elected MPs.

31 More, but not entirely proportional. At the 2011 Scottish Parliament election, for instance, the SNP won a majority (53 per cent) of seats, although they had less than 50 per cent of the vote – just 44 per cent in the regional contest. This is in part because there are more constituency than regional seats in both Scotland and Wales which reduces the proportionality of AMS.

32 J. Bradbury and J. Mitchell, 'The constituency work of members of the Scottish Parliament and National Assembly for Wales: approaches, relationships and rules', *Regional and Federal Studies*, 17 (2007), 117–145; T. C. Lundberg, 'Second class representatives? Mixed-member proportional representation in Britain', *Parliamentary Affairs*, 59 (2006), 60–77; D. C. W. Parker and C. M. Richer, 'Back from Holyrood: how mixed-member proportional representation and ballot structure shape the personal vote', *British Journal of Politics and International Relations*, 20 (2018), 674–692.

33 Some New Zealand MPs elected via the national list nonetheless have a 'constituency office' in that part of the country where they have the deepest political roots (some stand in both contests and if they lose in the constituency may then be elected through the national list).

34 A. Lijphart, *Patterns of Democracy: Government Forms and Performance in Thirty-Six Countries*, New Haven: Yale University Press, 1999, p. 153.

35 For a discussion of those used in national elections see A. Reynolds and B. Reilly, *The International IDEA Handbook of Electoral System Design*, Stockholm: International IDEA, 2005 – available at www.ifes.org/sites/

default/files/esd_english_o.pdf; and the ace project website at http://aceproject.org/ace-en/topics/es/annex/esy/esy_ie. For comparative studies see M. Gallagher and P. Mitchell (eds), *The Politics of Electoral Systems*, Oxford: Oxford University Press, 2005; and E. S. Herron, R. J. Pekkanen and M. S. Shugart (eds), *The Oxford Handbook of Electoral Systems*, Oxford: Oxford University Press, 2018.

36 Lijphart, *Patterns of Democracy: Government Forms and Performance in Thirty-Six Countries*; G. N. Powell, *Elections as Instruments of Democracy: Majoritarian and Proportional Visions*. New Haven: Yale University Press, 2000.

37 STV has been the electoral system deployed in what became the Republic of Ireland since its creation in 1922, the departing colonial power (the UK) insisting on it to ensure that the Protestant minority was represented in the Dáil Eireann. Its use was enshrined in the Republic's constitution in 1937; replacing it by FPTP was rejected at referendums in 1959 and 1968.

38 D. Farrell and M. Gallagher, 'British voters and their criteria for evaluating electoral systems', *British Journal of Politics and International Relations*, 1 (1999), 293–316.

Conclusion

1 See A. J. McGann, C. A. Smith, M. Latner and A. Keena, *Gerrymandering in America: the House of Representatives, the Supreme Court and the Future of Popular Sovereignty*, Cambridge: Cambridge University Press, 2016.

2 See Rodden, *Why Cities Lose. The Deep Roots of the Urban-Rural Political Divide.*

Index